# The Changing Tradition:
# Women in the
# History of Rhetoric

*Edited by*
*Christine Mason Sutherland*
*Rebecca Sutcliffe*

# The Changing Tradition: Women in the History of Rhetoric

*Edited by*
*Christine Mason Sutherland*
*Rebecca Sutcliffe*

© 1999 Christine Mason Sutherland and Rebecca J. Sutcliffe.
All rights reserved.

University of Calgary Press
2500 University Drive NW
Calgary, Alberta
Canada T2N 1N4

Canadian Cataloguing in Publication Data

Main entry under title:
The changing tradition

"Papers at the Conference of the International Society for the
History of Rhetoric at the University of Saskatchewan in July 1997" –
Pref.
Includes index.
ISBN 1-55238-008-4

1. Rhetoric–History. 2. Women–Language. 3. Women authors. 4.
Women orators. I. Sutherland, Christine Mason. II. Sutcliffe,
Rebecca J. (Rebecca Jane), 1963-   III. International Society for the
History of Rhetoric. Conference (1997: University of
Saskatchewan)
P301..C52N1999        808'.0082        C99-910334-2

All rights reserved. No part of this work covered by the copyrights hereon may be
reproduced or used in any form or by any means – graphic, electronic or mechanical –
without the prior permission of the publisher. Any request for photocopying, recording, taping
or reproducing in information storage and retrieval systems of any part of this book shall be
directed in writing to the Canadian Reprography Collective, 379 Adelaide Street West, Suite
M1, Toronto, Ontario M5V 1S5.

Printed and bound in Canada by Hignell Book Printing Limited.
∞  This book is printed on acid-free paper.

# Contents

| | |
|---|---|
| Acknowledgements | vii |
| Preface | 1 |

**PLENARY ADDRESS**

| | |
|---|---|
| Women in the History of Rhetoric: The Past and the Future<br>*Christine Mason Sutherland* | 9 |

**GROUP 1: EXCLUDED FROM THE RHETORICAL TRADITION**

| | |
|---|---|
| Plato's Women: Alternative Embodiments of Rhetoric<br>*C. Jan Swearingen* | 35 |
| Cutting Off the Memory of Women<br>*Jody Enders* | 47 |

**GROUP 2: ALONGSIDE THE RHETORICAL TRADITION**

| | |
|---|---|
| Ethos Over Time: The Ongoing Appeal of St. Catherine of Siena<br>*Margo Husby Scheelar* | 59 |
| Verbum inuisibile palpabitur: Les Sibylles dans la seconde moitié du XVe siècle: La répétition comme poétique de l'oracle<br>*Hélène Cazes* | 73 |
| Verbum inuisibile palpabitur: The Sibyls in the Second Half of the Fifteenth Century: Repetition as Oracular Poetics<br>*Hélène Cazes, translated by Nicholas Fairbank* | 85 |
| English Emblem Book Reception Theory and the Meditations of Renaissance Women<br>*Linda Bensel-Meyers* | 97 |
| Account of the Experience of Hester Ann Rogers: Rhetorical Functions of a Methodist Mystic's Journal<br>*Vicki Collins* | 109 |

## Group 3: Participating in the Rhetorical Tradition

Women and Latin Rhetoric from Hrotsvit to Hildegard  121
  *John Ward*

Lady Mary Wroth's *Urania* and the Rhetoric of Female Abuse  133
  *Victor Skretkowicz*

Mary Astell's Rhetorical Theory: A Woman's Viewpoint  147
  *Erin Herberg*

## Group 4: Emerging into the Rhetorical Tradition

The Public Woman: Women Speakers Around the Turn of the Century in Sweden  161
  *Brigitte Mral, translated by Malcolm Forbes*

Flora MacDonald Denison and the Rhetoric of the Early Women's Suffrage Movement in Canada  173
  *Andrea Williams*

Resisting Decline Stories: Gertrude Buck's Democratic Theory of Rhetoric  183
  *Suzanne Bordelon*

## Group 5: Engaging the Rhetorical Tradition

Re-inventing Rhetorical Epistemology: Donna Haraway's and Nicole Brossard's Embodied Visions  199
  *Philippa Spoel*

Feminist Epistemologies, Rhetorical Traditions and the *Ad Hominem*  213
  *Marianne Janack and John Adams*

Voice and the Inevitability of Ethos  225
  *Robert L. King*

Feminist Thoughts on Rhetoric  237
  *Lynette Hunter*


Afterword  249
  *Christine Mason Sutherland*

Notes on the Contributors  257

## *Acknowledgements*

The editors gratefully acknowledge the following: the Social Science and Humanities Council of Canada for a grant to make the publication possible; and a grant from the University of Saskatchewan. We thank Judith Rice Henderson of the University of Saskatchewan for initiating the project and giving help and encouragement throughout the editorial process. We also thank the following: Colette Nativel of the University of Paris for help in editing the French paper; Nicholas Fairbank for translating the French essay; Malcolm Forbes for translating the Swedish essay; Robert Schmiel of the University of Calgary for advice on editing; Suzanne Hathaway Rae for her invaluable help in dealing with various word-processing systems; and Sylvia Mills, Marion Hillier and Jo-Anne Kabeary for their secretarial assistance.

Christine Mason Sutherland (Editor)
Rebecca Sutcliffe (Editor)

# *Preface*

The essays in this collection were given as papers at the Conference of the International Society for the History of Rhetoric at the University of Saskatchewan in July 1997. Submitted to the editors in advance of the conference, and thoroughly revised, they make an important contribution to the subject under discussion.

It has long been accepted among rhetoricians that women have had no place in the history of rhetoric. But these are revisionist days, and during the past two decades or so, those who have studied the relationship between women and the rhetorical tradition have questioned this received wisdom from many points of view. Two collections of essays on the subject of women and the rhetorical tradition have already been published: *Reclaiming Rhetorica: Women in the Rhetorical Tradition*, edited by Andrea A. Lunsford, in 1995;[1] and *Listening to Their Voices: The Rhetorical Activities of Historical Women*, edited by Molly Meijer Wertheimer, in 1997.[2] These are discussed in the Afterword, where there is some evaluation of how they have contributed to this volume, and how it differs from both. The essays here continue and extend the work of exploration. Their authors do not present a united front; they are not all women; they would not all describe themselves as feminists; they certainly do not share one discipline, for rhetoric itself is interdisciplinary. But if there is no united front, there is yet unity of a kind, and that unity has to do with a commitment to discovering why, and to what extent, women have been excluded from rhetoric, and what contributions they have nevertheless made to it in the past, as well as what they are doing in it today. There is, therefore, unity in diversity.

There is unity in diversity, too, among the contributors. Two languages and seven different countries are represented. There is variety as well in the professional experience and standing of the contributors: some are researchers in rhetoric; some also teach it, its theory, and its practice. Some are established scholars with international reputations; others are graduate students. We are concerned to include not only the valuable scholarship and wisdom of seasoned scholars, but also the insights and fresh viewpoints of those just beginning their academic careers.

All the major periods in the history of rhetoric are represented: Greek, Roman, Medieval, Renaissance, Enlightenment, Nineteenth Century, Twentieth Century, and Contemporary. However, the papers in the collection are arranged to show the various ways in which received wisdom has been challenged, the rhetorical tradition revised. The headings for each group, therefore, do not identify particular periods, and the overall organization is not chronological. Within each group, however, the order is historical, since there is often some development, or some reversal, to be perceived. The fluctuations are in themselves interesting: women have not been so severely excluded in all ages, nor is their exclusion always to be attributed to the same causes. The first essay stands outside the organization of the rest and serves as an introduction to them, constituting a kind of overview of the field. It has been included at the request of the other contributors, who see it as a necessary positioning that enhances the value of their own essays. Because it was originally given as a plenary address, though it has since been revised, it is considerably, and unavoidably, longer than the rest. The groups are as follows:

### *1. Excluded from the Rhetorical Tradition*

Each of the essays in this first group takes a different attitude to the exclusion of women. C. Jan Swearingen's essay deals with women's rhetoric in ancient Greece. She questions the traditional assumption that they were wholly excluded, showing that some women did indeed practise rhetoric. Her discussion focuses on Aspasia and Diotima, both of whom are mentioned by Plato. Jody Enders' essay concerns the exclusion of women in a different period – the late fifteenth century. Her discussion of the demonization of the female memory in Heinrich Kramer's *Malleus Maleficarum* claims that the work contributed to a philosophical model that encouraged violence against women.[3]

## 2. Alongside the Rhetorical Tradition

The next group comprises four essays showing women's involvement in discourses that ran parallel to the rhetorical tradition itself. More than any other, this group challenges traditional definitions of rhetoric in a particularly fruitful way. Each of the essays concerns some aspect of religion. Margo Husby Scheelar's essay takes us beyond purely linguistic rhetoric: in her study of the ethos of Catherine of Siena, she fundamentally treats Catherine's life as text. One is reminded that Kenneth Burke includes behaviour in his definition of rhetoric. Hélène Cazes discusses representation of the mythical Sibyls in texts of the late fifteenth century, and their use in the repetition of the Christian gospel. The essay is especially interesting for raising issues of iconography, even of mythology, not often dealt with in traditional histories of rhetoric. Like Cazes, Linda Bensel-Meyers brings the study of the visual image within the scope of rhetoric. Her essay adds another point of view by including some discussion of reception theory. Vicki Collins' essay, like Husby Scheelar's, deals with a woman mystic, Hester Rogers. Here again, we find a challenge to the traditional definition of rhetoric, for although her journals were eventually published, their original audience was not public, but private: herself and God.

## 3. Participating in the Rhetorical Tradition

This group consists of three essays dealing with women who knew the rhetorical tradition and used it. John Ward discusses some of the medieval women who participated in the Latin rhetorical tradition of the Middle Ages, either as practitioners or as teachers. Although, as Ward notes, "nothing was so sidelined and marginalized in this period as the woman's voice," something of their work and achievement has survived. Victor Skretkowicz writes about Mary Wroth, a member of the famous Sidney family, who consciously used her knowledge of rhetoric in her feminist protest against the misogyny of her time. Skretkowicz describes Wroth as "the most explicitly rhetorically conscious of all late Renaissance English writers," and points out that "she had taken a conscious decision to enunciate publicly her adopted position as the foremost literary feminist of her epoch." Wroth has particular importance, therefore, both as a rhetorician and as a feminist. The final essay in this group, Erin Herberg's, introduces us for the first time in this collection to a woman who explicitly challenged rhetoric itself, as it was practised in her time. Herberg demonstrates how Mary Astell used both classical authors and Cartesian critics of rhetoric in her attempt to open up rhetorical practice to women.

## 4. Emerging into the Rhetorical Tradition

This group of essays shows us a number of women entering the rhetorical tradition on their own terms in the nineteenth and early twentieth centuries. Brigitte Mral discusses three Swedish women and the various strategies they adopted to cope with the problems they faced as woman speakers. While sharing the difficulties imposed by their sex, each of these women devised her own way of overcoming them. Andrea Williams brings to our attention a Canadian woman, one of the first to identify herself as a feminist. Williams' discussion of the varying ways in which Flora MacDonald Denison used rhetoric in her campaign for women's votes leads her to raise again the question of how rhetoric should be defined. The subject of Suzanne Bordelon's essay, Gertrude Buck, is a woman of a very different kind: one who made her contribution as a scholar, a theorist of rhetoric. With Buck, we come to a woman who is important simply as a rhetorician, aside from any considerations of gender. An English professor at Vassar, Buck was an educator of women, but her rhetorical theory is not a specifically feminist one: it applies to both sexes.

## 5. Engaging the Rhetorical Tradition

The last group of essays focuses on feminist issues in contemporary rhetoric. Philippa Spoel shows how the feminist critique leads to a redefinition of rhetoric. Specifically, she shows how a study of the rhetorical role of the body – which traditionally has been feminized in relation to masculine reason – contributes to a new sense of the nature of rhetoric itself. Like Spoel's, the essay contributed by Marianne Janack and John Adams deals with epistemology, in particular the feminist challenge to the traditional dismissal of the *ad hominem* argument as fallacy. Drawing upon recent work by feminist scholars, Janack and Adams offer a revised viewpoint on this question. Robert L. King's essay deals with a related issue: the tension between the concepts of voice and ethos. Are they different? How are they different? And does the idea of voice subjectivize and trivialize the idea of ethos? The final essay in the collection, Lynette Hunter's, like the others in this group, is concerned with epistemology. Questions of subjectivity versus objectivity, and of authority, which also engage Janack and Adams, and King, are considered from quite another angle. The focus of the paper is how standpoint theory and rhetoric might be brought together to critique aesthetics.

The collection is offered in the hope that it may serve to inform those interested in knowing more about the subject as well as assisting those already active in the field. We particularly wish that we may encourage others to join us in the study of this most interesting and important subject.

## *NOTES*

1. *Reclaiming Rhetorica: Women in the Rhetorical Tradition*, ed. Andrea A. Lunsford (Pittsburgh and London: University of Pittsburgh Press, 1995).
2. *Listening to Their Voices: The Rhetorical Activities of Historical Women*, ed. Molly Meijer Wertheimer (Columbia, South Carolina: University of South Carolina Press, 1997).
3. Heinrich Kramer's *Malleus Maleficarum*, 2 vols. (1949; reprint, Brussels: Culture et Civilisation, 1969).

# Plenary Address

# Women in the History of Rhetoric: The Past and the Future

CHRISTINE MASON SUTHERLAND

It has generally been assumed that women have played no part in the rhetorical tradition. Assuming for the moment at least that this is true, the first question we must ask, therefore, is simply: what is this rhetorical tradition from which we have been excluded? This question, which perhaps is seldom put by most rhetoricians because they assume that they know, must be asked by those of us who work in this particular field, so as to find out what we can legitimately study and write about. If it is true that for most of its history the rhetorical tradition has ignored women, and that women have for the most part ignored it, then it would appear that there is nothing to write about: that the relation between women and the rhetorical tradition is a blank. If there were indeed nothing, our only course would be to generate a continuous stream of lament for our erasure and silencing. But although there has been a certain amount of well-justified lament, there has been a great deal more that is not lament at all. It seems, therefore, that we have something more than a blank to work with.

In "Reinventing Rhetorical Traditions", his chapter in *Learning from the Histories of Rhetoric*,[1] Thomas Miller suggests that "[t]he rhetorical tradition is a fiction that has just about outlasted its usefulness." According to Miller, "Given the constitution of the canon, one must conclude that for a couple of thousand years the only people who used rhetoric were white male Europeans, a state of affairs that is at odds with our belief that every community uses rhetoric to put shared assumptions and values into social practice" (Miller 26). We must begin, then, by distinguishing between what we mean by the rhetorical tradition and rhetoric itself. Miller suggests that instead of studying the tradition of rhetoric, we need to study "the rhetoric of traditions.... If we adopt this more broadly engaged approach we can begin to make the discursive practices of marginalized traditions a central part of the history of rhetoric" (26). Opening up the tradition in this way apparently beyond the canon of established authority and practice – to what Hans Kellner calls "the unschooled practice of communication"[2] – is of course consistent with the approach of those most highly valued in the tradition itself: Plato defines rhetoric as the art of influencing the mind by words, and includes not only the public but also the private realm. Aristotle defines it as finding the available means of persuasion. Coming closer to the present, Burke identifies rhetoric with persuasion, and persuasion with meaning. Obviously the practice of rhetoric as defined by these giants embraces the whole of humanity, and the whole of time so far as humanity has experienced it. Yet the rhetorical tradition as it has developed over the centuries has carried a much narrower meaning, one which has confined it to the public discourse of men of the ruling classes. Other discourses, it is now often claimed, have been either absolutely excluded or at the very least marginalized. Miller recommends bringing these marginalized discourses into the centre, and this is no bad idea. However, I prefer to think of women in relation to rhetoric as belonging not to a margin but to a matrix: women have been an important – a vitally important– part of the human activity from which the particular rhetorical tradition has sprung. We are anterior to, rather than exiled from, that rhetorical tradition; our part in it has been to feed it, to support it, to enable it. Perhaps this is not enough, but I believe that we can serve our purpose better by acknowledging our ages-long connection with the tradition than by merely resenting our exclusion from it. Nothing will come of nothing: we cannot build upon absence and erasure.

An important reminder here comes from John Tinkler, whose essay in the summer 1987 issue of *Rhetorica* discusses the distinction between *contentio*, which is concerned with judicial rhetoric –

and is, as the word suggests, contentious – and *sermo*, which is not.³ *Sermo* has to do with private or semi-public unofficial discourse. As Tinkler sees it, much of the study of rhetoric has had to do with the theory of forensic practice. *Sermo* has often been ignored – marginalized, we might perhaps say. But *sermo*, too, belongs within rhetoric. Tinkler supports his argument with a quotation from Cicero's *De Officiis*: "*sermo* should find its natural place in social gatherings, in informal discussions, and in intercourse with friends; it should also seek admission at dinners. There are rules for *contentio* laid down by rhetoricians; there are none for *sermo*; and yet I do not know why there should not be" (284). *Sermo*, Tinkler reminds us, was a vitally important part of Renaissance rhetoric: the texts that the humanists imitated belonged to this branch of rhetoric rather than to *contentio*.

Now this kind of discourse has throughout the ages been practised by women: letters, diaries, works of devotion, in written discourse; conversation, story-telling, social exchange of all kinds in spoken. If, as Tinkler claims, *sermo* is a (now) neglected part of the rhetorical tradition, then the inclusion of women's discourse brings the tradition back to its own roots, rather than adding something new and alien. For the vast literature of *sermo* is part of that nourishing matrix to which I have referred, and without which the more formal and public parts of rhetoric might starve. Whether or not they have justified their practice with reference to *sermo*, scholars investigating the relationship of women to the rhetorical tradition have included texts of exactly this kind. To give just one example: *The Book of Margery Kempe*, a work discussed by Cheryl Glenn in *Reclaiming Rhetorica*,[4] was written by a woman so totally outside what we think of as the rhetorical tradition that she could not even read or write English, let alone Latin, and had to dictate her work.

So far as the objects of research are concerned, then, we deal with texts in a very wide range of genres, and can, I think, justify our practice in doing so. But what about the subjective? What about the scholars who study such works, the positions they take and the methods they use? And who are they? Although many of them are women, some are men. Some, both women and men, but by no means all, use feminist methods; others study the texts by more traditional means. Just as there is no specific kind of text or discourse, so there is no particular method that distinguishes those who study women and the rhetorical tradition. And this is as it should be. Here again, I think it is essential to keep the area as wide as possible. No doubt there are some who would like to confine the study to those who are professed feminists. But to do so would be to deplete and impoverish us. As Linda Gordon points out, "[t]here are traditions of female thought, women's culture and female consciousness that are not feminist . . . feminism is . . . a controversial political interpretation and struggle, by no means universal to women."[5] These "traditions of female thought," as they are evinced in texts, are very much part of what we who study women and the rhetorical traditions are concerned with.

Obviously such diversity can soon become confusing. Fortunately, some useful clarification has been provided by Amanda Goldrick-Jones, in an essay published in 1993/4 in the *Proceedings of the Canadian Society for the Study of Rhetoric*.[6] She distinguishes three streams: the first derives from the Neo Aristotelian movement, and is concerned with the recovery of neglected texts and other contributions by women. The second stream comprises mostly composition scholars, and grounds itself in the literature of the ethics of care, most notably represented by Carol Gilligan. This stresses women's (not specifically feminists') methods and practices which are grounded in cooperation rather than competition, which are dialogic and collaborative and resist the adversarial. (Let us note in passing that this kind of discourse belongs with *sermo* rather than with *contentio*.) It is issues of power and powerlessness that inform the third stream, postmodern feminism, that "calls into question how western thought and western rhetorical theory inscribes oppressive power relations" (Goldrick-Jones 32). Scholars in this stream extend the range of rhetorical study to include texts written by men, which are now re-read from a feminist perspective.

There is as yet, then, no consensus among us as to what is the appropriate position to take. Judging by Jane Donawerth's 1990 bibliography, we are now approaching the end of the second decade of the revisionist enterprise of integrating women within the rhetorical tradition.[7] An enormous amount of scholarship has been expended on the subject, but we have not yet established its boundaries.

So much for the past. But what of the future? Where are we going and how shall we get there? Obviously this is an even bigger and more amorphous question than that of where we have been and what we have done. Here I must acknowledge a great debt to Victor Vitanza's *Writing Histories of Rhetoric*,[8] it does not, of course, provide a satisfying answer to every question, but it at least clarifies for us where contemporary debate is situated – what some of these questions are. Obviously I cannot even begin to consider some of the larger issues raised in this important book; but one of the tensions identified in it, one that runs through the various discourses like a unifying thread, is particularly important for us who study women and rhetoric to address. Perhaps Sharon Crowley expresses the dilemma most clearly and fully. I quote from her "Let Me Get This Straight," the first essay in the collection:

> Constructionist historians argue that essentialist historians work backwards from current descriptions of reality, classifying similar but chronologically isolated or culturally diverse activities by means of contemporary categories. To put this another way: essentialist historians use currently privileged narratives to make sense of historical data that otherwise might seem unsavoury, inconsistent or unimportant. This fact accounts for the dominance of the current rhetorical tradition by texts written by males, as well as males' versions of women's lives and work.[9]

So far so bad, we may say; but Crowley goes on to assert, on the next page, "As far as I can see, however, the constructionist program offers no superior guarantee of historical accuracy since it assumes that historical materials are always read through contemporary lenses" (Crowley 16). Our choice, it then seems, is not between a disengaged and dispassionate objectivity and a politically and ideologically committed appropriation of the past: the only choice we have is between either recognizing the prejudiced nature of our scholarship or blinding ourselves to it and asserting naively that we are being objective. But is the situation really as bad as it appears to be? Are we possibly in danger of accepting as true a false polarization of the choices we have? Let us explore the situation a little further.

Postmodernists tell us that objectivity is both impossible and undesirable. But this, surely, is a matter of degree. While acknowledging that we can never be wholly disengaged, we might perhaps at least attempt some kind of disengagement. Rhetoric, after all, includes the art of listening, without predetermining what we are about to hear. What I am going to plead for is a sympathetic listening to the voices of the past – a listening which may well involve reading across the grain of our own preferences and political agendas. This is particularly difficult to do if one is a woman. Women look to the past, hoping to find, needing to find, affirmation, reflections of themselves. They are, many of them, anything but disengaged, dispassionate – and for good reason. Compared with what is known of men, so little is known of women; and inasmuch as they identify with other women, this is a great lack. Women today, whether feminist or merely female, seem to be focusing on their difference from men, not their similarity to them. It has not always been so. Thirty years ago they were chiefly concerned to prove that, aside from one or two irrelevant physical details, they were exactly like men. But the trend has now for some time been the other way; and because many women now think of themselves in this way, they feel cut off from a past that has for the most part not recorded them. Virginia Woolf refers to their quest for their grandmothers.[10] It is not just a question of discovery; it is also a question of recognition – finding, for example, in the seventeenth-century rhetorical theory of Mary Astell exactly that principle of caring, or nurturing, that scholars like Gilligan and Belenky have declared to be typical of women, though not, of course, exclusive to them.

Nevertheless, this search for ourselves is potentially dangerous. And it is especially dangerous to those who have renounced all belief in the possibility of taking a dispassionate, objective stance. The danger is the danger of anachronism: the ignorance of, or disregard for, cultural differences between our time and times past, amounting to cultural appropriation, which, I believe, operates not only in space but also in time. One of these anachronistic practices is identified, for example, by Juliet Fleming in a recent review of a book on Renaissance drama by women.

> Today literature is the domain of the individual; ... But the intellectual economy of early modern England was based on notions of authorship that were collective, aphoristic and non-subjective; excellence in the field of letters was understood, in the first instance, as skilled imitation, and not as the utterance of a distinctive voice. The writing by women that is being recovered from the archive reminds us that Renaissance literature differs from our own, and differs precisely over the question of modern subjectivity and its values. To read early modern women's writing according to the protocols of a liberal feminist search for woman's "oppositional voice" (or where that fails, for the "speaking silence") has its feminist point. But it has yet to give us serious critical purchase on the texts in question.[11]

The problem that Fleming identifies, then, is that of reading literature of the past according to the protocols of the present. To return for a moment to Sharon Crowley's essay, already quoted: "Essentialist historians use currently privileged narratives to make sense of data that might seem unsavoury, inconsistent or unimportant. This fact accounts for the dominance of the current rhetorical canon by texts written by males..." (14). True enough. But we must not disregard the possibility that we too have privileged narratives that equally distort what I will dare to call historical truth. A colleague of mine, for example, found, ironically, that the voice of a medieval woman was silenced, erased, not so much by the patriarchal voices of her own time as by the politically correct voices of ours. I have found similar problems in my own work on seventeenth-century women. Perhaps I can demonstrate most clearly what I mean by the problem of anachronism by going into some detail about how it has affected studies of Mary Astell.

Mary Astell, thinker, writer, educator, and political activist, lived from 1666 to 1731. Her work is important on any terms: hers was a splendid mind. She could, and did, take on any man, philosopher or theologian, John Locke or Francis Atterbury, without fear, and give a good account of herself. Her writing is superb – clear, direct, but fully voiced, conversational, but absolutely eloquent; and her eloquence and intellectual powers were recognized in her own time. Her work was rediscovered early in this century by Florence Smith; Astell scholarship has now been flourishing for some time. Part of her appeal to the twentieth century is that she appears to be an early feminist. It was not long, however, before scholars who studied Mary Astell discovered certain facts about her that puzzled them: progressive though she appeared to be, she was deeply conservative – in politics she was an ardent supporter of the Stuart monarchy; in religion, she was a high church woman. She believed in the divine right of kings. She was bitterly opposed to the Whigs. One of her longest and most important works is motivated by a burning desire to refute John Locke and his – as she saw it – secularist philosophy. This support of the "wrong" side has been immensely distressing and confusing to those women who wish to see in her an early example of their own position. Some scholars have been honest enough to acknowledge what they see as Astell's anomalous position, but there is a dangerous tendency simply to ignore her inconvenient beliefs, or worse still, to misunderstand her – to be unable to hear what she is clearly saying. One of the problems is, I believe, that modern feminism in most of its guises has been associated with liberalism. Since the 1960s there has also been a strong influence from Marxism. Conservatives have usually been seen as the enemy. How could one of the first English feminists have been so misguided as to support the wrong side? Astell's position is especially grievous to such feminists because of her political engagement, for she did not confine herself to works of peaceful scholarship, nor did she write books promoting a quiet devotion for women retired from the world. She was out there, fighting for her political beliefs, engaging in pamphlet warfare – in *contentio* rather than *sermo* –like any man of her time. John Locke, to whom liberals look back as a founder, was her abomination; Charles I, of whom the best that the twentieth century can find to say is that he was misguided, was her hero. And yet she sounds so much like a modern feminist; all her life was devoted to a struggle to win a proper education for women; and "proper" to her meant not only preparation for domestic duties, but also the study of philosophy. Descartes, for example, was on the curriculum for the women's college she tried so hard to establish. Furthermore, she evinced the twentieth-century virtue of solidarity with other women. Unlike another seventeenth-century woman also famous for her writing, Margaret Cavendish, whose ambitions were almost wholly selfish, Astell made common cause with other women, believed in them and worked for them. Her hostility to what we now call the patriarchy is unmistakable: she saw no evidence that women were in any way intellectually or morally inferior to men – quite the reverse, indeed: mothers, she asserts in *A Serious Proposal to the Ladies, Part II*, were properly the instructors of children because fathers set such a bad moral example. Astell was a firm believer in the importance of good ethos, and as far as she was concerned the typical man of her time had a very bad one.[12] And yet Mary Astell was inspired by the past, not the future, by a time when the unmarried woman could lead a useful life in a monastery. She resisted the modern democratic movement with all her might, and supported the failed cause of absolute monarchy. No wonder that our century finds it hard to make sense of her.

The problem, of course, is not hers, but ours. We have bought into the Whig view of history, which believes in progress, and believes, too, that there has been a trend of broadening liberation since the late seventeenth century. But as Joan Kelly established some years ago, at various points in history, an increase in political power for men has been accompanied by a loss of it for women. The aristocratic lady of the Middle Ages had considerable power, sometimes herself owning the land and the service of those who worked on it. The public and private areas in this earlier society were not so firmly distinguished. For the aristocratic lady, indeed, there was very little private life. The changes that began to take place in the fifteenth century increasingly withdrew power from the women of the highest class without doing anything to give more power to the women of the lower classes. "Imbued with the renascent ideas of civic virtue," says Joan Kelly, "humanism was unhappily far more narrow in its views of women than traditional Christian culture had been."[13] This assault upon the power of certain women was accompanied by "a sharp turn towards misogyny" at the end of the fourteenth century (Kelly 71). And the trend continued, and was of course strengthened by Reformation ideals of women which saw them as created wholly for the benefit of men, to be confined to an increasingly limited domestic world. Public and private drew further and further apart; the private was less and less significant and less and less valued. Interestingly, the move towards democracy in fifth century B.C. Athens had comparable effects, as Susan Jarratt and Rory Ong explain in their essay on Aspasia in *Reclaiming Rhetorica*:[14] men gained status and political power while women lost it. The hitherto politically underprivileged men seem to have gained their power at the expense of women. And the same phenomenon recurs at the time of the French Revolution: women were specifically excluded from liberty, equality, and fraternity. Rousseau, one of the fathers of that Revolution, is notorious for having devised for the little girl, Sophie (the counterpart of his typical boy, Emil) an education designed to prepare her only to be a good wife and mother, something for which Mary Wollstonecraft takes issue with him in *A Vindication of the Rights of Woman*.[15]

The reduction of opportunity for women, their enclosure within an increasingly restricted private life, affected not only aristocratic women, but in certain parts of Europe women of the middle classes, too. In an essay published in the journal *Dutch Crossing* in 1995,[16] Marijke Spies points out that the idea that women should be confined to the home was a relatively new one in the early seventeenth century. "Men act in the world, while women do the housekeeping. Traditional as this may seem to us, in Heinsius' time [that is, the early seventeenth century] it was a rather new conception, that was defended for the first time, and very seriously so, by humanists such as Erasmus and Vives. . . . In the Netherlands of the sixteenth century women did normally participate in social and economic life" (10). A contemporary account shows them travelling in public, buying and selling, and generally engaging in the same kind of commercial activity as men. "Given this situation," the essay continues, "you may understand that Heinsius' words – 'that the faithful nature and chaste behaviour of women have the thresholds of their houses as their boundaries' – implied the propounding of a new mode of behaviours" (11). The confinement of women to the domestic sphere did not, in Holland at least, imply that they ought not to be educated. Reformers allowed – indeed, insisted upon – a certain degree of literacy for women, though in England by the early seventeenth century learning among women was not so much encouraged, partly owing to the low view of them held by James I. But even in societies where woman's education was not discouraged, there was no suggestion that her educational powers ought to be put to public use: they were for the benefit of her husband and children only. If education made her a better wife and mother, then education was to be promoted. But let her not think that she might have any influence outside the home. Even her spirituality was subsumed under that of her husband: as Milton put it, in discussing Adam and Eve: "He for God only,/She for God in him."[17]

The trends in the seventeenth century, which brought about great political changes for the benefit of men, seem to have done nothing to enfranchise women: quite the reverse. We should not assume, therefore, that in supporting the Tories rather than the Whigs, Mary Astell was inconsistent with her own ideals and best interests. As she herself contends, the position of women in the Middle Ages was in some respects superior. In the Protestant, and increasingly secular, world of the late-seventeenth and eighteenth centuries, women had been demoted to the position of mere supporters of their husbands; and if they had no husbands, they had little social usefulness of any kind. There were no doubt more literate women at this time, but there was little opportunity for them to put their literacy to public use. Opportunities for scholarship that had been available to medieval nuns were simply not open to Mary Astell and other talented women of her time. Of course she looked back with regret and nostalgia to a time when provision had been made for women like herself.

In assuming that the development of democracy implies and finally entails the liberation of women, therefore, we as twentieth-century women may be deceived. To us it often seems that the emancipation of women was a necessary, a logical, progression from the liberation of men of the lower economic classes. But in fact, historically, democracy has often been inimical to women. Mary Astell's hostility to the new situation is more consistent than it appears to us.

Our mistaken assumption about political liberalism as helping to free women is just one example of the way in which we can misunderstand the past. Another, more subtle, but just as dangerous, is suggested in the review by Juliet Fleming from which I quoted earlier. It concerns our post-romantic idea that what everyone, women included, wants is recognition of our selves: fame, power, all that is implied in heroic individualism. Too often we assume that the motivation of any woman writer of the past was to be heard: to raise her own voice, to be listened to, to be taken seriously, for herself. It is true that there have been women in the past who did want just that. I have already mentioned Margaret Cavendish as being one of them: she prized her singularity; she wanted to be remembered for herself. But Margaret Cavendish is in most ways anomalous in her own time. The twentieth century, I believe, understands her better than the seventeenth did. Mary Astell, however, and many other seventeenth-century women were very differently motivated. For most of them, I would contend, the motivation for writing was not to have their voices heard; it was not recognition of themselves as individuals; it was not even the quest for personal freedom for its own sake. It was the desire to serve.

This point is most clearly set forth by Lynette Hunter in the introduction to her (as yet unpublished) transcription of the letters of Dorothy Moore.[18] Some of these letters document the plea of a seventeenth-century English woman who lived much earlier than Astell to be allowed some public function in the church. Her correspondent was Dr. André Rivet, an eminent Dutch theologian (Moore was living in the Netherlands at the time), who was well-known to that great seventeenth-century scholar, Anna Maria Van Schurman. Dorothy Moore was also a highly talented scholar, a gifted linguist and teacher. Her letters show her to be deeply concerned to make a strong public contribution to the good of the world, in particular, the church. Dr. Rivet has bought into the new ideas of confining women's activities to the home. Moore challenges him, bringing to bear arguments that he is unable to answer. Moore is not looking for personal recognition, for promotion, for political power. But she feels keenly the importance of not wasting her talents.

That this kind of compulsion lay heavily upon certain talented people of the seventeenth century we may deduce from Milton's sonnet on his blindness, where he complains of his inability to do the great work to which he has been called. What he laments here is not the loss of personal power and honour (to which he refers in *Lycidas* as "that last infirmity of noble mind")[19] but rather a circumstantial inability to do the work to which he feels called. Significantly, he refers to the parable of the talents, recorded in the Gospel according to Matthew: "That one talent which is death to hide,/ Lodged with me useless..."[20] The servant with one talent who kept it safely wrapped up in a napkin has it taken from him and is cast into outer darkness (Matt. 25:30). Responsibility to use one's talents for the public good was taken very seriously not only by men such as Milton, but also by women such as Dorothy Moore and Mary Astell. "Our Faculties were given us for Use, not Ostentation," says Astell in *A Serious Proposal*, "not to make a noise in the world but to be serviceable in it."[21] Nor did this serviceableness confine itself to private life: "The true Christian," asserts Astell in *The Christian Religion*, is concerned to practise "Vertues of a public, not a private nature" (353). And this was certainly Astell's practice: it is true that she held that women had no business preaching or engaging in legal practice in the law courts; but although they might not raise their voices in public, they could certainly contribute to the political debate in print. Indeed, for women such as Astell writing was a means of influencing their world for good while at the same time preserving a valued anonymity. Dorothy Moore rejects mere self-promotion. The advice she seeks from Dr. Rivet – and again I quote Lynette Hunter – concerns how women can "act modestly in public for the good of the body as a whole. Not to act as a member or in public service, is to act privately for personal advantage."[22] Similarly, Astell is seeking not to make herself famous but to do good in the world.

Behind this compulsion to use what one had been given lay a model of community life which again is very different from our own. Our own ideas are strongly conditioned by ideals of equality, a kind of political levelling that standardizes each of us in relation to the body politic. For Dorothy Moore and Mary Astell, the model was very different, informed by an ideal not of equality but of hierarchy. Freedom and fulfillment consisted in finding one's own unique place in the great chain of being, and of serving in it. To quote again from Lynette Hunter's introduction:

> Moore's use of the word "service" recalls a world view without "servants" as paid workers . . . . A late feudal structure would have depended upon the notion of "service" as a set of practices that paid respect to people to be honoured. Enacting various services also conferred honour on the practitioner. . . . Service was something one did for others in one's community; it was not a menial or humiliating action for which one had to be paid. (8)

Moore's and Astell's aspiration was thus to serve their fellows in the world, and in doing so to serve God.

How easily and how disastrously it is possible to misunderstand Astell's position is best illustrated with reference to her *Some Reflections Upon Marriage*, first published in 1700.[23] Mary Astell has come to our attention in the twentieth century primarily as a feminist: but in her own time, and in her own view (although it was certainly *A Serious Proposal to the Ladies* which established her reputation), her work went far beyond a defence of women and a plea for their education. True to her vision of being of service – of public service – in the world, Astell wrote political tracts and engaged in pamphlet warfare. Within the last few years, this aspect of her importance has been recognized by Patricia Springborg,[24] who has identified her as the first systematic critic of the political philosophy of Locke. Springborg reminds us that it is difficult, if not impossible, in dealing with seventeenth-century writers, to separate their philosophical principles from their religious convictions and their politics. I quote, in part, from Springborg's article of 1995: "Astell correctly saw that Locke's political philosophy was inextricable from his psychological and theological systems, addressing all three in works that were political, theological and homiletic" (621). The point I wish to make is that for Astell these various strands cannot be disentangled: each implies the others. Since for Astell politics and feminism are fundamentally connected, it is natural that she should incorporate politics within her feminist tracts, and use political analogies to demonstrate the injustice being done to women.

This is what she does in *Reflections Upon Marriage*. The work was originally published in 1700 as *Some Reflections Upon Marriage*, with a second edition in 1703. In the third edition of 1706, the title was changed to *Reflections Upon Marriage*, and a long preface was added. In this new preface, Astell addresses the criticism that the first edition of the work had received. Here Astell identifies the enemy with the Whig position. Indeed, Patricia Springborg believes that her prime object here is to attack Whig politics, using the analogy of the family as "a subversive stratagem" (621). How inconsistent it is, argues Astell, to proclaim political liberty while promoting domestic tyranny:

> [I]f absolute sovereignty be not necessary in a State, how comes it to be so in a family? or if in a Family, why not in a state; since no Reason can be alledg'd for the one that will not hold more strongly for the other? If the Authority of the Husband so far as it extends, is sacred and inviolable, why not of the Prince? (*Reflections* 17)

Now this is all very well; but as Hilda Smith has pointed out, what happens if we turn Astell's arguments back upon herself?[25] If absolute sovereignty is necessary in a state, is it not also necessary in a family? Astonishingly, Astell's answer is a firm yes. She believes not only in the divine right of kings but also in the divine right of husbands. And this in spite of all the ills and woes of wives that she spends so much time addressing, especially in this particular work. Nowhere is the tension between twentieth-century feminist views and those of Astell so apparent as here. It seems to our age that she is being outrageously inconsistent. Yet her own position was logically argued from her premises.

In some respects, Mary Astell was an Enlightenment rationalist. Certainly she was firmly on the rationalist side in the seventeenth-century dispute between rationalism and empiricism. But although in many ways she followed the rationality of Descartes, she was on the whole closer to that of Pascal, whom she also greatly admired. Let me explain. In referring to Pascal's theory of the three orders, A.J. Krailsheimer states: "The concept stemmed originally from mathematics . . . Just as lines, squares and cubes cannot be added together as being of different orders, so in the realm of human knowledge that which is proper to the body (the senses), the mind (the reason) and to the heart are of different orders and must be carefully distinguished if error is to be avoided."[26] Astell's address to this question of the grounding of human knowledge is not identical with Pascal's, but it does depend on making the same sort of distinction. Here is what Astell says about it in *A Serious Proposal to the Ladies, Part II*:

> There is not such a difference between Faith and Science as is usually suppos'd. The difference consists not in the Certainty but in the way of Proof; the Objects of Faith are as Rationally and Firmly Prov'd as the Objects of Science, tho by another way. As Science Demonstrates things that are Seen, so Faith is the Evidence of such as are Not Seen. And he who rejects the Evidence of Faith in such things as belong to its Cognizance, is as unreasonable as he who denies Propositions in Geometry that are prov'd with Mathematical exactness. (79)

So far as faith and moral behaviour are concerned, Astell's authority is the Bible. The premises from which she argues, therefore, are all drawn from the authority of Scripture. Her feminism, far from being at odds with Biblical revelation, is deduced from it. To return, then, to our question: how can Astell assert the intellectual and moral equality of women and yet support the authority of husbands?

Because marriage, in her view, comes under the domain of morals, her authority here is the Bible: "The Christian Institution of Marriage provides the best that may be for Domestic Quiet and Content, and for the Education of Children" (*Reflections* 37). However, although she is here drawing upon revelation rather than reason as her authority, Astell goes on to assert that the institution of marriage is entirely consistent with rational principles: "if we were not under the tie of religion, even the Good of Society and civil Duty would oblige us to what that requires at our hands" (36). Just as authority within the body politic is vested in the monarch (and let us remember that at the time Astell was preparing her second edition of this work the monarch was female) so within marriage authority is vested in the husband. Here again, what is enjoined by revelation is corroborated by reason:

> Nor can there be any Society great or little, from Empires down to private Families, without a last Resort, to determine the Affairs of that Society by an irresistible Sentence. Now unless this Supremacy be fix'd somewhere, there will be a perpetual Contention about it, such is the love of Dominion.... So that since Women are acknowledg'd to have least Bodily strength their being commanded to obey is in pure kindness to them, and for their Quiet and Security, as well as for the Exercise of their Vertue. (48)

The problem for Astell lies not in the divinely established authority of the husband (or the monarch), but in the unethical practices of those who fill such positions of authority. "She who elects a Monarch for Life, who gives him an Authority she cannot recall, however he misapply it . . . had need to be very sure that she does not make a Fool her Head, nor a Vicious Man her Guide and Pattern" (56). Consistently throughout the work she draws the analogy between public and private, insisting that the same standards be used for each sphere: "Nor will it ever be well either with those who Rule or those in Subjection, even from the Throne to every Private Family, till those in Authority look on themselves as plac'd in that Station for the good and improvement of their Subjects, and not for their own sakes" (57). And again, "He who shou'd say the People were made for the Prince who is set over them, wou'd be thought to be out of his Senses as well as his Politicks" (57).

It is her practice of thus using the same standards for both the public and private sphere that has led a modern feminist to assert that Astell subsumes the whole question of marriage under that of the subordination of women in general to men in general.[27] But this is a mistake: Astell goes to considerable trouble to detach the issue of wives' obedience to their husbands from that of the general subordination of women as a sex. For the one she believes there is unmistakable authority in Scripture; for the other, none. Even St. Paul, that bugbear of so many feminists, she exonerates from the charge of wishing to subjugate women to men. Here is, in part, what she says about his position:

> But scripture commands wives to submit themselves to their own husbands; True, for which St Paul gives a mystical reason (Eph. 5.22 etc.) and St Peter a Prudential and Charitable one (I St. Peter 3) but neither of them derive that subjection from the Law of Nature. Nay, St Paul, as if he foresaw and meant to prevent this Plea, giving Directions for their Conduct to Women in general (I Tim. 2), when he comes to speak of Subjection, he changes his Phrase from Women, which denotes the whole Sex, to Woman, which in the New Testament is appropriated to a Wife. (*Reflections* 20)

Much of what Astell has to say on this question of the subordination of women in general is to be found in the new Preface to the 1706 edition of *Reflections*. Here she takes issue with William Nicholls' book, *The Duties of Inferiors towards their Superiors in Five Practical Discourses*, in particular Part IV, "The Duty of Wives to their Husbands," a work published in 1701, a year later than her original edition.[28] What she objects to is not the duty but the inferiority. And she makes an important distinction between the fact of subjection and its legitimation.

"That the Custome of the World has put Women, generally speaking, into a State of Subjection, is not deny'd; but the Right can no more be prov'd from the Fact, than the Predominancy of Vice can justifie it" (*Reflections* 10). Nor does subjection in terms of power imply anything about capability. "Does it follow that Domestic Governors have more Sense than their Subjects, any more than that other Governors have? We do not find that any Man thinks the worse of his own Understanding because another has superior Power, or conclude himself less capable of a Post of Honour and Authority because he is not Prefer'd to it" (16). She then examines the scriptural evidence and shows that the injunction to wives to obey their husbands does not imply the inferiority of women in general to men in general. Citing St. Paul in I Cor. 11, she asserts: "No inequality can be inferred . . . [from his words] 'the Head of every Man is Christ and the Head of the Woman is the Man, and Head of Christ is God.' It being evident . . . that there is no natural Inferiority among the Divine Persons, but that they are in all things coequal" (p.11).

The question at issue, then, is not whether women should or should not be subjected to their husbands but whether that subjection is based upon a natural inferiority, or is simply a matter of designated authority; and whether women as a sex are inferior to, and ought therefore to be subjugated by, men as a sex. Granting the authority of husbands, she is nonetheless concerned to refute the claim of the Protestant reformers that women were created simply to serve men. Not so, she says; women were made to serve God:

> [T]is certainly no arrogance in a Woman to conclude that she was made for the Service of God, and that this is her End. Because God made all Things for Himself, and a Rational Mind is too noble a Being to be made for the Sake and Service of any Creature. The Service she at any time becomes oblig'd to pay a Man, is only a Business by the Bye. Just as it may be any Man's Business and Duty to keep Hogs; he was not made for this, but if he hires himself out to such an Employment, he ought conscientiously to perform it. (11)

We see, then, how the world view of our own time can come between us and a clear understanding of Mary Astell's work. As Patricia Springborg has said, the thought of the time did not distinguish clearly between philosophy and politics, nor between political philosophy and religion. When she is defending women's rationality, vigorously denying their supposed inferiority, and declaring their fitness to engage in works of public virtue, Astell sounds very much like a twentieth-century feminist: "If all men are born free, how is it that all women are born slaves?" she asks (18). As they are, if they are born merely to serve men. But for all that, the degree of autonomy she demands for women is conditioned by Biblical authority.

What conclusions may we draw from this example? So far as Mary Astell is concerned, we have to draw the conclusion that in many important respects she does not share the assumptions and values of feminists today, nor does she argue from the same premises. She grounds her arguments not only in reason but also, and predominantly, in revelation. The premises she uses are not those of political liberalism and individualism; her aim in liberating women from what she calls slavery is not that they may enjoy the pleasures of freedom, but that they may do their duty in serving God and the public community. True, she does not advocate public speaking for women; but she shows by her own example that women can and should take advantage of the anonymity of print to promote the public good. She herself did so. She wrote a number of pamphlets addressing, from the conservative point of view, important political issues of her time. Although she looked nostalgically back to the past for some of her ideals, she was nevertheless fully engaged in the present. In her longer works, she systematically provided a critique of Locke's philosophy that is being taken seriously today. We have to see Astell's feminism as part of that call to do good in the world which was so important to her. She fought to have a good academic education provided for women not only so that they might lead happier lives, and not primarily because she believed in their right to it, but because without it they could not fulfill the destinies of the fully reasonable beings that she held that they were. Her views on feminism, as on politics, were based on a world view radically different from ours in that it was grounded in a holistic set of ideas that included not only philosophy but also religion in its address to politics. Our own age sees the feminism, and connects with some of Astell's delicious satire on the patriarchy. But the very modern sound of some of this criticism leads us astray, and encourages us to assume that she shared all our values.

Where does this leave us? What I have been attempting here is to escape from the bias of our own time, an attempt that some contemporary historians of rhetoric may well see as ill-judged, and in the end not possible. To some extent I have to agree with them. I do not dare to claim that mine is a wholly disengaged and objective view: that somehow I have gained access to the whole truth about Mary Astell's feminism. No doubt I, like everyone else, am to some extent blinded by my own preferences and prejudices. But the important phrase is "to some extent." Without claiming for ourselves the possibility of what Donna Haraway calls the "god trick of seeing everything from nowhere"[29] – we can nonetheless at least attempt to listen with sympathetic understanding to positions very different from our own. What I am pleading for is a balance, the avoidance of two dangerous extremes. It is true that we can disconnect ourselves too radically from the past: recognizing the different values and assumptions of women such as Moore and Astell, we can take the position that they have nothing useful to say to us. To take this antiquarian approach is to cut ourselves off from the past, which is essentially the same thing as forgetting it, and therefore, perhaps, being condemned to repeat it – like Vladimir and Estragon in *Waiting for Godot*,[30] who must keep repeating the past because they cannot remember it. But it is the other extreme which I have addressed here: that of accepting and even celebrating our own bias: of using the writers of the past for our own purposes without regard for their own positions, the premises from which they argued and the conclusions which they drew. As I have tried to show, this too is disastrous: if it is really true that we see only what we have already decided to see, if our ideology entirely drives and determines our interpretation, if we are finally capable of nothing more than seeing the reflections of our own images and hearing the echoes of our own voices, then rhetoric has no point and humanity no hope: we are trapped inside ourselves. But I do not believe it. I still believe in the possibility of learning from the past, of using it, as Robert Connors says, "to make the world a better place,"[31] to promote good in our present without doing the past the injustice of misunderstanding and misrepresenting it.

And if this approach is to be recommended for all historians of rhetoric, it is particularly appropriate for women: we perhaps, more than others, need to find our roots in the past – to validate ourselves by discovering our own history; but also, according to some of our own theorists, we have as women a particular commitment to treat others with sympathy and understanding — to see the person, not just the position, to practise connected knowing. Surely this concern to treat others with justice and compassion can be, and must be, extended to the figures of the past.

## *NOTES*

1. Thomas P. Miller, "Reinventing Rhetorical Traditions" in *Learning from the Histories of Rhetoric: Essays in Honor of Winifred Bryan Horner*, ed. Theresa Enos (Carbondale and Edwardsville: Southern Illinois University Press, 1993), 26–41, p. 26.
2. Hans Kellner, "After the Fall," in *Writing Histories of Rhetoric*, ed. Victor J. Vitanza (Carbondale and Edwardsville: Southern Illinois University Press, 1994), 20–37, p. 23.
3. John F. Tinkler, "Renaissance Humanism and the genera eloquentiae," *Rhetorica*, 5, no. 3 (1987): 279–309.
4. Cheryl Glenn, "Re-examining the Book of Margery Kempe: A Rhetoric of Autobiography," in *Reclaiming Rhetorica: Women in the Rhetorical Tradition,* ed. Andrea A. Lunsford (Pittsburgh and London: University of Pittsburgh Press, 1995), 53–71.
5. Linda Gordon, "What's New in Women's History," in *Feminist Studies/Critical Studies*, ed. Teresa de Laurentis (Bloomington: Indiana University Press, 1986), 20–30, p. 30.
6. Amanda Goldrick-Jones, "Feminist (Re)Views and Re-visions of Classical Rhetoric," *Proceedings of the Canadian Society for the Study of Rhetoric,* 5 (1993–94), ed. Albert W. Halsall, 25–40.
7. Jane Donawerth, "Bibliography of Women and the History of Rhetorical Theory to 1900," *Rhetoric Society Quarterly,* 20, no. 4 (Fall 1990), 403–421.
8. See note 2 above.
9. Sharon Crowley, "Let Me Get This Straight," in *Writing Histories of Rhetoric,* 1–19, p. 14.
10. Virginia Woolf, *A Room of One's Own* (London: Penguin, 1928).
11. Juliet Fleming, "Absent Elizabethans," review of *Renaissance Drama By Women,* eds. S.P. Cerasano and Marion Wynne-Davies, *The Times Literary Supplement,* 23 August 1996, 12.
12. Mary Astell, *A Serious Proposal to the Ladies, Part II* (London: Rich Wilkin, 1697), 210.
13. Joan Kelly, *Women, History, and Theory* (Chicago and London: University of Chicago Press, 1984), 70.
14. Susan Jarratt and Rory Ong, "Aspasia: Rhetoric, Gender, and Colonial Ideology," in *Reclaiming Rhetorica: Women in the Rhetorical Tradition,* 9–24.

15. Mary Wollstonecraft, *A Vindication of the Rights of Woman* (1792: reprint, London: Penguin, 1992), 107ff.
16. Marijke Spies, "Women and Seventeenth-Century Dutch Literature," *Dutch Crossing*, 19, no. 1 (1995), 3–23.
17. John Milton, "Paradise Lost" Book IV, in *The Poetical Works of John Milton*, ed. H.C. Beeching (London: Oxford University Press, 1938), 173–448, p. 254.
18. Lynette Hunter, Introduction to *The Letters of Dorothy Moore*, unpublished manuscript.
19. Milton, "Lycidas," in *The Poetical Works of John Milton*, 38-42, p. 39, l. 71.
20. Milton, "To Mr Cyriack Skinner upon his Blindness," in *The Poetical Works of John Milton*, 85.
21. Mary Astell, *A Serious Proposal*, 62.
22. Hunter, 15.
23. Mary Astell, "Reflections Upon Marriage," in *Astell: Political Writings*, ed. Patricia Springborg (Cambridge: Cambridge University Press, 1996), 1–80.
24. Patricia Springborg, "Mary Astell (1666–1731), Critic of Locke," *American Political Science Review*, 89, no. 3 (September 1995), 621–633.
25. Hilda Smith, *Reason's Disciples: Seventeenth-Century English Feminists* (Urbana: University of Chicago Press, 1982), 118.
26. A.J. Krailsheimer, Introduction to *Pascal: Pensées* (London: Penguin, 1966), 22.
27. Smith, 135.
28. This work is cited in a note in Springborg, *Astell: Political Writings*, 9.
29. Donna Haraway, "Situated Knowledges," *Feminist Studies*, 14, no. 3 (Fall 1988), 575–599.
30. Samuel Beckett, *Waiting for Godot* (London: Faber and Faber, 1955).
31. Robert Connors, quoted in Sharon Crowley, "Let Me Get This Straight," in *Writing Histories of Rhetoric*, 1–19, p. 5.

# GROUP 1

# Excluded from the Rhetorical Tradition

# Plato's Women: Alternative Embodiments of Rhetoric

C. JAN SWEARINGEN

## Historiographical Headaches and Their Remedies

Persistent claimants assert that rhetoric is an historically male shop and that women cannot be added to it without distorting the integrity of the field beyond repair. The only study of women in the history of rhetoric, according to this view, is the study of their exclusion and suppression. Anything more will alter the very domain of rhetoric, which by definition has excluded women from training and practice. Others have argued on very different grounds – from post-feminist and postmodern positions – that women should not be added in to the history of rhetoric because history in general and the history of rhetoric in particular are based on a linear, male, venerate-the-great-ones model that feminists, as proponents of egalitarian, collective and collaborative modes of knowing, speaking, and writing, should want to repudiate. Though surely without intending to, post-feminist and postmodern positions amplify conservative warnings that to add women to rhetoric – for whatever reason and in whatever way – will alter the domain of the field of rhetoric, as revisionist history always does. So, do we close up shop? I think not.

Friskily surmounting theoretical impasses and other large obstacles, the project of feminist historiography in rhetoric has begun to diversify and shift the question, despite formidable protests, from *whether* women should be added to the history of rhetoric to *how* and *on what grounds* they should be recuperated and examined in different periods, and as a part of the ongoing definition of different rhetorical and literary genres. Do medieval women mystics, for example, belong in the study of medieval *poetria nova* or the study of preaching? Perhaps both. Should the tropes used by Sojourner Truth be examined as instances of the universality of rhetorical tropes in all human discourses, or as examples of oral instruction in rhetorical practices? Yes, both. When the history of a field is changed, its definition and subjects change – all to the better. Redefining both the domain and the definition of rhetoric, then, is and should be a goal of feminist historiography.

Lack of evidence, a common roadblock to studies of women in the ancient Near East, is not in the end a conclusive argument against the projects of recuperation and reinterpretation. As was said of the O.J. Simpson trial, absence of evidence is not evidence of absence. The same thing holds true of Diotima and Aspasia, indeed of any woman – or man – whose shade is glimpsed amidst the fragmentary papyri, shards, and distorted (by modern standards) literary-mythic histories of antiquity. Very exciting and sometimes troubling discussions are emerging among various formulations of feminist historiographies of rhetoric. For example, is any study of women or of a woman in the history of rhetoric a feminist project? Who defines that? *Should* we repudiate a heroine-list in the history of rhetoric? That discussion is by no means over. Why is it increasingly charged that looking at individual figures and practices of rhetoric, without concentrating on the historiographical problematics of such studies, constitutes "naive" history? Isn't it equally naive to ignore the long-standing teaching of history, *within* rhetoric, as *inevitably* revisionist and rhetorical? If this line of argument continues will we not end up in a position oddly like the arch-conservative philologist's – that all we can say is how it is we know that we cannot and should not know the history of figures or practices in the past? Asserting the absence of evidence is not evidence of absence – to borrow a chiasmus once again. Of special value to reappraisals of Diotima and Aspasia, a number of new methods and interpretive strategies have begun to amplify the methods we have for reconstructing the lives and experience of women in the ancient Near East and Greece.[1] In her recent translation and commentary on the *Homeric Hymn to Demeter*, Helene Foley observes that although there is no solid evidence that at one time women were the sole celebrants in Demeter cults, there is also no evidence to the contrary.[2] This proviso informs many recent reinterpretations of possible and probable roles held by women in ancient Near Eastern cultures. More precisely defined questions have been developed concerning social roles, identity, and status; the boundaries dividing public from private roles; and the difficulty of distinguishing political from religious leadership roles and discourses during the archaic and early classical periods. Foley's reappraisal of the Hymn to Demeter joins the recent work of Elaine Fantham and her colleagues scrutinizing the close links between Eleusinian and other rituals performed by women and the typical prominence of women in both wedding and funeral rituals that share – as Sappho's work reminds us – so many ceremonial images and lyrics. Examining the same period, Tikva Frymer-Kensky's study of women depicted in the Hebrew scriptures posits that although no solid or final proof may exist of women's roles different than those posited by longstanding Biblical scholarly traditions, a revisionist consensus now emphasizes that the evidence for the traditional views is equally unfounded and that the lack of firm evidence for either position is evidence of patriarchal bias in classical and Biblical scholarship. Absence of evidence is not evidence of the absence of women in antiquity.

Numerous parallels are emerging between feminist Biblical and Classical studies of the roles of women in the ancient Near East. Frymer-Kensky reviews archaeological reinterpretations of Israelite culture in the pre-monarchal era[3] that closely examine textual alongside archaeological evidence of women's prominence as religious leaders in such key cases as the songs of Miriam and Deborah, particularly Deborah's role as judge. New Testament counterparts include the prophetic speech portrayed in Mary's Magnificat, and Paul's representations of women leaders in the early churches.[4] The substantial overlap of women's roles in political and religious leadership, and objections to their presence, is taken up repeatedly in Greek drama; rebukes of strong-speaking women and of women's speech in inappropriate places are key themes in the *Antigone*,

*Hippolytus*, *Bacchae*, and *Agamemnon*, among other dramatic works. Research increasingly rejects the notion that women did not play public or ceremonial roles in the ancient world, and thereby leads to a reconsideration of how what they spoke can be examined rhetorically.[5] The wide range of topics developed in these studies provides an illuminating backdrop for the examination of Plato's dramatizations of Diotima's and Aspasia's speeches.

Contemporary feminist scholars are working on a functional and stylistic redefinition of rhetoric, such that the discourses of women past and present may be seen as rhetorical in some, and in some cases all, important senses of that definition.[6] Several studies of Aspasia, who is the "teacher of rhetoric" to Socrates in Plato's *Menexenos*, develop an analysis of her as an image of rhetoric in antiquity and in later times. The often-rebuked speech and public presence of Antigone and other female literary figures who speak politically and in public settings, including law courts, provide additional objects of analysis.

The broadest area of inquiry returns to the issue of women's prominence in mourning and religious rituals throughout the ancient Near East and examines the sequence of development in proto-rhetorical genres.[7] In the earlier stages of this sequence there has still been very little comparison of the texts and settings of funerary mourning and wedding songs composed and performed by women, with the earliest epitaphia.[8] Sappho's wedding and funeral songs, Aspasia's epitaphia in the *Menexenos*, Antigone's pleading for her brother's burial – and the recorded rebukes of these speeches – deserve much further study as evidence that women who once spoke were being silenced. For what reasons, in a number of places and periods, did such public women's roles become suppressed or sequestered as they did in Athens with laws forbidding women to mourn in public? How do women's funeral songs resemble or not resemble the earliest epitaphia?

To what extent is the marginalization of women's rhetorical roles a product of scholarly traditions and prejudices, some of it quite recent? That question returns us to the present. When the claim is made that what women do is not rhetoric because women have always been excluded from rhetoric, by its very nature and by its very territorial male practitioners, what is, or should be, the first line of rebuttal? We have already begun to dissolve the claim that "there weren't any." Let us now begin to scrutinize the corollary lines of exclusion: they weren't any good; and, if they were any good they were patronized or appropriated – in all of the ugly senses – by men. Otherwise, or so the story goes, they would never have been permitted to speak at all. How could they have gotten away with it? The question might now become: What on earth led them to practice an art for which they knew they would be rebuked and for which some, like Hypatia, were dismembered? Let us now begin to ask not why it is that women do not argue, why they are not agonistic, but what it is that happens to them when they are.

## *Aspasia's Forgery/Aspasia Forged: The Ethics of Historical Representation*

Having attempted to dispel, however momentarily, the widely held belief that the rhetorical women of antiquity are textual chimeras, jokes, or at best fictions, while the men of antiquity are not, I turn to an all-too-brief treatment of how we might approach representations of Aspasia in the classical period as something other than jokes on rhetoric and clear-cut attempts to denigrate Pericles. In addition to recovering information about the oral genres practiced by women in Greek and ancient Near Eastern antiquity, the study of Aspasia and others like her – teachers, symposiasts, authors as well as celebrants of poems and songs at births, weddings, and funerals – helps correct the ideas, rather recent in origin, that women were entirely sequestered in ancient cultures and that they were neither educated nor educators.

Between the seventh and fifth centuries B.C.E., chronological, cultural, and genre boundaries increasingly segregated the forms and practices of ritual funeral songs and processionals – traditionally performed and led by women – from the requisite state epitaphia – always composed and performed by men. Aspasia's shade lingers in this boundary, in a margin made even more complex by her status within Athens: a stranger, a non-citizen, and a female sophist presiding in a famous – or infamous – salon. Her representations in literature by historians, comic poets, Plato, and Cicero range from bawdy mockery to serious praise. In the *Menexenos* she is charged with forgery as the ghostwriter of Pericles' famed funeral oration. In the same dialogue, Socrates creates a second image of her that bears a more ambiguous import: the declaration that she taught him everything he knows about rhetoric. Cicero reports that her speech in the *Menexenos* was so highly regarded in his day that it was recited each year in Athens.

Charged with forgery, Aspasia is herself forged, represented, and recorded only in highly rhetorical chiaroscuro depictions.[9] Although we see her through a glass darkly, it cannot be said that we see her not at all. It is her voice, and not someone else's in the *Menexenos* that speaks through Socrates – and ultimately Plato – in a humorous counterpoint, and counterpart, to Pericles' famed epitaphios. Pericles, we seldom pause to note, speaks only through Thucydides. Many literary representations of Aspasia's shady seductive character seem to be written with a sidelong glance at Pericles and at rhetoric itself. Like gorgeous "Gorgias," who is also after all a literary artifice, "Aspasia" may refer to the growing Athenian suspicion that rhetoric as practiced by mysterious strangers beguiles and betrays its listeners. Yet "Aspasia" refers as well to an individual historical woman of whom we have many and varied reports, and to a figure who functions as a stand-in for generally held attitudes – most of them derisive – about educated women in the public sphere. To look upon the figure of Aspasia is to look upon the growing distaste the Athenians harbored toward Pericles' foreign imports, including the sophists, Aspasia herself, and rhetoric.

Two lines of interpretation of Aspasia's epitaphios in the *Menexenos* have been advanced in recent criticism: that it is a forgery crafted by Plato as a mockery of rhetoric, and alternatively that it is a representative and even exemplary piece of fifth-century sophistic rhetoric. Those critics who contend that Aspasia and her speech are merely literary and just a joke comprise two groups whose views are rarely consonant: traditional philologists[10] and postmodern feminist critics.[11] Critics who take the speech seriously as a sample of the rhetorical arts taught by the sophists focus on several elements in its composition: the metaphors of land, national identity, blood, birth, and soil through which Athenians are deemed true born, sons of Athens and Athena rather than of their birth parents. These readings of Aspasia's speech and roles, however, function reductively to dismiss serious importance or meaningful understanding.

Let us ask a slightly different question. What ethics of historical representation and of history-telling are at work in Pericles' and Aspasia's speeches, in epitaphic oratory more generally, and in the writers of the histories – Thucydides, Plato – in which we receive our only records of Pericles' and Aspasia's speeches? What ethical purposes, for example, might guide Plato's representation of Aspasia and her speech, including its delivery by Socrates? "The good," praise of valor as a guide for future actions, is explicitly defined in both speeches as a purpose of the ceremony and invites examination alongside similar practices of epitaphic and epideictic rhetorical histories today. What ethical purposes guide contemporary critics who interpret classical materials with two different goals: to emphasize that woman and rhetoric were alike victimized and demeaned in antiquity, and to redeem sophistic rhetoric as recorded in the representations of Plato, including his depiction of Aspasia?[12]

Plato's representations of Aspasia and Diotima as accomplished speakers and teachers can be viewed as reflections of the ritual and religious traditions from which he adapted many of his philosophical terms, and in which women were celebrants and practitioners. His depictions are less harsh and more god-honouring – in the case of Diotima – than those of many of his contemporaries. Yet his representations have often been interpreted solely as misogynist extensions of the rebukes directed at women – especially strong-speaking women – in the literature of the sixth and fifth centuries.[13] And there is more, after all, than Plato's representation to guide our interpretation of Aspasia. Plutarch reports that Aspasia was an associate of Protagoras in the mid-fifth century and was known as a student and colleague of Anaxagoras. Their relationship, frequently reported in classical histories, implicates Aspasia in Anaxagoras' crime of impiety through guilt by association, but in so doing proves an association between a woman and a philosopher – a relationship whose very possibility has often been scoffed at.

In the argot of the time it was one thing for the poets to lie – that's entertainment and art. But for the sophists to teach openly an art of distorting history was quite another matter. Eric Havelock's characterization of this similarity remains a provocative point of debate: "The sophists mistakenly sought to retain for oratory the magical spell cast by the epic poets."[14] The practice of rhetorical history within epitaphia – the practice allegedly taught by Aspasia – was licensed, I suggest, by a psychology consonant with Anaxagoras' view that there is neither coming-into-being nor passing away; neither birth nor death; only change, mixing, and separating. In the case of words, and rhetorical histories, there are *many* versions of the *same* thing, each of them true – probabilistically, contingently, in its own way, in its own time. It is through the vehicle of rhetorical history – a forgery? and a forging – that Aspasia herself characterizes epitaphia and her own epitaphios. And it is through Plato's equally rhetorical portrait of her speech that we receive our most ample, if ambiguous, portraits of what she said and of how she taught. Although nothing Plato writes can be taken at face value, it is without precedent for him to refer to something that was not there at all. It is a very deep irony indeed that shrouds the tone of Plato's depiction of Aspasia: foreigner in Athens, yet creator of a speech that praises the Athenians' differences from and superiority to all other states and races; woman and teacher in a male political domain whose mythology and history by her own crafting made the men of Athens motherless sons of the Athenian soil.

## *Diotima from Mantinea:*
## *The "God-Honoring" Priestess from "God Town"*

Plato's Diotima, too, merits re-examination as a trace of women teachers, speakers, and religious celebrants. In the *Symposium*, Socrates reports that she was called in to avert a plague during the Peloponnesian war and at that time taught him many matters concerning love, discourse, and rhetoric. Her speech, he says, was "spoken like one of our best sophist's." Diotima may be technically more purely fictional or literary than Aspasia, who is recorded in other histories of the time. Regardless, the two roles she is given in the

*Symposium* were commonly available to women in the period. They are intriguingly unlike one another at first glance. A priestess and teacher of the art of love, who speaks like a sophist?

The mythic history of the Athenian race that Aspasia relates provides an example of the ceremonial political oratory taught by some of the sophists, a political mythic history which was impious because it supplanted the Demeter cult of the Eleusinian mysteries. The newer Olympian gods were war gods, patrons of the city-state of Athens embodied in Athena, and established a shared political and national identity not defined by biological parentage but by legal citizenship in the land of Athens, land sanctified not only by its birth-giving quality but just as importantly by the blood of the war dead. The citizen-men of Athens are motherless, sprung directly from the earth, just as Athena is a motherless child of Zeus, sprung directly from his forehead.

Diotima, priestess though she is, represents none of the new state mythology, none of the gods of the state religion. Instead, she interrogates Socrates' mysterious Daimon, and asks him which god of love he honours. She examines at length the passion that is stirred by discourse, among the various media of human intercourse, and asks Socrates about his refusal to accept the earlier or "lesser" Eleusinian mysteries, which introduce initiates into the ways of physical desire and sexuality. The power and validity of his teachings are called into question on the grounds that he has refused this required introductory course in the deeper powers of divine and human passions. Finally, she chides him for his abstemious and austere prose, with which he teases his interlocutors as with the hint of hidden beauty and riches beneath a plain surface. But when Alcibiades enters the discussion to affirm this rebuke of Socrates for being a tease and a professional beloved, Diotima suddenly seems rebuked as well, the calm courtliness of her decorous teaching suddenly seems to be altogether too much spoken like a sophist of the methodical, didactic sort – of Socrates' sort.[15] Her teacherliness at this point gives us one glimpse of the meaning of "sophist," and an intriguing hint that Socrates' reputation as both a tease and an austere opponent to the sophists was well-deserved. The many-faceted crystal of Plato's representations of Diotima via

Socrates as priestess and sophist has by no means lost its shine, or its multiplicity.

I close by returning to the question of the ethics of our examinations of representation. What are we to make of our glee upon discovering or inventing forgery, the deep satisfaction that often accompanies sneering, dismissive announcements that Aspasia is merely literary? To announce that classical evidence is literary, a textual chimera, a fragment, a forgery, a fiction, is not news. Directing the announcement selectively at studies of women in antiquity is an act of pseudo-objectivity that should not go unremarked. "There is no such thing as the totally objective recovery of history, for something informs our choice of questions to ask and our selection of data that seems significant to us."[16] So, let us listen once again to the epitaphios of Aspasia, and to Diotima's intriguing teachings on love and desire, discourse and procreation. And then, to echo Virginia Woolf, we may hear once again the voices of the women who died arguing, and who died for the right to argue, against all odds – and who have somehow survived even in the absence of evidence.

## NOTES

1. See in particular the range of recent studies examining women's public ritual roles as celebrants and composers of songs for births, weddings, funerals, and other holy days: M. Alexiou, *The Ritual Lament in Greek Tradition* (Cambridge: Cambridge University Press, 1974); Sue Blundell, *Women in Ancient Greece* (Cambridge, MA: Harvard University Press, 1995); Phyllis Culham, "Ten Years After Pomeroy: Studies of the Image and Reality of Women in Antiquity" in *Rescuing Creusa: New Methodological Approaches to Women in Antiquity*, ed. Marilyn Skinner (Special Issue of *Helios*, 13, no. 2; Texas Tech University Press, 1987), 9–30; Elaine Fantham, Helene Peet Foley, Natalie Boymel Kampel, and Sarah B. Pomeroy, *Women in the Classical World* (Princeton, NJ: Princeton University Press, 1994); Helene Peet Foley, *The Homeric Hymn to Demeter: Translation, Commentary, Essays* (Princeton, NJ: Princeton University Press, 1994); Tikva Frymer-Kensky, *In the Wake of the Goddesses: Women, Culture and the Biblical Transformation of Pagan Myth* (New York: Macmillan/Free Press, 1992); Cheryl Glenn, "sex, lies, and manuscript: Refiguring Aspasia in the History of Rhetoric," *College Composition and Communication* 45, no. 2 (1994): 180–200; Madeleine Henry, *Prisoner of History: Aspasia of Miletus and Her Biographical Tradition* (New York: Oxford University Press, 1995); R.S.

Kraemer, *Her Share of the Blessings: Women's Religions Among Pagans, Jews, and Christians in the Graeco-Roman World* (New York: Cambridge University Press, 1992) and "Women in the Religion of the Greco-Roman World," *Religious Studies Review* 9 (1983): 131–32; Jennifer Larson, *Greek Heroine Cults* (Madison: University of Wisconsin Press, 1995); Nicole Loraux, *The Children of Athena: Athenian Ideas About Citizenship and the Division Between the Sexes,* trans. Caroline Levine (Princeton, NJ: Princeton University Press, 1993); C. Meyers, *Discovering Eve: Ancient Israelite Women in Context* (New York: Oxford University Press, 1988); Donovan Ochs, *Consolatory Rhetoric: Grief, Symbol, and Ritual in the Greco-Roman Era* (Columbia, SC: University of South Carolina Press, 1993); I. Morris, *Death Ritual and Social Structure in Classical Antiquity* (New York: Cambridge University Press, 1992); Sarah Pomeroy, ed., *Women's History and Ancient History* (Chapel Hill: University of North Carolina Press, 1991); Dora Pozzi and John Wickersham, eds., *Myth and Polis* (Ithaca, NY: Cornell University Press, 1991).
2. *The Homeric Hymn to Demeter,* xii–xiii, 65–75, 138–42.
3. E.g., Meyers.
4. E.g., Kraemer, *Her Share of the Blessings,* and see Nigel Watson, "Reconstructing the Other Half of the Telephone Conversation," review of *The Corinthian Women Prophets, Australian Biblical Review* 40 (1992): 58–63; Antoinette Clark Wire, *The Corinthian Women Poets: A Reconstruction through Paul's Rhetoric* (Fortress, 1991).
5. Lisa Ede, Cheryl Glenn, and Andrea Lunsford, "Border Crossings: Intersections of Rhetorics and Feminisms" *Rhetorica* 13, no. 4 (1995): 401–42, examines this.
6. Andrea Lunsford, ed., *Reclaiming Rhetorica: Women in the Rhetorical Tradition* (Pittsburgh: University of Pittsburgh Press, 1995).
7. See for example the continuing, valuable examination of literacy and oral genres in the archaic and early classical period, and a widening of the boundaries defining "poetry" and "rhetoric": Walter Burkert, *The Orientalizing Revolution: Near Eastern Influence on Greek Culture in the Archaic Age,* trans. Margaret Pinder and Walter Burkert (Cambridge, MA: Harvard University Press, 1992); Claude Calame, *The Craft of Poetic Speech in Ancient Greece,* trans. Janice Orion (Ithaca, NY: Cornell University Press, 1995); Thomas Cole, *The Origins of Rhetoric in Ancient Greece* (Baltimore: Johns Hopkins University Press, 1991); Michael Gagarin, "Oral Poetics and Early Greek Oratory," International Society for the History of Rhetoric, Edinburgh 1995; and Kevin Robb, *Literacy and Paideia in Ancient Greece* (New York: Oxford University Press, 1994). However, there is virtually no attention to the question of women as teachers or performers in these studies.
8. However, studies by Alexiou (*The Ritual Lament*), Loraux (*The Children of Athena*), and Ochs (*Consolatory Rhetoric*) provide the materials to begin to make these comparisons, as does Aspasia's epitaphios.

9. Madeleine Henry's *Prisoner of History* addresses this issue with painstaking detail and subtlety.
10. For an overview of these attitudes see Edmund Bloedow, "Aspasia and the Mystery of the Menexenos," *Wiener Studien* 9 (1975): 32–48, and Mary Ellen Waithe's chapters on Aspasia and Diotima in Waithe, *A History of Women Philosophers*, vol. 1, *600 B.C.-500 A.D.* (Boston/The Hague: Martinus Nijhoff, 1987), 75–116.
11. For example, Barbara Biesecker, "Coming to Terms with Recent Attempts to Write Women into the History of Rhetoric," *Philosophy and Rhetoric* 25 (1992): 140–61; Susan Jarratt, "Performing Feminisms, Histories, Rhetorics," *Rhetoric Society Quarterly* 22 (1992): 1–6; Linda Lopez McAlister, "Some Remarks on Exploring the History of Women in Philosophy," *Hypatia* 4, no. 1 (1989): 1–8; and John Poulakos and Susan Jarratt, "Forum," *Rhetoric Society Quarterly* 22 (1992): 66–70.
12. I am thinking in particular of Page duBois, *Sowing the Body* (Chicago: University of Chicago Press, 1988); David Halperin's "Why Is Diotima a Woman?" *Before Sexuality: The Construction of Erotic Experience in the Ancient World*, eds. David M. Halperin, John Winkler, and Froma Zeitlin (Princeton, NJ: Princeton University Press, 1990); and Susan Jarratt's *Rereading the Sophists: Classical Rhetoric Refigured* (Carbondale: Southern Illinois University Press, 1991).
13. Described in detail by Halperin ("Why Is Diotima a Woman?"), Jarratt (*Rereading the Sophists* and "Forum"), and Waithe (*A History of Women Philosophers*), 75–116.
14. Eric Havelock, *Preface to Plato* (Cambridge, MA: Belknap Press of Harvard University Press, 1963), 161, n. 25.
15. There is a longer, more detailed account of these relationships in my discussion of Diotima's teaching on language in "A Lover's Discourse, Diotima, Logos, and Desire," *Reclaiming Rhetorica*, ed. Lunsford, 25–52.
16. Frymer-Kensky, *In the Wake of the Goddesses*, ix.

# *Cutting Off the Memory of Women*

## Jody Enders

"By the power of devils," writes Heinrich Kramer in his notorious fifteenth-century inquisitorial treatise, the *Malleus Maleficarum*, "and with God's permission, mental images long retained in the *treasury* of such images which is the *memory*, are drawn out, *not from the intellectual understanding* in which such images are stored, but from the *memory*, which is the *repository of mental images*, and is situated at the back of the head and are presented to the imaginative faculty."[1] At issue in this remarkable statement are illusions, imagination, persecutions, power, impulses, deceit, God, and the Devil – all of which come together in a vivid discussion of a female memory which Kramer opposes to intellect: "and so strongly are they impressed on that faculty, that man has an inevitable impulse to imagine a horse or a beast, when the *devil* draws from the memory an image of a horse or a beast; and so he is compelled to think that he sees with his external eyes such a beast when there is actually no such beast to see; but it seems to be so by reason of the impulsive force of *the devil working by means of those images*" (146 47; emphasis mine). Rife with such classic mnemonic terms as "thesaurus," "effigies," and "imagines," Kramer's manual clearly identifies the fourth rhetorical canon as a topic particularly relevant to the diabolical acts of women and to the legal redress that might be effected to regulate and punish them. The question is: What does memory have to do with the prosecution and persecution of witches?

In this essay, I endeavour to answer it by analyzing Kramer's marshalling of the mnemotechnical lore of his day as a means to anathematize and, literally, to "demonize" the female memory as the birthplace of intellect and speech. Touching on questions of anthropology, biology, pedagogy, and the cultural construction of gender, Kramer explains that there are more female than male witches because women "have weak memories (*defectum in memorativa potentia*); and it is a natural vice in them not to be disciplined, but to follow their own impulses without any sense of what is due; this is her whole study, and that she keeps in her memory" (124). In that sense, he does considerably more than insist on the literal Latin meaning of "education" as "leading out" (*educere*) with the woman as the passive receptacle of her own education and the Devil doing the leading. When he targets the female memory, his intervention is scarcely confined to epistemology: he also justifies a larger attack on the female bodies which house that faculty, conveniently somaticized above as a bodily organ.[2] In what follows, I argue that his vision of the female memory helps to create a philosophical model that normalizes and naturalizes violence against women – all with God's permission (*Deo interdum permittente*) – which then extends to the torture of women.

According to a long tradition well known to the Middle Ages and Renaissance thanks to such texts as the widely disseminated *Rhetorica ad Herennium*, *memoria* was the "treasure-house of the ideas supplied by Invention [and] the guardian of all the parts of rhetoric" (nunc ad *thesaurum* inventorum atque ad omnium partium rhetoricae *custodem*, memoriam, transeamus).[3] Moreover, such theorists as Longinus, Augustine, Martianus Capella, Geoffrey of Vinsauf, and Hugh of Saint Victor all stressed its capacity for performance insofar as the purpose of the mnemonic treasure chest and its imagistic contents served, for Longinus, to "engender speech" or, for Geoffrey, to translate "wandering images" into "languages [that] should be heard in reciting."[4] Memory was a virtual performance, even a virtual reality in which "the arrangement and disposition of the images [was] like the script."[5] But where one of the canonized rhetorical functions of memory was ostensibly to "set the stage" for the delivery of a speech or for the performance of law and literature, memory also had a dark underside: namely, how to set the stage for violence – and specifically, violence against women.

Perhaps most germane of all, however, to the history of women and the rhetorical tradition was the belief that one of the most important things memory could script was the larger cultural performance of social control and civilized behaviour. Ever since Plato equated lawyers with dramatists by reason of their shared capacity to create memorable illusions that influenced judicial and poetic communities, memory had served as a primary means by which to control and correct the misguided mental pictures of society by "persuad[ing] people that their notions of justice and injustice are illusory pictures."[6] In his own mode of legalistic persuasion, Kramer's is one of the most illusory pictures of all as he reverses the positive valence of the very category invoked as the supposed means for understanding woman: her memory. Agency becomes passivity, birth becomes death, natural becomes unnatural, desire becomes fear, preservation becomes extermination.[7] Although memory had been institutionalized as the birthplace of speech, it was not desirable that women, who naturally possessed memories, should speak or act in the various arenas of law, politics, education, religion, and literature. Rhetorically speaking, the faculty designed to engender speech was *not* to engender it in women.

As it happens, the very notion of a mnemonic treasure-house for women posed a series of truly thorny problems in rhetoric, law, politics, religion, and literature. It was perfectly clear – even to Kramer – that women possessed memories which were theoretically capable of engendering speech. Under certain grim medieval circumstances like those of the Black Death, their memories even functioned as a kind of village register.[8] Nor is it any surprise to anyone familiar with misogynistic literature to learn from the so-called romantic perspective of the *Poissance d'amor* (once attributed to Richard de Fournival) that the female memory was a perceived source of recalcitrance, rebelliousness, lack of discipline, and failure to submit. Women's bodies take their cues from their unruly memories: "on voit souvent avenir ke, quant hom prie une femme k'ele soit acline a se volente, li *memoire* et li raisons de cheli ne s'i acordera mie" (it often happens that when man bids woman to yield to his will, her memory and reason do not agree).[9] So it is that, in a casuistic sleight of hand, Kramer constructs a rationale according to which an active male memory is a good thing while the presumably identical entity in women is a danger. He manages to transmute the theoretically *active* faculty of memory into one that is necessarily *passive* if possessed by women. Because female power was effective, because the behaviour of the alleged witch was difficult to control, and because men fell victim to her illusions, Kramer attributes that power not to the women who exercise it but to the Devil. As the creator of pernicious memory images, woman is recast as the passive, mnemonic receptacle of the Devil, which renders any power she herself might possess diabolical:

> All these things are caused by devils through an illusion or glamour in the manner we have said, by confusing the organ of vision by transmuting the mental images in the imaginative faculty. . . . And the reason is that they effect this thing by an easier method, namely, by drawing out an inner mental image from the repository of the memory, and impressing it on the imagination (*ex conservatoria seu memorativa potentia ad imaginativam ista facere possunt*). (151–52; 130-31)

Here, man is seduced only because of woman. Kramer acknowledges the power of the female memory to confuse and frighten men – but only in order to argue that it is *because* of her weak and undisciplined memory that woman is really disempowered. As in so many medieval retellings of the Fall with its simultaneously persuasive and scapegoated Eve, Kramer finds a way to argue that a potent female mnemonic faculty is but a form of impotence.[10] Hers is a "disempowered power" of which she is both origin and non-origin – even in the realm of impotence itself, as when witches are accused of stealing male organs in the middle of the night "in great numbers, as many as twenty or thirty" (151). Therefore, if woman does possess a memory, it is opposed to intellectual understanding, relegated to governance by the diabolical imagination, and dangerous to the men who are exposed to the Devil in her. Violence, torture, and even death become legitimate responses to the manufactured problem about her memory as inquisitors like Kramer seek to ensure that her bedeviled speech and behaviours never occur.

Since *memoria* was a virtual performance, it was but a step to move from virtual to actual persecution and, in Kramer's case, to torture of the accused witch, which he advocates throughout the *Malleus*. Metaphorical violence to her memory then serves as a catalyst for real violence to her body. Should various forms of "questioning" fail (including threats or promises to spare her life), Kramer gives the following advice to the interrogator: "if she refuses to confess the truth, he should have the engines of torture brought before her, and tell her that she will have to endure these if she does not confess. If then she is not induced by terror to confess, the torture must be continued on the second or third day, but not repeated at that present time unless there should be some indication of its probable success" (166–68).[11] In fact, in one of the premier strategies of torture, the victim is abused, disenfranchised, and de-intellectualized — even as it is she who is accused of abusing, absconding with property, and compromising male intellect and potency.[12] In nearby Toulouse, for example, a similar prosecution associated with disenfranchisement was being waged against Catherine, wife of Delort. In a manipulation of another classic memory image made famous by Plato, Catherine is indicted for persecuting her aunts "whose heir she was" by means of a physical concretization of a waxen block: "heating waxen figures dressed in one of their blouses over a slow fire, so that their unfortunate lives wasted away as the waxen figure was melting in the brazier."[13] Women are persecuted as witches: yet it is they who are configured as powerful tormenters of men and women alike.

Nor was the torture of the female body confined to witchcraft alone. In one of the more ominous culminations of the regulation and punishment of the female memory as the birthplace of speech, the early modern period saw the invention of a gendered torture device known as the brank or gossip's bridle. Fashioned to, quite literally, "hold the tongue" of women, the brank is described by William Andrews as "an instrument employed by our forefathers for punishing scolds":

> The brank may be described simply as an iron framework; which was placed on the head, enclosing it in a kind of cage; it had in front a plate of iron, which, either sharpened or

> covered with spikes, was so situated as to be placed in the mouth of the victim, and if she attempted to move her tongue in any way whatever, it was certain to be shockingly injured.[14]

Blinding a woman's eyes, blocking out the visual component of her *phantasia*, and forcing her to "hold her tongue" by physically pinning it, the brank constituted an effort to stifle the dangerous speech of women. Whether it was employed frequently, seldom, or not at all, it remains, at the very least, a hyper-real, iron incarnation of a threat to sever the female cerebral connection between memory and speech – the same rupture advocated by Kramer in the *Malleus*. Even so, its very existence hyper-corrects the connection between the female intellect and speech which Kramer denies. One cannot "cut off" the memory of women if there is no memory to cut off; the best bet is a memorable image of infamy. The brank possessed all the dramatic potential for public humiliation of the pillory, and the commentator Andrews displays all the even-handed sensitivity to female pain of the medieval writer of farce:

> With the brank on her head she was conducted through the streets, led by a chain, held by one of the town's officials, an object of contempt, and subjected to the jeers of the crowd and often left to their mercy. In some towns it was the custom to chain the culprit to pillory, whipping-post, or market-cross. She thus suffered for telling her mind to some petty tyrant in office, or speaking plainly to a wrongdoer, or for *taking to task a lazy, and perhaps a drunken husband.*[15]

Ultimately, whether the attack on women be spiritual, physical, or the sinister combination of both in which the rhetorical Middle Ages excelled, the various indictments of the female memory are cast in terms of their goals: to sever the female cerebral connection between memory and speech, to cut off what the rhetorical tradition should otherwise shore up. Nowhere, of course, is that goal more eloquently expressed than in the permanent silencing of thousands of female voices through the questionable death-sentences they received during "the great European Witch-craze of the

Sixteenth and Seventeenth Centuries."[16] In that quintessential persecution in which exterminating the intellect became as urgent as destroying the body, memory became for the medieval and early modern woman a literal "prison house of language," a metal (not a mental) guardian of speech, a jailer of language.[17] Although Friedrich Nietzsche once wrote that "whenever man has thought it necessary to create a memory for himself, his effort has been attended with torture, blood, sacrifice,"[18] it seems that efforts to create a memory for women were even bloodier.

## NOTES

1. Authorship of the *Malleus* has often been attributed jointly to Kramer and Jakob Sprenger, but historians have largely determined that the latter's participation was relatively minimal. Unless otherwise stated, Latin citations are from the *Malleus Maleficarum*, 2 vols. (1949; reprint, Brussels: Culture et Civilisation, 1969); and further English citations are from the readily accessible translation by Alan C. Kors and Edward Peters, eds., *Witchcraft in Europe 1100–1700: A Documentary History* (1972; reprint, Philadelphia: University of Pennsylvania Press, 1986), who follow the earlier translation by Montague Summers (London, 1928). Heightening the notion that it was God giving permission for prosecution is the fact the *Malleus*, which was written in 1485 or 1486, was published in 1486 with the *Summis desiderante* of Innocent VIII as a preface (see Jeffrey Burton Russell's discussion in *Witchcraft in the Middle Ages* [Ithaca, NY: Cornell University Press, 1972], 230–34]). I expand the present discussion considerably in an essay, "Violence, Silence, and the Memory of Witches," in *Violence Against Women in Medieval Texts*, ed. Anna Roberts (Gainesville: University of Florida Press, 1998).
2. For a fascinating discussion of concomitant developments in medicine about the structure of the brain, see editor George Mora's discussion of the "Memorative Function of the Brain" in *Witches, Devils, and Doctors in the Renaissance: Johann Weyer's* De praestigiis daemonum (Binghamton, NY: Medieval and Renaissance Texts and Studies, 1991), 728–31.
3. Cicero, *Ad C. Herennium* (hereafter *RAH*), ed. and trans. Harry Caplan, Loeb Classical Library (1954; reprint, Cambridge, MA: Harvard University Press, 1977), III, 28. In the twelfth century, John of Salisbury agreed, calling it the "mind's treasure chest, a sure and reliable place of safe-deposit for perceptions" (*The* Metalogicon *of John of Salisbury: A Twelfth-Century Defense of the Verbal and Logical Arts of the Trivium*, ed. and trans. Daniel D. McGarry [Berkeley: University of California Press, 1955], I, 11).
4. Longinus, "On the Sublime," ed. and trans. W. Hamilton Fyfe, in *Aristotle, Longinus, Demetrius*, Loeb Classical Library (1927; reprint, Cambridge, MA:

Harvard University Press, 1946), 15, 1–2; Geoffrey of Vinsauf, *Poetria Nova*, in *The Poetria Nova and its Sources in Early Rhetorical Doctrine*, trans. Ernest Gallo (The Hague: Mouton, 1971), 2036. I argue for the status of memory as virtual performance and even protodrama in my *Rhetoric and the Origins of Medieval Drama*, Rhetoric and Society, no. 1 (Ithaca, NY: Cornell University Press, 1992), 44–54. Exemplary introductions to the art of memory in general include Frances Yates, *The Art of Memory* (Chicago, IL: University of Chicago Press, 1966); Mary Carruthers, *The Book of Memory: A Study of Memory in Medieval Culture* (Cambridge, MA: Cambridge University Press, 1990); and Janet Coleman, *Ancient and Medieval Memories: Studies in the Reconstruction of the Past* (Cambridge: Cambridge University Press, 1992).

5 Cicero, *RAH*, III, 30.

6 Plato, *Laws*, ed. and trans. Harold North Fowler, Walter Lamb, and Robert Bury, 2 vols., Loeb Classical Library (1926; reprint, Cambridge, MA: Harvard University Press, 1942), 663b-c.

7 I make this argument at greater length in Chapter 2 of Jody Enders, *The Medieval Theater of Cruelty: Rhetoric, Memory, Violence* (Ithaca, NY: Cornell University Press, 1999).

8 This was the subject of a conference paper presented by Daniel L. Smail, "Archives of Knowledge and the Coming of the Black Death," International Congress of Medieval Studies (Kalamazoo, Michigan, 5 May 1994); see also Patrick Geary, *Phantoms of Remembrance: Memory and Oblivion at the End of the First Millennium* (Princeton, NJ: Princeton University Press, 1994), 63–73.

9 *La Poissance d'amours dello Pseudo-Richard de Fournival*, ed. Gian Battista Speroni, Pubblicazioni dell Facolt di Lettere e Filosofia dell'Universit di Pavia 21 (Florence: La Nuova Italia, 1975), 237–40; quoted, translated, and discussed by Helen Solterer in *The Master and Minerva: Disputing Women in French Medieval Culture* (Berkeley: University of California Press, 1995), 53.

10 After all, Eve is both the origin of the Fall and (because of her successful persuasion of Adam in various medieval versions) the first human rhetorician, the Devil being the first "divine" one.

11 For helpful introductions to torture, see Edward Peters, *Torture* (New York: Basil Blackwell, 1985); Page duBois, *Torture and Truth* (New York: Routledge, 1991): esp. Chapter 14, "Women, the Body, and Torture"; and Robert Bartlett, *Trial by Fire and Water: The Medieval Judicial Ordeal* (1986; reprint, Oxford: Clarendon, 1988).

12 For Scarry's argument, see *The Body in Pain: The Making and Unmaking of the World* (1985; reprint, New York: Oxford University Press, 1987), 27.

13 This text is reproduced in translation by Kors and Peters, *Witchcraft in Europe*, 96–97. Among many other places, the wax tablet image appears in Plato's *Theaetetus*, trans. Francis MacDonald Cornford (1957; reprint, Indianapolis, IN: Bobbs-Merrill, 1977), 191D. For the history of this image, see also Carruthers, *The Book of Memory*, 16–32. For an interesting feminist analysis of

the complex relationships among women accusers and victims, see Deborah Willis, *Malevolent Nurture: Witch-Hunting and Maternal Power in Early Modern England* (Ithaca, NY: Cornell University Press, 1995).

14 William Andrews, *Old-Time Punishments* (London: Simpkin, Marshall, Hamilton, Dent, 1890), 38–39.

15 Ibid., 39.

16 Here I invoke the title of Chapter 3 of H. R. Trevor-Roper's *The Crisis of the Seventeenth Century: Religion, the Reformation, and Social Change* (1956; reprint, New York: Harper and Row, 1968). Estimates on this "gynocide" vary, but Kors and Peters (*Witchcraft in Europe*) remark, p. 13, e.g., that, for the period from the fourteenth through the seventeenth centuries, "few begin guessing below the range of 50,000–100,000."

17 Here I suggest a literal meaning for two metaphoric book titles: Fredric Jameson's *The Prison-house of Language: A Critical Account of Structuralism and Russian Formalism* (Princeton, NJ: Princeton University Press, 1972); and R.A. Kaster's *Guardians of Language: The Grammarian and Society in Late Antiquity* (Berkeley: University of California Press, 1988).

18 Friedrich Nietzsche, *The Birth of Tragedy and the Genealogy of Morals*, trans. Francis Golffing (Garden City, NY: Doubleday, 1956), 192–93.

# GROUP 2

# Alongside the Rhetorical Tradition

## *Ethos Over Time: The Ongoing Appeal of St. Catherine of Siena*

### Margo Husby Scheelar

The ethos of someone like St. Catherine of Siena is hard to examine at any time. Six hundred years separate her from us, six hundred years that make her as foreign as though she were from a non-Western culture. At times, from our late-twentieth-century viewpoint, her actions seem quite irrational. However, as Habermas points out, the interpreter of another person's life must grasp the reasons allowing the "author's utterance to appear as rational" in order to begin to understand what was meant by that utterance.[1] The researcher cannot merely subject the historical person's life to the researcher's standards[2] but has to endeavour to understand how the person being studied interpreted her actions within the context of her own life. This is a difficult task at any time and undoubtedly more difficult because of the vast differences in culture and belief systems between Catherine and the modern academic researchers. Such a task is worth the effort, however, not only for what it reveals about Catherine but also for what it reveals about those who reacted to her ethos as mystic, as daughter of God, as intermediary, as crusader, both in her time and since her death.

Catherine di Iacopo di Benincasa was born in Siena, Italy in 1347 and died a mere thirty-three years later. She had her first mystical experience at the age of six, at which time she devoted herself to God, not an entirely unusual idea in the late Medieval period. When she was fifteen and of marriageable age, her parents sought a spouse for her despite her objections. In an act of self-determination, she cut all her hair off in order to be less beautiful and less valuable in the marriage market. Her infuriated parents then turned her into the family servant, a role she thrived on as she developed the discipline of meditation even as she toiled. After a mystical experience of St. Dominic, she persuaded her parents and the Sisters of Penance of St. Dominic to allow her to join this lay order. For the next three years, she lived alone in her room, praying, studying, and meditating, beginning the ascetic practices that she would continue for the rest of her life. She ate very little; she slept on planks rather than soft beds; she wore a chain around her waist; and she trained herself to go without sleep for long periods.[3] Another mystical experience in 1368, this time a mystical marriage with Jesus, caused her to emerge from her private world of prayer to work in the public world of illness, poverty, church corruption, and politics. Over the next twelve years, she corresponded with people from all classes of society, challenged popes, nursed plague victims, and dictated her *Dialogue*, a text containing her conversations with God. She had "no formal schooling" and "there is nothing new or original" in her theology, yet even after her death her influence was "a major force in Dominican reform."[4] She had no diplomatic training, yet she corresponded with royalty, spoke with authority to popes, and worked tirelessly for peace within Italy and within the fragmented fourteenth-century Church.[5] Her mystical experiences are the stuff of legend and her practical assistance to those in need undoubtedly contributed to her being called "blessed Mama" by her confessor and her followers.[6] All who confessed their sins to Catherine were granted special dispensation to receive absolution from her confessor and his companions, an authority generally reserved for bishops,[7] and certainly not granted to a woman and her followers. She narrowly escaped martyrdom in 1378 and died in Rome in 1380. Canonized in 1461, St. Catherine of Siena is one of only three women[8] who have been granted the title, "Doctor of the Roman Catholic Church," an honour granted her on October 4, 1970 by Pope Paul VI. She shares with St. Francis of Assisi the role of patron saint of Italy. Her *Dialogue* and the biography written by her confessor "were among the first books to see print . . . in Italy . . . Spain, Germany and England."[9]

## *Ethos of the Mystic*

Catherine's multi-faceted ethos begins with the ethos of the mystic. In his 1978 essay, Michael N. Nagler discusses the difficulty modern researchers have understanding mystical experiences. He writes, "[In the West] we have been generally reluctant to believe that a regular, systematic method for the acquisition of spiritual awareness is either necessary or possible."[10] But, as a result of his examination of the spiritual practices of early Stoicism, and of Hinduism, Buddhism, and Christianity, he comes to the conclusion that "mysticism is real, it is reached by controlling the mind through unremitting spiritual and mental discipline."[11] The mystic "sees all creatures, indeed all of creation not as we do, as separate and at times conflicting entities, but as participating always in a spectacular heart-rending unity."[12] The mystic has an "uncanny tendency to succeed ... [in] ... carrying out a stubborn political campaign against injustice ... by a compelling appeal to truth without recourse to force."[13] A major mystical experience, Nagler says, causes one "to undergo ... a permanent overhaul of one's way of perceiving, one's character, conduct and consciousness."[14] Individuals who live in the world of mystical experience have "[a] part of their consciousness ... already rooted in the eternal."[15] Medieval Catholicism had a comprehension of the eternal and mystical in which Catherine moved, albeit not without some challenge. During her mystical experiences, she would often become unconscious to the world around her and, if this happened while she was at church, she would be carried outside and left in the street where people would kick or slap her as they went past.[16] On the other hand, she spoke with such authority that, when a Franciscan and an Augustinian came to quiz her on her theology, they ended up transforming their self-indulgent lifestyles into lives of service to the poor.[17]

Because Catherine saw herself as being rooted in an eternity defined in Christian terms, she believed that the "action of the will" in conjunction with the entire human spirit should move in response to the love of God that is revealed in Jesus.[18] The human response to the love of God, therefore, frames one's character – good sense, goodness and good will, the elements of ethos, are all defined in relationship to the holiness of God and made evident in relationship with other people. In her *Dialogue* Catherine recorded what she believed to be God's words to her on this topic:

> You then are my workers. You have come from me, the supreme eternal gardener, and I have engrafted you onto the vine by making myself one with you. Keep in mind that each of you has your own vineyard. But everyone is joined to your neighbours' vineyards without any dividing line. They are so joined together in fact, that you cannot do good or evil for yourself without doing the same for your neighbours.[19]

Catherine's sense of this intense and intimate relationship with God is essential to understanding her ethos; the latter does not exist for her apart from the former. Indeed, it cannot, for Catherine's life reflects the ethos of one who saw herself, both grounded in eternity and alive in temporality, functioning as an intermediary for the Church.

### *Ethos of Daughter/Intermediary*

According to Christian thought, the major intermediary between God and humanity is Jesus Christ, the one Christians believe to be the Son of God. Catherine never presumed to be equal to Jesus, but in her *Dialogue* she records God using the descriptor, "daughter," more than any other when addressing her.[20] According to her biographer, Catherine recounted that it was the first descriptor God used after her mystical encounter with Jesus, during which He encouraged her to "act courageously [and] accomplish without fear the works" He would give her.[21] The early years of Catherine's life indicate that she was well aware of what the role of daughter involved. When her parents were angry with her for cutting her hair in defiance of their desire to beautify her in preparation for marriage, she worked as their servant in obedience to their wishes. She knew that, if she continued to refuse to consider marriage, she would have to give them a good reason, and her vow to serve God was that reason. She had to choose between obedience to her eternal parent, God, and obedience to her human parents. Although her behaviour may be interpreted as a reaction against an authoritarian patriarchal family structure, it is also reminiscent of the behaviour of the Son of God when the roles of earthly son and heavenly Son collided. The Gospel of Luke records the story of Joseph and Mary taking Jesus to Jerusalem to celebrate the Passover.[22] After the festivities ended, Joseph, Mary, and their various friends and relatives packed up and headed for home. Jesus had not rejoined the group but his parents did not know that; they thought he was with one of his relatives or friends. When they realized that he was not with the group, they headed back to Jerusalem and searched the city for three days before they finally found Jesus, sitting in the temple, chatting with the elders. When Mary asked her son why he had behaved in this fashion, he replied, "Why is it that you sought me? Did you not know that I must be about my Father's business?"[23] After this, Luke records that Jesus went home with his earthly parents and "was subject to them."[24] When Catherine's parents demanded that she work as their servant, she was subject to them. Her model was Jesus. As it was with Jesus, so Catherine believed it should be with her. The daughter had the same priorities as the Son, which is not surprising given that her devotion to God was a result of the vision of the Son of God.

One could argue that Catherine's equating of herself with Christ was arrogant, hardly a trait that would impress either God or man. It is seen as arrogant only if Catherine is endeavouring to appropriate the power and status of Jesus Christ. Such is most definitely not the case. Catherine's theology was traditional: Jesus is the Son of God who was born, lived, suffered, and died in order to redeem fallen humanity. So, if Catherine sees herself as being called God's daughter, then her role is not about power but about sacrifice, just as Jesus' role was. At one point, she told her confessor that she believed Jesus had called her to suffer as He had:

> If thou wishest to become powerful against thy enemies, take the Cross for thy safeguard ... Choose, therefore, to have trials and afflictions; endure them not only with patience, but embrace them with delight; they are lasting treasure,

for the more thou wilt suffer for me, the more thou wilt be like me, and according to the doctrine of the Apostle,[25] the more thou wilt resemble me in sufferings, the more, also, thou shalt be like unto me in grace and glory.[26]

Her final reward would be a "heavenly crown,"[27] but not power.

As far as Catherine was concerned, her role as daughter/intercessor was chosen for her by God, just as Jesus' role as Son/intercessor was chosen for Him by God. From her point of view, therefore, her ethos as daughter/intercessor was not one of her construction; it had been constructed in that eternal realm in which she was grounded. Because it was constructed there, she had a duty to fulfill it because she believed it would only be through her and others like her that the Church would be reformed.[28] Therefore, in her rhetorical role as intermediary, she had a duty to pray, to suffer, to teach, to be as active as necessary in order to get the Church back onto the path of virtue. This was the driving reason behind her persistent communication with Pope Gregory XI, exhorting him to be a strong disciplinarian of the clergy, to set an example of holy obedience and fearlessness, to be focused on Christ rather than on material goods, and to return to Rome where he belonged.[29] She was absolutely clear that she stood between eternity and temporality, speaking to each on behalf of the other and doing so with an authority that she saw as coming from eternity. In a powerful letter to Pope Gregory, she writes, "My dearest *babbo*,[30] forgive my presumption in saying what I've said – what I'm compelled by gentle First Truth[31] to say."[32] After delivering a strong call to the pope to lead the Church with the authority given to him by God, she writes, "Don't make it necessary for me to complain about you to Christ crucified. (There is no one else I can complain to, since there is no one greater [than you] on earth.)."[33] Just as an intermediary involved in a temporal dispute talks to both parties, not just one, Catherine talked to both the temporal world and the eternal world – to the former via letters and to the latter via prayers and sufferings.

Living out the ethos of intermediary almost cost Catherine her life. At one point the pope sent her to Florence to settle a dispute, and those who were in opposition to the pope decided that

Catherine should die. Catherine heard soldiers looking for her as she was praying one night, so she went up to them and offered her life to them if they would spare her followers. For reasons unclear to anyone, the soldiers did not kill her. The fact that she wept over having missed the opportunity to give her life "for the love of Him who redeemed me at the price of His own"[34] indicates the depth of her identification with the suffering of the one she believed to be the Son of God. This identification with Jesus extended to her deathbed where one of her followers recorded her last words: "Father, into Thy hands I commend my soul and my spirit,"[35] a clear repetition of Jesus' last words: "Father, into Thy hands I commend my spirit."[36]

## Ethos of Crusader

Catherine the daughter of God was also Catherine the fourteenth-century European who believed that one sure way to bring unity to fragmented Christianity was for all Christians to band together against a common enemy, namely the Muslims who held Jerusalem.[37] In this, she was not alone. Pope Gregory had long been urging the feuding powers in the Christian west to unite against the Turks and Saracens.[38] Catherine's support for this endeavour was in direct opposition to the warnings of a Swedish mystic, Birgitta,[39] who viewed a Crusade as a papal excuse to ignore immediate problems and a military excuse for "plundering and ravaging on a more extensive scale than was possible in Christendom."[40] Birgitta may have had a more temporally pragmatic view of war, but Catherine believed that sending soldiers to the Holy Land would mean that they would be fighting for something of eternal, rather than temporal, value. It was not to be; although Gregory declared a Crusade in 1373, plans for it collapsed and Catherine's dream of a united Christian Europe did not come to fruition. In this case, her ethos may be seen as flawed, indicating an ethnocentrism unpopular in our late twentieth century. However, opposition to the Crusade was not based upon ideas of racial and religious equality; it was based upon conflicting political desires within Europe. Since Catherine's political correspondence includes repeated eternal referents, repeated calls for spiritual purity and holiness on the part of everyone from king to commoner, one could argue that her focus on eternity blinded her to some of the political realities of the temporal world.

Seventy-five years later, in 1448, the pope who ultimately canonized Catherine, Pope Pius II, campaigned for another Crusade, again unsuccessfully. Catherine's ethos as daughter/intermediary/crusader undoubtedly contributed to Pius II writing in the Bull of Canonization: "We . . . have contemplated . . . with joy the virtues, the genius, the greatness of soul, the strength and fortitude of this blessed Catherine . . . "[41] He may also have felt a kinship with this holy woman who shared his yearning to see Jerusalem in Christian hands. However, although he may have felt an affinity for her at the time of her canonization, he must have lost it by the time he died. It is reported that, on his deathbed, "Pius II . . . repented bitterly of three things: of having written the book of 'The Two Lovers;' of having preached a crusade; and of having canonized that sovereignly contemptible woman, Catherine of Siena."[42] Precisely why he decided that she was so contemptible is uncertain. It is possible that, when Pius II really examined Catherine the daughter of God, the intermediary, the crusader, he found the Catherine who had no fear of chastising the head of her Church, the man she believed to be the greatest man on earth. Pius II had an "untiring quest for adventure, [a] fondness for travel and hunger for knowledge . . . [that] . . . imposed marked limits upon his introspectiveness"[43] and, for Catherine, introspection was the key to self-knowledge, knowledge of God, and knowledge of one's duty before God.[44] Since Pius II certainly had not known Catherine personally, he could only have heard her voice through her *Dialogue* and letters and, even across the distance of time, found her both appealing and problematic.

Pius II was not the first pope to find Catherine both appealing and problematic. Gregory XI had a very high regard for Catherine's spiritual insights but, in the end, wondered if he had paid too much attention to her. In 1376, when someone wrote him an anonymous letter telling him not to return to Rome because of a plot against his life, Gregory sent the letter to Catherine for analysis and response. She urged him to hold fast to his plan to return the papacy to Rome, assuring him that "peace with [his] rebellious children and the reform of holy Church" would follow this move.[45] Neither peace nor reform ensued. Political intrigue and division continued. When Gregory became ill and realized he was dying, his fear that chaos would erupt upon his death led him to say that he regretted "having listened to the advice of meddling women."[46] The ethos of Catherine, the mystic, the daughter of God, the intermediary, had been so powerful that Gregory now wondered if it had overshadowed his own good sense.

Catherine's ethos continues to be appealing and problematic in the twentieth century. The appeal seems to be confined to the Church, though, not reaching the world at large as it did in her time. In 1921, Pope Benedict XV commended Catherine for being the major force behind the papacy's return to Rome and for her hard work on behalf of Urban VI, who had been elected pope after Gregory's death.[47] In 1970, when Pope Paul VI declared Catherine to be a Doctor of the Church, he commended her sacrifice, her doctrine, her faith, her love for Christ, and the illuminating example she is to the glory of the servants of the Church.[48]

In the academy, however, the trend appears to be to examine the lives of medieval female ascetics such as St. Catherine, and pronounce their behaviours "strange": [49] they are victims of patriarchy[50] who live in imaginary worlds of freedom[51] and their self-denial is be seen as symptomatic of anorexia.[52] In rhetorical terms, the ethos of women such as Catherine is flawed. Their good sense is questionable; if they were sensible, they would not deny themselves to the point of death. Their goodness may not be questioned but it is framed within the rubric of 'victim' which automatically puts them in a position inferior to that of the modern, 'empowered' woman. Their goodwill is disputed: historian Rudolph Bell describes Catherine as "a girl totally dedicated to the spiritual welfare of her family" but one who is "a troubled young woman" who pitted her will against God's, "committed the sin of vainglory and . . . starved herself to death."[53] A troubled, rebellious, proud anorexic does not have a positive ethos. She is effectively silenced, shelved as having nothing to say to our modern world, silenced by modern scholarship and not by the patriarchy of medieval Roman Catholicism.

Reducing the complex life of a medieval religieuse to a paradigm that allows us to silence her is a fascinating exercise in "revisionist history"[54] and it reveals a great deal about the culture in which it arises. As Nagler (p. 37) mentions, the mystical way of knowing and being is foreign to most of us in the modern West. We pride ourselves on that which is scientifically provable and question the validity of that which does not fall under our definition of rational. We identify more easily with the individual struggling to climb the corporate ladder than with the individual who sees herself as a daughter of God and struggles to live a life that straddles both eternity and temporality. Modern Western society also tends to pride itself on individualism rather than interdependence, on self-actualization rather than self-denial; it emphasizes self-esteem rather than sin. McDonald's ubiquitous "You deserve a break today!" has greater appeal than the sentiment expressed so often by Catherine, "I long to see you engulfed and drowned in the sweet blood of God's Son."[55] Thus, although we may understand Catherine's mourning over the fourteenth-century Church, her asceticism and suffering on behalf of that Church are distant from our way of being in the universe. Our pluralistic society finds us embarrassed by the ethos of an advocate of a Crusade and of a particular religion. So we explain her with our own paradigms; but those are problematic, too. One is hard-pressed to see Catherine as another female victim of a patriarchal church when she was addressing cardinals, fearlessly rebuking one pope and being consulted not only by him but also by his successor. Noffke points out that many people accused Catherine of having precipitated the Great Western Schism.[56] If this is even partly true, it is a charge that cannot be laid against a powerless victim, either of patriarchy or of anorexia.

Given that Catherine was grounded in eternity, that her main audience was God, that her entire life was spent seeking to live out what she believed was a call from God, perhaps she has little to say to the modern secular academy which is focused on an entirely different version of truth and actually finds her truth to be uncomfortable, irrelevant, and politically incorrect. Nevertheless, as we use rhetorical tools to analyze her writings and the things written about her by her contemporaries and by others who have studied her, we find a dynamic, determined woman who lived her ethos as a mystic, a daughter of God, an intermediary until the day she died. Her actions, however unusual they may seem to us, made sense to her in the framework of that multifaceted ethos in relation to her main audience, God. And, for better or worse, that ethos made sufficient sense to two popes and thousands of other people to cause them to see her as spiritually credible and persuasive. Catherinian scholar, Suzanne Noffke, writes, "Catherine was a teacher and a preacher, and a good one, but she was even more an uncompromisingly honest searcher after the Truth and Love that is God in Jesus crucified."[57] Whether or not we share her spiritual goal, her uncompromising determination to continue to search and to continue to work for the betterment of her world may say something to our world after all.

## *NOTES*

1. Michael Pusey, *Jürgen Habermas*. Key Sociologists, series ed. Peter Hamilton (London: Ellis Horwood Limited & Tavistock Publications Limited, 1987), 63.
2. Ibid., 62.
3. Raymond Capua, *Life of Saint Catherine of Siena,* ed. E. Cartier, trans. Ladies of the Sacred Heart (1395; reprint Philadelphia: Peter F. Cunningham, 1859), 27, 45, 113; Suzanne O.P. Noffke, trans., *The Letters of St. Catherine of Siena, vol. 1* (Binghamton: Medieval & Renaissance Texts & Studies, Volume 52, 1988), Letter 19: 79.
4. Suzanne Noffke, in Catherine of Siena, *The Dialogue*, trans. Suzanne Noffke (New York: Paulist, 1980), 9, 10, 1.
5. After a dispute between the French king and Pope Boniface VIII, Philip of France kidnapped Boniface and took him to Avignon in 1302. From then until 1377, popes lived in Avignon, an event known as the Babylonian Captivity, which distressed Italians and split the Roman Catholic Church. Healing this rift was the focus of much of Catherine's life work. However, even after Pope Gregory XI returned to Rome, struggles continued and there were, at one time, three different popes. This schism was not resolved until 1417.
6. Capua, *Life of Saint Catherine.*
7. Capua, *Life of Saint Catherine,* 173.
8. St. Teresa of Avila and St. Teresa of Lisieux are the other two, so named in 1970 and 1998 respectively.

9. Noffke, *Dialogue*, 1.
10. Michael N. Nagler, "Mysticism: A Hardheaded Definition for a Romantic Age," *Studia Mystica* 1, no. 1 (Spring 1978): 37.
11. Ibid., 54.
12. Ibid.
13. Ibid.
14. Ibid., 46.
15. Ibid., 47.
16. Edmund G. Gardner, *Saint Catherine of Siena: A Study in the Religion, Literature and History of the Fourteenth Century in Italy* (London: J.M. Dent & Co., 1907), 50.
17. Ibid., 93.
18. Suzanne Noffke, *Catherine of Siena: Vision Through a Distant Eye* (Collegeville: Liturgical, 1996), 11.
19. Noffke, *Dialogue*, 62.
20. "Daughter" is used 95 times in 167 chapters.
21. Capua, *Life of Saint Catherine*, 76.
22. Luke 2:41–50.
23. Luke 2:49.
24. Luke 2:51.
25. Possible reference to Romans 8:16–18.
26. Capua, *Life of Saint Catherine*, 68.
27. Capua, *Life of Saint Catherine*, 68.
28. Noffke, *Dialogue*, 362.
29. Noffke, *Letters*, 69, 71, 74, 76, 77, 80, 81, 88.
30. A term of endearment that cannot be accurately translated.
31. Catherine often uses this term when talking about God.
32. Noffke, *Letters*, 71: 222.
33. Ibid., 223.
34. Capua, *Life of Saint Catherine*, 311.
35. Gardner, *Saint Catherine of Siena*, 351.
36. Luke 23:46.
37. Noffke, *Letters*, 30, 35, 40, 41, 64, 78, 79.
38. Gardner, *Saint Catherine of Siena*, 117.
39. Birgitta of Sweden (St. Bridget) also wrote Pope Gregory XI about visions she had regarding his need to reform the Church and return to Rome. In Gardner, *Saint Catherine of Siena*, 103–105.
40. Gardner, *Saint Catherine of Siena*, 118.
41. Josephine E. Butler, *Catherine of Siena: A Biography* (London: Dyer Brothers, 1878), 130.
42. Ibid., 333.
43. Kenneth M. Setton, *The Papacy and the Levant (1204–1571)*, vol. 2 (Philadelphia: The American Philosophical Society, 1978), 258.

44　Noffke, *Dialogue*, 25.
45　Noffke, *Letters,* 81:247.
46　Noffke, *Vision Through a Distant Eye,* 62; Gardner, *Saint Catherine of Siena,* 253. The other woman to whom he referred was St. Bridget.
47　Claudia Carlen, IHM, ed., "Fausto Appetente Die: Encyclical of Pope Benedict XV on St. Dominic, June 29, 1921," *The Papal Encyclicals 1903-1939* (McGrath Publishing Company, n.d.), 217–20.
48　Pope Paul VI, "Acta Pauli PP. VI," *Acta Apostolicae Sedis: Commentarium Officiale* (Palazzo Apostolica, Citta del Vaticano: Libreria Editrice Vaticana, An. et vol. LXII (10): October 31, 1970).
49　Martha Grace Reese, "St. Catherine of Siena: The Way of Mystic Madness," *Religious Traditions* 11 (1988): 40.
50　Rudolph M. Bell, *Holy Anorexia* (Chicago: University of Chicago, 1985); Renee Neu Watkins, "Two Women Visionaries and Death: Catherine of Siena and Julian of Norwich," *Numen* 39, no. 2 (1993): 196; Gail Corrington, "Anorexia, Asceticism and Autonomy: Self-Control as Liberation and Transcendence," *Journal of Feminist Studies in Religion* 2, no. 2 (Fall 1986): 51-62; Reese, "The Way of Mystic Madness."
51　Ulrike Weithaus, "Sexuality, Gender and the Body in Late Medieval Women's Spirituality," *Journal of Feminist Studies in Religion* 7, no. 1 (Spring 1991): 51.
52　Bell, *Holy Anorexia.*
53　Bell, *Holy Anorexia,* 49, 50, 51.
54　Mary Lassance Parthun, quoted on the jacket of Bell's book.
55　Noffke, *Letters,* 31: 108.
56　Noffke, *Vision Through a Distant Eye,* 62.
57　Ibid., 64.

## *Verbum inuisibile palpabitur:*
## *Les Sibylles dans la seconde moitié du XVe siècle: La répétition comme poétique de l'oracle*

HÉLÈNE CAZES

Certains aimaient à disserter sans fin du sexe des anges; ils auraient pu, aussi bien, disserter du nombre des Sibylles, de leur âge ou de leurs prophéties respectives. En effet, l'extraordinaire fortune des oracles sibyllins, à la fin du Moyen-Age et au début de la Renaissance, se développe dans le désordre et la confusion des sources, sans grand dommage, d'ailleurs quant au message messianique délivré par les anciennes devineresses. Il semblerait au contraire que l'imprécision et la pauvreté lacunaire des textes transmis ait aidé à leur succès et à leur multiplication.

### *Des livres-phénix*

De fait, le mythe originel, comme les vicissitudes de la transmission manuscrite des textes, autorisaient, dès la fin de l'Antiquité, toutes les reconstructions et manipulations souhaitées, si bien que les livres grecs, connus sous le nom d'*Oracles Sibyllins*, se présentaient déjà comme les fragments et les conjectures d'un corpus dispersé et disparu. Et c'est bien dans l'anéantissement préliminaire des livres et personnages relaté par les mythes, que se joue l'immense succès des prédictions: quelle plus grande liberté espérer que celle laissée par l'absence et la rareté des traces? Tout commence en effet par la destruction de six des neuf livres d'oracles.

Dans les anciennes annales, on relate cette histoire sur les livres sibyllins: Une vieille femme, étrangère et inconnue, vint trouver le roi Tarquin le Superbe avec neuf livres. Elle affirmait que c'étaient des oracles divins et voulait les vendre. Tarquin s'enquit du prix: la femme réclama une somme exorbitante. Le roi pensa que, du fait de son âge, la femme déraisonnait, et il se mit à rire. Alors, elle installe devant lui un petit foyer, l'allume et brûle trois des neuf livres. Et la voilà qui redemande au roi s'il veut acheter les livres restants, toujours pour le même prix. Tarquin éclata de rire et dit que la vieille radotait. Aussitôt, sans bouger de sa place, la femme brûla trois autres livres et, tranquillement, elle lui reposa la question: veut-il acheter les trois derniers livres, toujours au même prix? Tarquin change; le visage grave, prêt à entendre, il comprend que cette obstination sûre d'elle n'est pas à prendre à la légère. Il acquiert les trois derniers livres, sans marchander, au prix demandé pour le lot initial.[1]

Que dire ensuite des incendies répétés par lesquels le sort s'acharnerait à réduire en poussière les précieuses prédictions? En 83 avant JC,[2] sous le règne d'Auguste,[3] en 64 après JC,[4] en 408,[5] les trois malheureux tomes échappés au feu de Tarquin brûleraient à nouveau dans leur sanctuaire et leur renaissance à l'image du phénix est déjà un miracle. L'on suivrait de miracle en miracle les rédactions et redécouvertes successives de ces livres muets jusqu'au temps qui nous occupe: la fin du XVe siècle. A cette époque, deux traditions distinctes se sont établies séparément: la première, plus proche de la mythique vérité et de la falsification messianique de l'Empire, est constituée par un corpus en grec, en huit livres, et non traduit en latin avant la Renaissance. C'est sur cette branche que se greffera la recherche érudite des humanistes du XVIe siècle comme Sixtus Birken, qui en donne édition et traduction latine en 1545[6] ou Sébastien Châteillon qui en propose une version métrique en 1546. Peu connus au Moyen-Age et peu utilisés, ces oracles semblent bien moins servir les différents lecteurs que les fragments rassemblés par Lactance, dans les *Institutions Divines*,[7] pour démontrer l'universalité de la révélation chrétienne, puisque la bonne nouvelle aurait été répandue même auprès des Païens; le Père de l'Eglise établit ainsi une série de dix Sibylles, dont chacune porte un nom et est attachée à un lieu, et il compile les sources antiques pour élaborer le premier canon de ce second corpus. Augustin, dans la *Cité de Dieu*,[8] traduit les textes grecs choisis par Lactance, y adjoint une citation virgilienne sur la Sibylle de Cumes, et offre alors un ensemble cohérent de courtes prédictions qui seront transmises, enrichies et citées durant tout le Moyen Age.

C'est cette seconde branche de la tradition qui m'intéresse ici: constituée de fragments, de traductions, de citations de deuxième ou troisième main, elle permet la floraison durant plusieurs siècles de prédictions adjacentes et se retrouve, vers le milieu du XVeme siècle, sous la forme d'un canon hétéroclite mais accepté. En effet, l'on connaît le succès des séries de Sibylles dans l'art religieux de cette période: en France, en Italie, en Allemagne, stalles, vitraux et fresques font défiler les Sibylles, phylactères en main, pour célébrer la venue du Christ. Ces processions féminines, composées le plus souvent de douze prophétesses grâce à l'adjonction de nouvelles devineresses, semblent avoir été conçues pour faire pendant aux séries de prophètes de l'Ancien Testament, dans une pensée somme toute fort proche de celle de Lactance: l'universalité de la bonne parole. Mais les Sibylles ont changé depuis le premier canon: jeunes pour la plupart, belles, respectées comme le montrent riches vêtements et niches d'apparat, elles ne ressemblent plus guère à la vieille femme échevelée que méprise Tarquin ou qui effraie Énée. Même lorsque mention expresse est faite de leur laideur ou de leur âge avancé, comme pour Démophile ou la Sibylle de Cumes, la représentation ne vise pas à repousser le spectateur: elles n'inspirent plus l'horreur originelle de leur fonction sacrée.

## *Des femmes qui rajeunissent avec les siècles*

Cette nouvelle jeunesse, qui se laisse admirer dans les églises ou sur les murs de riches mécènes, a souvent été commentée sans qu'une interprétation en ait pu être proposée car les textes qui accompagnent parfois ces belles figures et qui circulent à la même période n'en donnent aucune explication. Peut-être faut-il y voir la représentation, par la chair elle-même, de la joie de la révélation: interprètes du monde d'en dessous dans l'univers païen, filles de rois vaincus telle Cassandre, ou vieilles étrangères sans nom ni amis, les devineresses antiques ne seraient reconnues que dans le contexte chrétien. Aussi, peu importe le sort des livres perdus, brûlés, dédaignés dans les siècles d'ignorance impie: le visage tourné vers l'avenir, fortes de leur jeunesse éternelles, les Sibylles chrétiennes ne sont comprises et entendues qu'en l'âge nouveau de l'ère chrétienne. Le corpus élaboré par Lactance, Augustin et les ajouts médiévaux est, dans cette perspective, le seul pertinent puisque, justement, il ne retrace que l'essentiel et garde souvenir du mépris initial des peuples sans foi.

L'on voit bien, dès lors, comment ces femmes en procession, charmantes et inspirées à la fois, méritent l'attention des prédicateurs et des artistes religieux: sujet de choix pour la figuration et la représentation concrète de la révélation, elles ne sont pas seulement le pendant des prophètes, elles sont en elles-mêmes la manifestation de la vie éternelle accordée aux croyants. Car, malgré l'abondance d'exemples où, jusqu'à la chapelle Sixtine, les prophétesses font face aux prophètes, aucun parallèle n'est fixé, aucun canon ne s'établit pour arrêter de façon convaincante une mise en «couples» des annonciateurs du Messie. Dans «Quelques séries italiennes de Sibylles», C. de Clerq compare quatre séries: les Sibylles du palais Orsini (avant 1438), la procession du mystère de l'*Annunziazione* de Feo Belcari donné à Florence en 1471, les gravures de Baccio Baldini (Florence, avant 1460) et un traité de Barbieri.[9] Or les symétries proposées entre figures de l'Ancien Testament et les devineresses antiques ne concordent pas entre les séries; dans les fresques, disparues, du palais Orsini et qui sont connues par des descriptions manuscrites, on trouve en effet les appariements suivants: Abraham-Persica / Mycheas-Libica / Jacob-Delphica / Moyses-Chimeria / Sophonias-Ericthea / David-Samia / Ysaias-Cumana / Iheremias-Elespontia / Daniel-Frigea / Ysaias-Tiburtina / Yhohel-Europhila / Abacuc-Agripa / Micheas.[10] Dans le mystère de Feo Belcari, on trouve au contraire, la conjonction d'un ange, d'un patriarche et d'une Sibylle dont le groupe forme chaque rang de la procession: Noé, Giacobe-Eritrea / Mosé, Giosué-Sofonia / Samuele, David-Persica / Elia, Eliseo-Pontica / Malachia, Amos-Samia / Isaia, Gionas-Michea / Geremia, Ezechiele-Osea /

Daniele, Abacuch-Cumana / Egeo, Abias-Tiburtina. Quant aux gravures de Baldini, elles ne proposent aucun parallèle.

Enfin, en 1481, paraît un traité sur les Sibylles, dû à la compilation et à la plume de Filippo Barbieri (Philippus de Barberiis); dans la première version de cet ouvrage, une série de gravures apparie chaque devineresse à un prophète selon une combinaison encore différente: Persia / Osias-Libica / Ieremias-Delphica / Ieremias-Emeria / Ioel-Erithrea / Ezechiel-Samia / David Rex-Cumana / Daniel-Phrigia / Malachias-Europea / Zacharias-Agrippa / Isaias-Tiburtina / Micheas.

Les discordances entre les combinaisons relevées, tout autant que l'existence de séries autonomes de Sibylles, telle la série de gravures exécutée par Baldini,[11] indiquent ainsi que la piste des analogies entre personnages de la Révélation ne suffit pas pour expliquer le succès ni les infléchissements de la fortune des Sibylles. Il semblerait bien plutôt que les Sibylles constituent une série indépendante à la fin du XVe siècle et que la cohérence des prophéties et prophétesses soit intrinsèque à leur procession toute féminine. Selon cette hypothèse, qui résout les flottements dans les analogies entre devineresses antiques et prophètes, patriarches ou anges de l'Ancien Testament, les douze figures de femmes ne seraient appariées à des personnages masculins que pour satisfaire à une symbolique de la symétrie, sans autre support théorique.

Pour présomption d'une lecture des séries sibyllines, indépendamment de tout mariage avec les séries de patriarches, je reprendrai ce court traité de 1481, première dissertation publiée sur les sibylles et leurs prophéties; certainement issu de la compilation de manuscrits italiens circulant au XVeme siècle et détaillant les prophétesses, leurs noms, leurs origines et leurs prédictions, le texte est dû à Filippo Barbiéri, homme d'Eglise.[12] Comme en réponse à la fameuse lettre du Pogge qui déclare l'inextricable complexité de la «question sibylline» en 1554,[13] en écho également à la publication en 1465 de l'édition princeps des *Institutions Divines* de Lactance, Barbiéri propose sous le titre *Des Douze Sibylles qui annoncèrent la venue du Christ* un exposé concis et documenté, qui reprend les sources antiques et modernes et les fond dans une présentation fort rassurante: chaque chapitre est constitué par la présentation de la prophétesse, de son nom, des sources qui témoignent de son existence, des éléments remarquables de sa représentation et du texte de sa prédiction. Pour chaque Sibylle, est jointe au texte une gravure où un phylactère reprend les phrases marquantes de sa prophétie. Ce traité s'inscrit ainsi dans le droit fil de la tradition médiévale et renaissante où les Sibylles forment un thème iconographique abondamment représenté.

Dans la première édition de 1481, les gravures de Sibylles sont couplées à celles de prophètes de l'Ancien Testament, selon la liste indiquée plus haut. Or, dès la seconde édition, par Herolt et Riessinger à Rome en 1482, les prophètes disparaissent, pour ne plus revenir: les couples de célibataires sacrés sont défaits comme ils furent faits, sans un mot.

### *Un opuscule peut en cacher un autre*

De fait, l'examen des prophéties sibyllines recueillies par Barbiéri ne saurait être mené sans une mise en contexte: quoique formant un livre indépendant par la présence d'un titre et d'un *explicit*, le traité sur les Sibylles est la deuxième partie d'un ensemble cohérent constitué de quatre traités de Barbiéri. Leur regroupement, constant dans les éditions et rééditions successives, est attesté par l'étude des cahiers composant les volumes finaux du livre complet et dont je donne les éléments en annexe: le texte sur les prophétesses est matériellement indissociable du premier des traités: les *Discordances entre saint Augustin et saint Jérôme*. En effet, le jeu des cahiers et des pages empêche absolument d'imaginer une publication indépendante de la seconde pièce – même si le traité sur les «Discordances» fut, en 1479, publié seul dans une édition napolitaine perdue et citée par sa réédition en 1490, par Francesco del Tuppo.[14] Aussi, l'on peut lire dans le premier des textes du recueil comme une introduction à l'exposé sur les Sibylles, puisque le lecteur passe, sans grande solution de continuité, d'une compilation de témoignages païens et antiques attestant d'une révélation chrétienne à la collection de gravures et de prédictions sibyllines. La cohérence est d'autant plus forte que le seizième point de désaccord entre Augustin et Jérôme porte précisément sur les prophétesses du monde antique et que, selon la compilation inspirée de Thomas d'Aquin, Barbiéri commence dès ce passage à énumérer les prédictions sibyllines, les sources qui nous les ont transmises et leur accomplissement par la venue du Sauveur.

## *Répéter et répéter encore*

Dès lors, ce n'est plus dans la mise en regard de figures symétriques et scripturaires qu'il faut lire la cohérence sibylline, c'est, fort précisément, dans la continuité que constitue leur série. Car, si prophéties et noms s'échangent selon les auteurs, si lieux et nombres se chevauchent et se contredisent, l'on découvre en revanche une remarquable similitude entre toutes les prophéties des différentes demoiselles. Oui, l'Hellespontica de Barbiéri reprend les prédictions de l'Erythréenne du palais Orsini; et son Erythréenne reprend la fin d'une prophétie italienne du XIIIeme attribuée à la Tiburtina chez Orsini et dans la cathédrale de Sienne. Mais, à bien écouter, elles disent toutes la même chose et peu importe laquelle emploie quel mot exact; toutes vierges, toutes étrangères et disparues, elles annoncent la naissance d'un Messie né sans enfantement humain.

C'est dans ce goût de la répétition que me paraît résider la fascination pour les séries de Sibylles: tout d'abord, la prophétie en elle-même ne saurait exister sans présenter l'événement – lequel, hélas, est le plus souvent antérieur à la rédaction des prédictions – comme la répétition du texte. La force du futur de la prophétie est de se conjuguer au passé: le sens est donné par la réalisation de la prédiction qui structure alors des vers fort obscurs, les éclairant par un contexte réel et avéré. En effet, comment comprendre les poèmes célébrant le règne de l'enfant, si ce n'est en proposant une référence qui précise le large, trop large signifié? Et que faire de prophéties portant sur le lointain avenir? La prophétie n'intéresse que le passé, à qui elle donne une résonance messianique et qu'elle parsème de repères textuels.

Rééditer la prédiction, c'est déjà entrer dans la magie de la répétition: répéter le texte qui fut réalisé. Dans le cas des devineresses qui se multiplient et se paraphrasent l'une l'autre, le jeu de miroirs s'enrichit encore, puisque la répétition est renvoyée d'une Sibylle à l'autre, comme dans le montage d'un kaléidoscope. Et, pareillement, la représentation et la personnification des prophétesses renforcent les jeux de redites: jeunes filles ou vieilles demoiselles, elles clament leur virginité avant d'annoncer la venue de l'autre Vierge, la sainte mère du Messie.

Répétitions, redites, représentations, les séries sibyllines tendent alors vers le ressassement dont, mystérieusement et merveilleusement, jaillit le sens. C'est d'ailleurs l'une d'elles qui annonce l'avènement de l'*inuisibile verbum* porté par une femme: *Inuisibile uerbum palpabitur*, dit Agripa, le Verbe invisible se fera chair. Le verbe secret, crypté, difficile de la prophétie s'éclaire et fut éclairé par l'avènement du Verbe.

Le livre, dès lors, devient le support et la matière de cette incantation de la répétition et des répétitions: jusqu'en 1514, date de la dernière édition connue du traité de Barbiéri, toutes les Sibylles sont représentées, selon un modèle graphique cohérent sur le volume et le livre se transforme ainsi en album d'emblèmes, que l'on pourrait imaginer détachables si leur valeur ne tenait, justement, à la réitération et à l'accumulation. En tant que recueil d'opuscules, le livre joue également le jeu des ressassements, groupant dans le même volume des textes similaires et congruents, comme le traité sur les «discordances» et sa continuation. C'est ainsi que, loin des cathédrales et des palais, indépendamment de toute contingence d'ordre architectural, décoratif ou artistique, la série des Sibylles, au sein du livre, grandit encore par l'adjonction d'une treizième compagne: Falconia Proba, poétesse du IVe après JC, qui composa en citations virgiliennes une Histoire Sainte fort appréciée durant tout le Moyen Age et la Renaissance. Représentée par une gravure, elle porte sur un phylactère dans les éditions citées, non pas le texte d'une prédiction mais son nom et son statut de femme de consul: comment la femme mariée ne dépare-t-elle donc pas la série? C'est que sa parole est uniquement répétition: son œuvre est d'avoir «remis Virgile en ordre» pour chanter la foi chrétienne. Le sens, alors, naît de la seconde énonciation des mots virgiliens, tout comme celui de la prophétie qui n'apparaît qu'avec l'accomplissement.

Treize femmes perdent leurs livres, délirent ou prennent les mots des autres, treize gravures donnent chair et beauté, pour un livre qui ne parle que de relectures et, ainsi, célèbre la magie du Livre: la répétition virtuellement infinie.

### Annexe: Éditions du traité de Barbiéri

*1ère édition: 1er décembre 1481, Rome*

En fait, deux tirages sous la même date, le second datant probablement de 1482.
Exemplaires consultés de l'éd. de 1481: Paris, BN Res D 3650; BN Res D 6445; Arsenal T. 4523; Lucques, Biblioteca Guvernativa, Inc n° 229.
Références bibliographiques: *Gesamkatalog der Wiegendrucke*, III, Leipzig, 1928, p. 401 n° 3385; M. Pellechet, *Catalogue général des Incunables des bibliothèques publiques de France*, I, p. 455, n° 1843; Hain-Copinger 872; BMC 2, 320 IA 19262; IGI 1245. Sanders, *Le livre à figures italien*, n° 772.

Edition de 1481/1482.
Selon Sanders (773), l'imprimeur a repris les cahiers 1 et 2, une partie du 3. Il a joint 16 autres bois. Le registre, identique, ne correspond plus aux cahiers.
GW 3386 Hain-Copinger-Reichl 2455; BMC 4, 131, IA 19263

Description: Huit cahiers in 8° et un cahier in 4°, (13 x 18 cm) non paginé, non signé. a2, b-i8, k4 pour le premier tirage ; a-b8, c6, d-k8, l4 pour le second. Car. rom.

Contenu: [A1-2v°]: préface de I. P. de Lignamine.
[A3-6v°]: traité sur les «Discordances», sans titre. Première ligne en majuscules, place d'attente pour initiales.
Incipit: *Duo luminaria magna que deus fecit: id est duos sacrosancte ecclesie doctores egregios: Eusebium uidelicet Hieronymum & aurelium Augustinum quos deus elegit (…)*
[A 10 v°] *Nunc afferamus in medium dicta propria Sibyllarum, et que unaqueque earum dixerit, nec seruabimus in hunc ordinem temporis nec dignitatis excellentiam sed secundum quod nobis occurrerit (…)*

[Passage au deuxième cahier. Gravures: Sibylle sur la page de droite, représentée comme un emblème avec l'illustration surmontant le texte de la prophétie, prophète sur la page de gauche, avec le même dispositif d'illustration et de texte.]
[p. 32] *Probe centone clarissime foemine excerptum e Maronis carminibus ad testimonium ueteris nouique testamenti opusculum sequitur.* (…)

*2ème édition: Rome, 1482, Georgius Herolt et Sixtus Riessinger*

Exemplaires consultés de l'éd. de 1482: Florence, BN, Inc M 6. 23
Références bibliographiques: GW , III, Leipzig, 1928, p. 401 n° 3387; Pellechet, I, p. 455, n° 1841. Hain-Copinger-Reichl 2453; Proctor 3854; BMC IV, 129, IA 29240.
Sanders, 774.

Description: Huit cahiers in 4°, non signés ; a10, b-g8, h10. Car. rom et riche ornementation.
[A1] table
Tractatus solemnis et utilis editum per religiosum uirum magistrum Philippum Syculum Ordinis predicatorum Sacre theologie possessorem integerrimum in quo infrascripta perpulchre compilauit.
In primis discordantias nonnullas inter sanctos Eusebium Hieronymum et Aurelium Augustinum sanctosancte ecclesie doctores circha quas plurimas doctorum aliorum opiniones adducit. Secundo duodecim sibillarum uaticinia que de christo ediderunt cum earum figuris proporciona.
*Tercio Carmina Probae Centone Clarissime foemine Romae que ex Maronis carminibus ad corroborationem ueteris nouique testamenti diuino ingenio excerpsit.* (…)

*3ème édition: Oppenheim [Jacob Koebel, 1514]*

Exemplaire décrit: Paris, Mazarine, 31581, Réserve.
Bibliographie: J. Benzing, *Jacob Köbel zu Oppenheim 1494–1533*, Wiesbaden, 1952 n° 55. Donne la date de 1517. P. Hohenemser, *Flugschriften-Sammlung Gustav Freitag*, Nieuwkoop, 1966, n° 33 et 34. Donne 1514. Hain Copinger 2454. Pellechet 1842.

Recueil de quatre pièces homogènes dont la publication séparée n'est pas attestée. Oppenheim, sd, in 4°
[1ère pièce]: *DUO magna luminaria...*
[2ème pièce]: *OPUSCULUM DE VATICINIS SIBILLARUM* Car. rom pour le texte, titres en car. goth. Organisation en album d'emblèmes: un chap. par page, sur le recto et la gravure correspondante au verso de la page, annoncée par un bandeau *SEQUITUR IMAGO* ou *SEQUITUR SCHEMA* ou *SEQUITUR FIGURA*; l'illustration est donc au dos du texte auquel elle correspond.
[3ème pièce]: *OPUSCULUM uariis iudeorum et gentilium de Christo testimoniis.* Même impression.
[4ème pièce]: *CENTONES PROBE FALCONIE DE UTRIUSQUE TESTAMENTI HISTORIIS EX CARMINIBUS VIRGILII SELECTI CUM ANNOTATIONE LOCORUM EX QUIBUS DESUMPTI SUNT.*

## NOTES

1 Aulu-Gelle, *Nuits Attiques*, 1, 29; anecdote rapportée également par Lactance, *Institutions Divines*, 16, 5 et Servius, *Commentaires*, Aen. 6, 72.

2 Denys d'Halicarnasse, *Antiquités Romaines*, 4, 62.

3 Tacite, *Annales*, 6, 12 ; Suétone, *Auguste*, 31.

4 Tacite, *Annales*, 15, 44.

5 Rutilius Namatianus, *Sur son retour*, 2, 52.

6 *Sibyllinorum oraculorum libri octo, multis huc usque seculis abstrusi, nuncque primum in lucem editi (...)*, Bâle, 1545.

7 Lactance, *Institutions Divines*, 1, 16.

8 Augustin, *Cité de Dieu*, 18, 23.

9 C. de Clerq, «Quelques séries italiennes de Sibylles«, *Bulletin de l'Institut Historique Belge de Rome*, 48-49 (1978-1979), 104-27.

10 Les traits d'union unissent les couples. Les appariements sont ainsi corrects, même si, dans les fresques, Micheas reste seul, et, dans le traité de Barbieri, Persica et Micheas sont seuls.

11 J. Philipps, *Early Florentine Designers and Engravers* (Cambridge, MA: Harvard University Press, 1955), 56 sq. Chaque gravure comporte la figuration d'une sibylle assise, son nom, une inscription latine (proche de la description manuscrite des fresques du palais Orsini) et huit vers italiens (proches des prophéties de l'*Annunziazione* de Feo Belcari).

12 Selon le *Dizionario Biografico degli Italiani*, 4 (Rome: Edizioni Nazionali, 1964), 217-21, né à Syracuse en 1426, où il fut professeur prédicateur de l'ordre des

Dominicains à Catane. En 1475, Inquisiteur général de Sicile, Sardaigne et Malte, il persécute les Juifs. Nommé vicaire du couvent de Messine en 1478, il fut suspendu pendant un an en 1479, accusé d'avoir composé un libelle diffamatoire contre quelques grands (dont Paul II et Sixte IV). Il réintègra sa charge «propter humilitatem et poenitentiam factam». Il est également l'auteur d'une *Cronaca dei papi è imperatori* (de 1316 à 1469), publiée anonymement à Rome en 1479 et attribuée à Giovanni de Lignamine (Cf. Muratori: *Rerum Italicarum Scriptores IX* [Mediolani: 1726], coll. 263-276).

13  Cf. S. Settis, «Sibilla Agrippa», dans *Etudes de Lettres* (1985), 89-123: le «mémoire de Sagramori», 1454, évoque, à propos des Sibylles de Sienne, «l'affaire des Sibylles». Une lettre du Pogge, en réponse à une demande d'éclaircissement de Vulturio sur les noms et le nombre des Sibylles, renvoie aux fresques du palais Orsini en ces termes: «De Sibyllis quod petis, non est mihi nunc otium talia exquirendi; sed quod re nequeo, consilio adiuuabo. Bonae memoriae Cardinalis de Ursinis (...) in aura palatii sui, quae paramenti camera appellatur, Sibyllas omnes summa cum diligentia pingi fecit cum inscriptione eorum, quae suis temporibus, quaeque de Christo praedixit. Quare scribas Romama licet, ut et formam picturae, et nomina Sibyllarum, et epigrammata notentur ab homine erudito, tibique mittantur. Nam nullo loco reperies quod quaeris exquisitius, et simul effugies molestum laborem. Non enim parua cura haec res est aut nunc confici potest, aut tunc confecta est summa cum doctissimorum uirorum diligentia.» (Lettre citée par S. Settis, «Sibilla Agrippa», 99, d'après l'éd. *Epistolae*, 40, 41, par Th. de Tonellis, 3, Florence, 1861).

14 [Naples, Francesco del Tuppo, 1490]: GWK 3888; IGI 1244. Exemplaire consulté: Bibliothèque Angelica, Rome, Inc 483. La dernière pièce, le traité sur les «Discordances», donné sans titre, porte l'inscription: *Sequens hoc opusculum Rome impressum est: qu[od] //Reuerendissmo Cardinali Neapolitano dicaui: S[ed] //quia impressorum uicio et negligentia plures me[n]do//sitates co[m]misse sunt: Eam ob rem dedi op[er]am ut ite//rum imprimeret[ur]: >per uirum doctum: qui materia[m] intelligeret.*

# *Verbum inuisibile palpabitur: The Sibyls in the Second Half of the Fifteenth Century: Repetition as Oracular Poetics*

### Hélène Cazes
#### Translated from the French by Nicholas Fairbank

Those who liked to argue endlessly about the sex of angels could just as well have argued about the number of Sibyls, their age, or their respective prophecies. In fact, the extraordinary fortune of the sibylline oracles at the end of the Middle Ages and the beginning of the Renaissance developed in disorder and a confusion of sources but, nevertheless, without much damage with respect to the messianic message delivered by these ancient seers. It would seem, on the contrary, that the inaccuracy and deficiency of the surviving texts have added to their success and to their multiplication.

## *Phoenix Books*

In fact, the original myth, like the difficulties of copying manuscripts by hand, allowed, from the end of Antiquity, any and all reconstructions and manipulations, such that the Greek texts, known as *Sibylline Oracles*, were already presented as the fragments and the conjectures of a work divided and dispersed. And it is because of the very destruction of the books and of the characters related by the myths that the predictions enjoyed their immense success – who could hope for a greater freedom than that created by the absence or the scarceness of traces? Everything begins, in fact, with the destruction of six of the nine books of oracles.

In the ancient annals the following story is told about the sibylline books: an unknown woman of great age comes to the king Tarquin the Proud with nine books. She affirms that they are the divine oracles and wishes to sell them. Tarquin asks the price; the woman demands an exorbitant sum. The king believes that, because of her age, the woman has lost her senses, and he laughs at her. She then builds a small fire and, in front of the king, burns three of the nine books. She asks him if he wishes to buy the remaining books, still for the same price. Tarquin bursts out laughing, saying that the woman is senile. Without further ado the woman burns three more books and calmly asks the question: Does he wish to buy the last three books, still at the original price? Tarquin's expression changes. Serious now, he understands that the woman's tenacity is not to be taken lightly. He buys the last three volumes without bargaining, at the price asked for the original nine.[1]

What can be said of these repeated fires which relentlessly reduce the precious predictions to ashes? In 83 BC,[2] in the reign of Augustus,[3] in 64 AD,[4] in 408,[5] the three volumes that escaped Tarquin's fire would burn again in the sanctuary where they were kept, their rebirth in the image of the phoenix already a miracle. One can follow the series of miracles through the successive rewritings and rediscoveries of these silent books up to the time that interests us – the end of the fifteenth century. In this period, two distinct traditions were established separately: the first, closer to the mythical truth and to the messianic falsification written during the Roman Empire, consists of a Greek corpus in eight volumes which was not translated into Latin before the Renaissance. Onto this branch was grafted the erudite research of the sixteenth-century humanists, such as Sixtus Birken, who produced an edition with a Latin translation in 1545,[6] or Sebastianus Castalio, who proposed a metrical version in 1546. Little known in the Middle Ages, and little used, these oracles seem to have served the different readers less than did the fragments reassembled by Lactantius in *Institutiones Divinae*[7] in order to demonstrate the universality of the Christian revelation (because the Good News would have spread even among pagans); this Church Father thus established a series of ten Sibyls, each one with a name and attached to a place, and his compilation of the ancient sources developed the first canon of this second corpus. Augustine, in *The City of God*,[8] translated the Greek texts chosen by Lactantius, and attached to it a Virgilian quotation on the Sibyl of Cumes, thus offering a coherent set of brief predictions that were transmitted, enriched, and quoted throughout the Middle Ages.

It is this second branch of the tradition that interests me here. Made up of fragments, translations, and second- or third-hand quotations, it allowed new predictions to flourish for several centuries, and, near the middle of the fifteenth century, existed in the form of a heterogeneous but accepted canon. We are familiar with the success of the series of Sibyls in the religious art of the period; in France, Italy, and Germany stalls, stained glass, and frescoes are decorated with the Sibyls, phylacteries in hand, to celebrate the coming of Christ. These female processions, composed most often of twelve prophetesses, thanks to the creation of new ones, seem to have been conceived to match the series of Old Testament prophets in a manner of thinking very close to that of Lactantius – the need to spread the Good News throughout the world. But the Sibyls have changed since the first canon: young for the most part; beautiful; respected, as shown by the richness of their clothing and the luxuriousness of their alcoves; they scarcely resemble any longer the dishevelled, solitary woman who scorned Tarquin or who frightened Aeneas. Even when express mention is made of their ugliness or of their advanced age, as with Demophile or the Sibyl of Cumes, their representation is not intended to repulse the spectator; they no longer inspire the original awe of their sacred function.

## *Women Rejuvenated with the Centuries*

This new youth, which can be admired in churches or in the houses of wealthy patrons, has often been commented on without any further interpretation being proposed, for the texts that sometimes accompany these figures, and that circulated in the same period, give no explanation. Perhaps this new outer appearance reflects the inner spiritual bliss of the Revelation: interpreters of the pagan underworld, daughters of conquered kings, like Cassandra the daughter of Priam, or old women from afar, nameless and friendless, these ancient seers of the pagan world would only be recognized in the Christian context. The Christian Sibyls were to be understood and listened to only in the new age of the Christian era. Their rejuvenated faces were turned towards the future; what happened during centuries of ignorant impiety – the fate of the lost, burned, or discounted books – was of little importance. The corpus compiled by Lactantius and Augustine, with its medieval additions, is, in this perspective, the only pertinent one precisely because it retraces only the essential and retains the memory of the initial disdain of a people without faith.

One can well see how, since that time, these women in procession, both charming and inspired, merit the attention of clergy and religious artists: subjects of choice for a concrete representation of the revelation, they are not only counterparts of the prophets, they are in themselves the manifestations of eternal life granted to believers. For despite the abundance of examples where, even in the Sistine Chapel, the prophetesses are face to face with the prophets, no parallel is drawn and no law is established to convincingly put a stop to the image of "couples" announcing the coming of the Messiah. In "Quelques séries italiennes de Sibylles," C. de Clerq compares four series: the Sibyls in the Orsini palace (before 1438), the procession of the mystery of the *Annunziazione* by Feo Belcari in Florence (1471), the engravings by Baccio Baldini (Florence, before 1460), and a treatise by Barbieri.[9] But in fact the proposed symmetries between the Old Testament prophets and the Sibyls are not the same for each series; in the Orsini palace frescoes, now lost but known by their written description, one finds the following pairings: Abraham-Persica / Mycheas-Libica / Jacob-Delphica / Moyses-Chimeria / Sophonias-Ericthea / David-Samia / Ysaias-Cumana / Iheremias-Elespontia / Daniel-Frigea / Ysaias-Tiburtina / Yhohel-Europhilia / Abacuc-Agripa / Micheas.[10] In the mystery of Feo Belcari, one finds, on the contrary, the grouping of an angel, a patriarch, and a Sibyl forming each line of the procession: Noé,

Giacobe-Eritrea / Mosé, Giosué-Sofonia / Samuele, David-Persica / Elia, Eliseo-Pontica / Malachia, Amos-Samia / Isaia, Gionas-Michea / Geremia, Ezechiele-Osea / Daniele, Abacuch-Cumana / Egeo, Abias-Tiburtina. As for the carvings by Baldini, no groupings are suggested.

Finally, in 1481, a treatise on the Sibyls appeared from the pen of Filippo Barbieri (Philippus de Barberiis); in the first version of this work a series of carvings pairs each prophetess with a prophet in yet another set of combinations: Persia / Osias-Libica / Ieremias-Delphica / Ieremias-Emeria / Ioel-Erithrea / Ezechiel-Samia / David Rex-Cumana / Daniel-Phrigia / Malachias-Europea / Zacharias-Agrippa / Isaias-Tiburtina / Micheas.

The discrepancies between the above groupings, as much as the existence of simple series of Sibyls such as the engravings executed by Baldini,[11] indicate that the path of the analogies between the characters of the Revelation suffices to explain neither the success of the Sibyls nor their change in fortune. It would seem, rather, that at the end of the fifteenth century the Sibyls constituted an independent series, and that consistency between prophecies and prophetesses is intrinsic to their all-female procession. According to this hypothesis, which resolves the problem of loose analogies between Sibyls and prophets, patriarchs, or angels of the Old Testament, the twelve female figures were paired to male figures only to satisfy a wish for symmetry, without any other substantiation.

For a reading of the sibylline series independent of any connection with series of patriarchs, I will refer to the short treatise of 1481, the first dissertation published on the Sibyls and their prophecies. The text is by cleric Filippo Barbieri,[12] and is most likely the product of a compilation of Italian manuscripts circulating in the fifteenth century and detailing the Sibyls – their names, their origins, and their predictions. As if in reply to the famous letter of Pogge, who declares the inextricable complexity of the "sibylline question" in 1554,[13] which in turn echoes the publication in 1465 of the first edition of the *Institutiones Divinae* of Lactantius, Barbieri proposes a concise and documented exposé under the title *Of the Twelve Sibyls who announced the coming of Christ*, which returns to the sources ancient and modern and blends them in a convincing format: each chapter presents a prophetess – her name, the sources that witness her existence, and particular elements of her representation and of the text of her predictions. For each Sibyl there is an engraving showing a phylactery that bears the prominent phrases of her prophecies. This treatise is thus part of the direct line of medieval and Renaissance tradition where the Sibyls form an iconographic theme that is abundantly represented.

In the first edition of 1481, the engravings of the Sibyls are paired with those of the Old Testament prophets, according to the list above. However, beginning with the second edition by Herolt and Riessinger in Rome (1482), the prophets disappear; the sacred couples leave as they appeared – without a word.

## *One Opuscule Can Hide Another*

In fact, one cannot examine the sibylline prophets gathered by Barbieri without putting them in context: although by presence of a title and an *explicit* the treatise on the Sibyls ranks as an independent book, it is, in fact, the second part of a coherent ensemble consisting of four treatises by Barbieri. Their grouping, found consistently in subsequent editions and re-editions, is attested by a study of the quires that make up the final volumes of the complete book and whose elements are listed in the appendix. The text on the prophetesses is materially indissociable from the first treatise, the *Discrepancies between Saint Augustine and Saint Jerome*. In fact, the arrangement of the quires and the pages absolutely prevents one from imagining any independent publication of the second section, even if the treatise on the *Discrepancies* was, in 1479, published alone in a now lost Naples edition quoted in its second edition in 1490 by Francesco del Tuppo.[14] Thus one can read the first of the texts in the collection as something like an introduction to the account of the Sibyls, because the reader moves, without discontinuity, from a compilation of ancient pagan testimonies attesting to Christian revelation, to the collection of engravings and sibylline predictions. The coherence is even stronger when one takes into account that the sixteenth part of the *Discrepancies* between Augustine and Jerome is concerned precisely with the prophetesses of the old world and that, according to the compilation inspired by Thomas Aquinas, Barbieri begins, from this passage, to enumerate the Sibylline predictions, the sources that have transmitted them to us, and their fulfilment by the coming of the Saviour.

## *Repeat, and Again, Repeat*

It is then no longer in the visual placement of symmetric and scriptural figures that one must understand the revival of the Sibyls. It is precisely in the continuity that constitutes their series, because although prophecies and names change according to the authors, although places and numbers overlap and contradict each other, one discovers, on the contrary, a remarkable similarity between all the prophecies of the different maidens. Certainly, Barbieri's Hellespontica repeats the predictions of the Erythrea of the Orsini palace, and his Erythrea repeats the end of an Italian prophecy from the thirteenth century attributed to the Tiburtina of the Orsini palace and in Siena Cathedral. But, if we listen carefully, they all say the same thing and it matters little who used exactly which words. All virgins, all strangers, all passed away, they announce the birth of a Messiah not of human conception.

It is in this taste for repetition that the fascination for the series of Sibyls seems to reside. First of all, prophecy in itself would not exist without the presentation of the event (which, alas, more often than not precedes the predictions!) as the repetition of the text. The strength of the prophecy's future is that it is in the past tense: the meaning is given by the realization of the prediction which thus gives structure to otherwise obscure verses, clarifying them by means of an actual and recognized context. In effect, how can we understand the poems celebrating the reign of the Child if not by proposing a reference? And what does one do with prophecies of the distant future? Prophecies involve only the past, to which they give a Messianic resonance strewn with textual landmarks.

To reissue the prediction is to enter into the magic of repetition: to repeat the prediction that has already come true . . .

In the case of the seers who multiply and paraphrase each other, the play of mirrors is enriched again, as the repetition is kaleidoscopically reflected from one Sibyl to another. Furthermore, the representation and personification of the prophetesses reinforce the repetition: as young maidens or old maids, they appear as promises of the Virgin to come, the holy mother of the Messiah.

As the same images are repeated in the sibylline series, their sense mysteriously and marvellously appears. One of them announces the coming of the *inuisibile uerbum* carried by a woman: *Inuisibile uerbum palpabitur*, says Agripa, the invisible Word will be made flesh. The secret, encoded, complicated word of prophecy lights up and is illuminated by the coming of the Word.

The book, from this point on, becomes the means and source of this incantation of repetition and repetitions: until 1514, the date of the last known edition of Barbieri's treatise, all the Sibyls are represented according to a consistent graphic schema, and the book is thus transformed into an album of emblems which one might imagine as detachable if their value did not lie in the very fact of their reiteration and accumulation. As a collection of opuscules, the book also plays on repetition, the way in which similar and congruent texts are grouped, like the treatise on *Discrepancies* and its continuation. Thus, far from cathedrals and palaces, independent of architectural order, decorative or artistic, the sibylline series within the book grows in number again with the addition of a thirteenth companion: Falconia Proba, poet of the fourth century AD, who composed a Sacred History in Virgilian quotations, which was much appreciated throughout the Middle Ages and the Renaissance. In an engraving in the editions cited, she bears a phylactery which shows, rather than the text of a prediction, her name and her status as wife of a consul. How does a married woman not detract from the series? Her words are also repetition; her work is to have "put Virgil in order" so as to declaim the Christian faith. The sense, then, comes from a second enunciation of the Virgilian word, like that of a prophecy which appears only with its realization.

Thirteen women lost their books, became delirious, or borrowed words from others; thirteen engravings gave them flesh and beauty; and all came from one book which spoke only of rereadings and thus celebrated the enchantment of the one Book: repetition that is virtually infinite.

## Appendix: Editions of the Barbieri Treatise

*1st edition: 1 December 1481, Rome*

In fact, two printings with the same date, the second probably from 1482.
Copies of the 1481 edition consulted: Paris BN Res D 3650; BN Res D 6445; Arsenal T.4523; Lucques, Biblioteca Guvernativa, Inc no. 229.
Bibliographic references: *Gesamkatalog der Wiegendrucke,* III, Leipzig, 1928, p. 401 np. 3385; M. Pellechet, *Catalogue général des Incunables des bibliothèques publiques de France,* I. p. 455, no. 1843; Hain-Copinger 872; BMC 2, 320 IA 19262; IGI 1245. Sanders, *Le Livre à figures italien,* no. 772.

1481/1482 Edition.
According to Sanders (773), the printer took sections 1 and 2 and a part of 3 and joined 16 other woodcuts. The register, being identical, no longer corresponds to the quires.
GW 3386 Hain-Copinger-Reichl 2455; BMC 4, 131, IA 19263
Description: Eight sections in 8° and one section in 4°, (13x18 cm not paginated, unsigned. a2, b-i8, k4 for the first impression; a-b8, c6, d-k8, 14 for the second. Roman characters.)

Contents: [A1-2v°]: preface by I.P. de Lignamine.
[A3-6v°]: Treatise on the "Discordances," untitled. First line in upper case, blank space left for initial letters.
Incipit: *Duo luminaria magnaque deus fecit: id est duos sacrosancte ecclesie doctores egregios: Eusebium uidelicet Hieronymum & aurelium Augustinum quos deus elegit (...)* [A 10 v°] *Nunc afferamus in medium dicta propria Sibyllarum, et que unaqueque earum dixerit, nec seruabimus in hunc ordinem temporis nec dignitatis excellentiam sed secundum quod nobis occurrerit (...)*
[Continuation to the second section. Engravings: Sibyl on RH page, represented as an emblem with the illustration above the text of the prophecy, prophet on the LH page, with same arrangement of illustration and text.]

[p. 32] *Probe centone clarissime foemine exerptum e Maronis carminibus ad testimonium ueteris nouique testamenti opusculum sequitur. (...)*

*2nd edition: Rome, 1482, Georgius Herolt & Sixtus Riessinger*

Copies of the 1482 edition consulted: Florence, BN, Inc M 6.23
Bibliographic refs.: GW, III, Leipzig, 1928, p. 401 no. 3387; Pellechet, I, p. 455, no. 1841. Hain-Copinger-Reichl 2453; Proctor 3854; BMC IV, 129, IA 29240.
Sanders, 774.

Description: Eight quires in 4°, unsigned; a10, b-g8, h10. Roman characters, richly decorated.
[AI] table
Tractatus solemnis et utilis editum per religiosum uirum magistrum Philippum Syculum Ordinis predicatorum Sacre theologie possessorem integerrimum in quo infrascripta perpulchre compilauit.
In primis discordantias nonnullas inter sanctos Eusebium Hieronymum et Aurelium Augustinum sanctosancte ecclesie doctores circha quas plurimas doctorum aliorum opiniones adducit.
Secundo duodecim sibillarum uaticinia que de christo ediderunt cum earum figuris proporciona.
Tercio Carmina Probae Centone Clarissime foemine Romae que ex Maronis carminibus ad corroborationem ueteris nouique testamenti diuino ingenio excerpsit.
(...)

*3rd edition: Oppenheim [Jacob Koebel, 1514]*

Copy described: Paris, Mazarine, 31581, Reserve.
Bibliography: J. Benzing, *Jacob Köbel zu Oppenheim 1494–1533*, Weisbaden, 1952 no. 55. Gives date of 1517. P. Hohenemser, *Flugschriftyen-Sammlung Gustav Freitag*, Nieuwkoop, 1966, no. 33 & 34. Gives date of 1514. Hain Copinger 2454. Pellechet 1842.

Collection of four homogeneous items whose separate publication is not attested.

Oppenheim, no date, in 4°
[1st section]: *DUO magna luminaria ...*
[2nd section]: *OPUSCULUM DE VATICINIS SIBILLARUM*
Text in Roman characters, titles in gothic. Organized as an album of emblems: one chapter per page recto, with corresponding engraving verso announced by a band *SEQUITUR IMAGO* or *SEQUITUR SCHEMA* or *SEQUITUR FIGURA*; the illustration is thus on the back of the text to which it corresponds.
[3rd section]: *OPUSCULUM uariis iudeorum et gentilium de Christo testimoniis.* Same printing.
[4th section]: *CENTONES PROBE FALCONIE DE UTRIUSQUE TESTAMENTI HISTORIIS EX CARMINIBUS VIRGILII SELECTI CUM ANNOTATIONE LOCORUM EX QUIBUS DESUMPTI SUNT.*

## NOTES

1. Aulu-Gellius, *Noctes Atticae*, 1, 29; the anecdote is also reported by Lactantius, *Institutiones Divinae*, 16, 5 and by Servius, *Commentarii*, Aen. 6, 72.
2. Denys of Halicarnassus, *Roman Antiquities*, 4, 62.
3. Tacitus, *Annals*, 6, 12; Suetonius, *Augustus*, 31.
4. Tacitus, *Annals*, 15, 44.
5. Rutilius Namatianus, *De Reditu Suo*, 2, 52.
6. *Sibyllinorum oraculorum libri octo, multis huc usque seculis abstrusi, nuncque primum in lucem editi (...)*, Basel, 1545.
7. Lactantius, *Institutiones Divinae*, 1, 16.
8. Augustine, *The City of God*, 18, 23.
9. C. de Clercq, "Quelques séries italiennes de Sibylles," in *Bulletin de l'Institut Historique Belge de Rome*, 48–49 (1978–1979), 105–27.
10. The hyphens link the couples. The pairings are correct; however, in the Orsini frescoes Micheas stands alone and in the Barbieri treatise both Persia and Micheas are alone.
11. J. Phillips, *Early Florentine Designers and Engravers* (Cambridge, MA: published for the Metropolitan Museum of art by Harvard University Press, 1955), 56 ff. Each engraving depicts a seated sibyl, with her name, a Latin inscription (similar to the handwritten description of the Orsini palace frescoes), and eight verses in Italian (similar to the prophecies of the *Annunziazione* of Feo Belcari).
12. According to the *Dizionario Biografico degli Italiani*, 4 (Rome: Edizioni Nazionali, 1964), 217–21, he was born in Syracuse in 1426, where he was predicator in the Dominican order at Catane. In 1475, as General Inquisitor of Sicily, Sardinia, and Malta, he persecuted the Jews. Named vicar of the convent of

Messina in 1478, he was suspended for a year in 1479, accused of having written a defamatory statement which libeled certain important people (among them Paul II and Sixtus IV). He took on his charge again "propter humilitatem et poenitentiam factam." He was also the author of *Cronaca dei papi è imperatori* (from 1316 to 1469), published anonymously in Rome in 1479 and attributed to Giovanni de Lignamine (Cf. Muratori: *Rerum Italicarum Scriptores IX* [Mediolani: 1726], coll. 263–276).

13 Cf. S. Settis, "Sibilla Agrippa," in *Etudes de Lettres* (October–December 1985): 89–123: the "mémoire de Sagramori," 1454, evokes, with regard to the Sibyls of Siena, "l'affaire des Sibylles." A letter of Pogge, written in response to a request for clarification from Vulturio on the names and the number of Sibyls, refers to the Orsini palace frescoes in these terms: "De Sibyllis quod petis, non est mihi nunc otium talia exquirendi; sed quod re nequeo, consilio adiuuabo. Bonae memoriae Cardinalis de Ursinis (...) in aula palatii sui, quae paramenti camera appellatur, Sibyllas omnes summa cum diligentia pingi fecit cum inscriptione eorum, quae suis temporibus, quaeque de Christo praedixit. Quare scribas Romama licet, ut et formam picturae, et nomina Sibyllarum, et epigrammata notentur ab homine erudito, tibique mittantur. Nam nullo loco reperies quod quaeris exquisitius, et simul effugies molestum laborem. Non enim parua cura haec res est aut nunc confici potest, aut tunc confecta est summa cum doctissimorum uirorum diligentia." (Letter quoted by S. Settis, "Sibilla Agrippa," 99, according to the edition *Epistolae*, 40, 41, by Th. de Tonellis, 3, Florence, 1861.)

14 (Naples: Francesco del Tuppo, 1490): GWK 3888; IGI 1244. Copy consulted: Angelica Library, Rome, Inc 483. The last section, the treatise on the "Discordances," given without title, carries the inscription: *Sequens hoc opusculum Rome impressum est: qu[od] //Reuerendissimo Cardinali Neopolitano dicaui: S[ed] //quia impressorum uicio et negligentia plures me[n]do//sitates co[m]misse sunt: Eam ob rem dedi op[er]am ut ite//rum imprimeret[ur]:>per uirum doctum: qui materia[m] intelligeret.*

# English Emblem Book Reception Theory and the Meditations of Renaissance Women

LINDA BENSEL-MEYERS

Middle-class women of the English Renaissance are too often dismissed from the rhetorical tradition. It is true that these domestic women were unprepared to contribute scholastic treatises: expected to be silent and obedient wives and mothers, Renaissance middle-class women were excluded from the formal rhetorical training reserved for more public lives. If publicly silent, however, they were not privately so, and the rhetorical dimension of their private meditations can contribute greatly to our understanding of the habits of mind that shaped the rhetorical treatises of the age. This is particularly true for our understanding of Renaissance rhetorical theories that sought to explain the imagistic reasoning of the English emblem books. As Michael Bath has articulated the problem, we know more about how Renaissance theorists "set about the business of defining a genre system" to encompass the popular emblem books than "the place which such books occupied in the *episteme* of English Renaissance culture."[1] Consequently, as modern scholars of the form, we know much about the translation and adaptation of emblem books for English audiences, but we know little about how these books were actually read.[2]

The meditations of Renaissance women are particularly fertile ground for the investigation of common practice in reading and writing imagistic rhetoric: emblem collections, as our earliest conduct books, were for a large part read by women; Renaissance women, save for royalty who were trained in rhetoric, were largely unconscious of the hermeneutics they used when engaged in figural reasoning; the meditation was a popular method for women to engage in practical rhetoric on a daily basis; and, perhaps most importantly, the iconic meditation form drawn from St. Ignatius' *Spiritual Exercises* directly influenced Francis Quarles and other Baroque emblem writers, underscoring the inherent parallels in the two forms.[3] A particularly illuminating representation of the unconscious hermeneutics behind the meditations of Renaissance women is the meditation written at the age of 17 by the future Lady Elizabeth Delaval. (Conflicting evidence would date the work some time between 1662 and 1671.) This work, entitled "Upon the haveing wormes in my gum's and the takeing of them out," can be examined as a form of imagistic reasoning internalized from a culture's practice in reading emblem books. When we compare an early English emblem from Whitney's 1586 collection, *A Choice of Emblemes*, to Delaval's practical exercise written almost eighty years later, we discover how the open-ended *copia* of arguments behind the early emblem form not only problematized the normative didactic purpose but fueled the hermeneutic power behind English Renaissance syncretism, a complex of signifying systems that enabled the young Elizabeth both to engage in a highly conventionalized figural meditation and to subvert the form in an ingenuous ideological critique of the moral reasoning available to her.

## *Problematizing the Reception of Whitney's Emblems*

The habits of mind reflected in Delaval's figurative meditation can be traced in an examination of how the English Renaissance's century-long love affair with the emblem book contributed to a rhetorical practice in imagistic reasoning not accounted for in the scholastic theories. A cursory review of emblem books held in the British Library reveals every so often a curious emendation, annotation, or synoptic rebuttal from a Renaissance hand, evidence of not just active engagement with the text but of actual attempts to redirect the argument, leaving intriguing evidence of how contemporary readers interacted with the tripartite emblem form.[4] These interpolations do not respond to the motto or the emblematic woodcut (features of the form that were more often controlled by the printer than the author) but to the epigram, the extended commentary that Mario Praz has described as the argument that resolves the engima introduced by the other two parts.[5] How that tension is resolved is precisely what is at issue here. Michael Bath singles out our problem as one of not fully comprehending the multiple signifying practices of the period: "Put quite simply the issue is whether the emblem depends on the invention of original but arbitrary connections between image and meaning, or whether the relation between sign and referent depends on some deeper and more intrinsic ('natural') affinity."[6] Whether we view the epigram's argument as a witty invention or as a discovery of the truths inherent in the book of nature, though, we still tend to view it as "resolving" the tension, completing the form in a manner that closes it to reader interaction. In fact, the implication has been that emblem books were not worthy of scholarly investigation because they were no more than conduct books, self-evident arguments for the moral training of the less literate.[7] This pervasive normative view of the emblem makes the occasional responses of Whitney's readers more curious; they are partial evidence of a different kind of reception of emblematic rhetoric, exposing how the epigram problematized the emblem form with intentional verbal ambiguity.

An early emblem with a curious annotation is Whitney's emblem 56.[8] The motto is "*Alius peccat, alius plectitur*" ("One sins, the other is beaten"), and the emblematic picture depicts a man preparing to throw a stone at a dog, who is biting another stone, as birds fly away in the background. Here is the epigram that follows:

> The angrie dogge doth turne vnto the stone,
> When it is caste, and bytes the same for ire,
> And not pursues, the same that hathe it throwne,
> But with the same fulfilleth his desire:
> Euen so, theyr are that doe bothe fighte, and brall,
> With guiltlesse men, when wrathe dothe them inflame,
> And mortall foes, they deale not with at all,
> But let them passe, to theire rebuke, and shame:
> And in a rage, on innocentes do ronne,
> And turne from them that all the wronge haue donne.[9]

The epigram resolves the tension between the motto and emblematic picture by revealing the truth about human nature that leads us to blame the messenger and not the sender (the parallel to Shakespeare's Cleopatra and her handling of Antony's messenger shows the lesson to be a commonplace). For an understanding of the normative reading, it does not matter whether Whitney's epigram is a product of clever invention learned through rhetorical training in the commonplace books, or is discovered through an Augustinian hermeneutic that uncovers nature's truths behind the specific images. What does matter for the normative reading is that we comprehend an overt moral that the poet wants us to be aware of as we move about the world.

This reading of the emblem as a self-contained, didactic form does not consider how the contemporary reader might have experienced, and even participated in, the process of resolving the tension between the commonplace motto and the affective appeal of the emblematic picture. However, the reader's emendation in this copy of emblem 56 — merely the change of one word — shifts our attention to the many other shapes the epigram's argument can take. For just as Erasmus set the goal of figurative amplification as "to turn one idea into more shapes than Proteus himself is supposed to have turned into," the poet's goal appears to have been to amplify the epigram's argument by forcing the reader to apply as many hermeneutic systems as the Renaissance had available.[10] On line three of the epigram, the reader has crossed out "same" and written in "man," attempting to distinguish this instance of "same" from those two in the surrounding lines (where the word signifies "stone"). As normative readers, we tend to overlook these ambiguous pronouns, dismissing them as the accidental inconsistencies of a fledgling vernacular, and we read through them to find one logical path of semantic relationships. However, the reader's emendation brings the ambiguity into focus, dramatizing in the emblem form the Renaissance attitude toward Scriptural hermeneutics that Barnett has defined as "immeasurable fecundity rather than a token of any ambiguity."[11] The reader consciously chose to read the emblem as being about "the angrie dogge" who bites the stone rather than the man who threw it (an option that clashes with the picture, since anger is depicted in the man rather than the dog).

In the second half of the epigram, however, the perspective of "the angrie dogge" becomes that of a man who fights and brawls with guiltless men (who, in turn, could be seen as a transformation of the "same" stone in the preceding line). At this point, we could go back and change all of the instances of the word "same" to "man" just as we could change all of the instances of the third person plural pronoun to mean either the persecutor or the persecuted (particularly line six). The fact that we can do this on the second reading reinforces the underlying circularity of the motto: "One sins, the other is beaten, who then sins, and another is beaten, who then . . ." The circularity is similarly highlighted in the emblem, for if we read it as signifying a visual gloss on the Chain of Being, the man is lower than the stone he holds above his head.

Perhaps most important for the emblem form's meditative dimension is the generative effect of the typological reading, which not only problematizes the reader's experience further but creates a moral dilemma. An Augustinian hermeneutics could lead us to collapse the unfolding associations we make as we read in time into an experience of the providential eye: "the angrie dogge" of the first half prefigures the appearance of the "guiltlesse men, when wrathe dothe them inflame" in the second, and the moral fulfillment is pictured in the turning away from those "that all the wronge haue donne." But the conclusion is unclear: Will God turn away from those "that all the wronge haue donne," and does that mean they will escape divine retribution? Or lose grace? Or both, if we see these meted out on earth and in heaven, respectively? (This also offers a possible explanation for the other dimension of the woodcut not mentioned in the epigram: Are the birds who fly away in the background representing souls freed of Satan's snare, flying up to heaven while the souls of the "angrie" are bound to earth and stone? Or do they represent the liberation of those "that all the wronge haue donne?"[12]) The ambiguity is furthered by line eight, where it is unclear whom "theire" refers to: will the "guiltlesse men" or the "mortall foes" feel "rebuke, and shame" when the guilty pass by? The experience is no longer one of logical argument but of what Waswo refers to as "affective semantics."[13] The images in the emblematic picture, when viewed after an experience of the "immeasurable fecundity" of arguments evoked by the epigram, pose a rhetorical resolution: the image of the man evokes rebuke; that of the dog, shame. The final rhetorical effect of the emblem form is to actualize our humility.

According to Hecksher, "(s)ince most emblems were made to inspire, to warn, to encourage, to persuade, the emblematic picture should, wherever possible, show present and future action."[14] To problematize the reading with multiple signifying systems, we engage in an associative process of figurative reasoning that enables us to read backward as well as forward, not to stop with the epigrammatic conclusion but to return to the emblematic woodcut as an embodiment of typological time set out for our meditation. It is not difficult to see how the emblem's figurative signification of past, present, and future tapped into the three powers of the mind – the memory, the understanding, and the will, respectively.

Raspa, in discussing Ignatius' *Spiritual Exercises*, describes how "[t]ogether, the three powers of the mind came to be looked upon in the meditation as organizing sensations in the shape of imagery in the imagination" in order to "provoke the experience of a new world view."[15] The process of figurative reasoning used in the meditation parallels what we have seen in the English emblem, but the meditation's rhetorical end of "experiencing a new world view" does not appear to explain the rhetorical end of emblems collected as commonplace books. How the educated elite used the emblem books does not necessarily tell us how the common reader experienced them, though. The practice of imagistic rhetoric in the worldly meditations of middle-class women, on the other hand, reveals just how powerful the providential eye of imaginative figuration became for the common reader of the later Renaissance.

As Kahn has observed, the power of linguistic ambiguity produced by figurative speech did not go unnoticed at the time: Puttenham and, later, Jonson and Hobbes all complained "that linguistic ambiguity has been known to lead to rebellion."[16] It is not surprising, then, that we find in the highly figured meditations of Renaissance women both a practice of conventional forms and a simultaneous subversion of the moral codes that threatened to confine them.

## Emblematic Reasoning in the Meditations of Renaissance Women

The middle-class Renaissance woman did not receive a formal education except insofar as it gave her the moral training necessary for her domestic roles as mother and wife. Her moral education exposed her primarily to figurative forms: euphuistic romances as well as spiritual meditations and emblem books. What we have of her writing is primarily autobiographical in the form of spiritual meditations that are more worldly than doctrinal. Often, these meditations can be read as overt records of the Renaissance woman's daily struggles with her conscience. As Simonds has pointed out, at this time an Augustinian view of the workings of conscience prevailed: it was not seen as the guide of one's reason in choosing the path of virtue (since reason could not control the already corrupted will) but "to remind the sinner subconsciously of a continuing need for repentance."[17] Often, the meditations follow a tripartite, pseudo-emblematic structure that enables this "repentance" while simultaneously keeping before us the palpable image of someone or something that excuses her sin. Paradoxically, the image set out for her meditation often becomes figuratively transformed into both the cause of her spiritual struggle and the promise of redemption for her sin. For example, when Lady Grace Mildmay (1552-1620) meditates on the corpse of her husband, she begins, "Let me behold *my* corpse which lieth folden in searclothes" and proceeds to meditate on her past life as a wife, her present as a widow, and her future as a resurrected soul rejoining her husband in heaven.[18]

Lady Elizabeth Delaval's adolescent meditation is an intriguing example of just how embedded in the culture the hermeneutics of figurative reasoning had become. Written when Elizabeth was 17, between 1662 and 1671, the meditation contains the emblematic structure of the Ignatian meditation but is less formal. Imagistically, it is one meditation, but, formally, it is in two parts: "Upon the haveing wormes in my gum's and the takeing of them out" and "Meditations the next day affter the worm's were taken out."[19] It also contains numerous parenthetical asides, most of which reveal her own skepticism (e.g., "or at least they make us believe so" or "as some people do foleishly imagine"). The discourse meditates on the worms which "a poor unlearn'd woman" has taken out of Elizabeth's gums to remove her pain. Working with the commonplace that only God can give and cure pain, she wrestles with the dilemma of whether the worms are merely a witch's trick or proof of God's mysterious grace. In the process, she effectively transforms the verbal image of the worms in the basin into an emblem for how the Worm of Conscience has been extracted from her.

The first part of the meditation serves as the motto in the proto-emblematic structure: it introduces the commonplace that God punishes her with pain and it can be cured only with his blessing, "makeing me smart under his rod, even till I humble kiss it, by suffering willingly." Knowing what we do about Elizabeth's overforward flirtations,[20] the sexual allusion is a revealing comment on her attitude toward the meditative act: too naive to be blasphemy, her linguistic gestures of contrition could be described as a flirtation with God, petitions based on her desire rather than her repentance. Similarly, after she stoically claims that the pain she endures cannot be described, she indulges in a very graphic and pathetic description of her pain. The effect is to justify how the "suffering willingly" can be redefined as mere "patience till tomorrow" when she will let the "poor unlearn'd woman" try what physicians could not do. Here, as elsewhere, the effect of evoking conventional and doctrinal attitudes serves to validate rebellious behavior.

The next day's meditation sets forth the picture to be contemplated: "behold here is no less than 200 worm's in this basin." The meditation itself is the argument, which formally deduces a resolution to the enigma of the worms: 1) (The emblematic picture) Were the worms the cause of my pain or are they evidence of witchcraft? 2) (The commonplace motto) "God forbid I shou'd ascribe such power to a wicked creture, as is only due to our gloryous creator." 3) (The proto-epigram) "In fine, affter all criticall arguments I dare afrime [sic] it for a truth that worm's have caused those torturing paines my God has punish'd me withall and in his good time mercyfully removed." Her deduction is self-justifying: If the worms exist, then I must say they are from God, because God would punish me if I called them signs of witchcraft. (The assumption, of course, is that she will say whatever needs to be said to be forgiven.) The discourse itself is amplified with acts of contrition: "Most wellcome then be all my aflictions." "... he that hateth reprofe shall die." The logic works only in the providential eye of typological time: the worms in the basin, signifiers of her past suffering, are also a *memento mori* image of her destined future as a corpse devoured by worms; and meditating on both enables her to perform an act of contrition that, only by the end of the meditation, linguistically recreates the worms in the basin into an emblem for the Worm of Conscience that had pricked her throughout and is now "mercyfully removed" by God.

Elizabeth was a strong-willed, flirtatious beauty, raised by an aloof aunt and indulgent governesses (who let her read romances in lieu of schoolbooks). Because of her willfulness and youth, this meditation dramatically demonstrates how she practices emblematic reasoning and typological hermeneutics to simultaneously repent and rationalize her behaviour, enabling her to subvert those cultural norms that could make her feel guilty for acting on her own behalf. Her interpretive process and her meditation's imagistic structure of typological associations reveal just how English Renaissance syncretism could fuse a complex of signifying systems into an *episteme* for a culture intrigued with emblems but unwilling to be controlled by them.

## NOTES

1 Michael Bath, *Speaking Pictures: English Emblem Books and Renaissance Culture* (London and New York: Longman, 1994), p. 2.
2 Some of the most important work published recently includes the *Index Emblematicus: The English Emblem Tradition*, vol. 1 (van der Noot, Giovio, Domenichi, Whitney), ed. Peter M. Daly, Leslie T. Duer, Anthony Raspa, and Paola Valeri-Tomaszuk (Toronto: University of Toronto Press, 1988) and Michael Bath's *Speaking Pictures*. The latter is particularly thorough and current in its discussion of the reception of individual emblem books. However, it necessarily restricts its discussion to source evidence which reveals how the emblem books influenced future writers or commonplace textbooks. Bath's thorough synthesis of scholarly work on Renaissance England's "untidy body of signifying practices," however, does pave the way for further investigation in how the emblem was received by the contemporary reader.
3 For a very thorough discussion of the influence of the Ignatian meditation form on seventeenth-century poetics, see Anthony Raspa's *The Emotive Im-*

*age: Jesuit Poetics in the English Renaissance* (Fort Worth, TX: Texas Christian University Press, 1983).

4  I would like to thank the John C. Hodges Better English Fund at the University of Tennessee for supporting my research at the British Museum during the summer of 1995. The handwritten annotations of the epigrams appear to be roughly contemporaneous with the Renaissance due to the style of letter formation and orthography. They are also in a less literate dialect that combines vulgar Italian, English, and Latin constructions.

5  See the first of the two volumes of Mario Praz's *Studies in Seventeenth Century Imagery* (London: Warburg Institute, 1939; reprint 1964).

6  *Speaking Pictures*, 3 ff. Bath discusses this debate as being as old as Plato's *Cratylus*, and a representation of the curious nature of Renaissance syncretism, where the debate over the nature of signs was carried out in the clash of poetic conventions. Petrarchan love poetry and Metaphysical conceits, for example, represent a view of resolving the tension between the motto and the emblem as a witty display of invention, whereas Scriptural hermeneutics justifies viewing the epigram as a discovery of the truths contained in the images as part of nature's book. Bath concludes, rightly I think, that the Renaissance view collapses both positions, leading me to the view that the emblem form embodies a copia of possible arguments, a dialectic fueled by the possibilities of both representation and interpretation, signifier and signified.

7  See Peggy Munoz Simonds, *Iconographic Research in English Renaissance Literature: A Critical Guide* (New York: Garland Publishing, 1995), xvi. A similar assessment has been offered by others.

8  British Library C57 12. Two possible owners of this copy of *A Choice of Emblemes* can be identified. On the top of the title page is written "Tho. Goodnike" (twice in succession), and on the underside of the same leaf, what appears to be "John Yoedna is my name."

9  Following the epigram is a couplet in italics from Alciato: "*Sic plerique sinunt veros elabier hostes,/Et quos nulla grauat noxia, dente petunt.*" ("Thus many let their true enemies elude them, and with bared teeth, hunt those that are not guilty.") Bath discusses Whitney's penchant for this kind of interpolation: "[I]t is precisely the untidiness of such marginal citations that make them something of an embarassment to normative models of the emblematic sign" (*Speaking Pictures*, pp. 74–5). The identification of the reference to Alciato's emblem 175 is made in *Index Emblematicus*.

10  The quotation comes from Erasmus's *De copia* as translated by Betty I. Knott in Vol. 24 of *Collected Works of Erasmus* (Toronto: University of Toronto Press, 1978), 302.

11  See Mary Jane Barnett, "Erasmus and the Hermeneutics of Linguistic Praxis," *Renaissance Quarterly* 49, no. 3 (Autumn 1996): 542–72.

12  Whitney might be drawing upon the same iconography as that used in the Caged Bird emblem. Although this emblem for the soul in captivity was used

by Whitney, Alciato, and several others (including Shakespeare in *King Lear*) to refer to the loss of freedom at court, it indicates the commonplace use of the bird image as a symbol for the soul.

13 See Richard Waswo, *Language and Meaning in the Renaissance* (Princeton, NJ: Princeton University Press, 1987), 229.

14 See William Hecksher, "Renaissance Emblems: Observations Suggested by Some Emblem-Books in the Princeton University Library," *Princeton University Library Chronicle* 15 (1954): 57.

15 Raspa, *The Emotive Image*, 37.

16 See Victoria Kahn, "Humanism and the Resistance to Theory," in *Literary Theory/Renaissance Texts*, ed. Patricia Parker and David Quint (Baltimore, MD: Johns Hopkins University Press, 1986), 385.

17 See Peggy Munoz Simonds, "Some Images of the Conscience in Emblem Literature," in *Acta Conventus Neo-Latini Guelpherbytani: Proceedings of the Sixth International Congress of Neo-Latin Studies*, ed. Stella P. Revard, Fidel Radle, and Mario A. Di Cesare (Binghamton, NY: Medieval Renaissance Texts & Studies, 1988), 315.

18 *With Faith and Physic: The Life of a Tudor Gentlewoman, Lady Grace Mildmay (1552-1620)*, intro. and ed. Linda Pollock, (London: Collins & Brown, 1993), 40-42. The italics are my emphasis.

19 *The Meditations of Lady Elizabeth Delaval: Written Between 1662 and 1671*, ed. Douglas G. Greene, *The Publications of the Surtees Society*, vol. 190 (Gateshead: Northumberland Press Ltd., 1978), 76-79.

20 See Greene's biographical introduction to *The Meditations of Lady Elizabeth Delaval*, which he has gleaned, for the most part, from the meditations themselves.

# Account of the Experience of Hester Ann Rogers: Rhetorical Functions of a Methodist Mystic's Journal

VICKI COLLINS

> *La mysterique* is the only place in the history of the West in which woman speaks and acts so publicly.
>
> Luce Irigaray

In *Speculum of the Other Woman* Luce Irigaray makes significant rhetorical claims for the speech of female mystics, calling their language "*la mysterique*," which combines the notions of mystical discourse and *l'hysterique*.[1] Irigaray's claims are theoretical, leaving to other scholars the challenge of identifying specific historical examples of *la mysterique* and determining why women's mystical discourse has been privileged in cultures that otherwise required women to remain silent. This work has been begun by historians of rhetoric like Cheryl Glenn in her writings on Margery Kempe[2] and by literary scholars like Karma Locherie in her work on body and flesh in the writing of medieval women mystics.[3] However, little attention has been paid to mystical discourse in the Protestant tradition.

The purpose of this essay is to extend the study of women's mystical discourse into Protestantism by recovering the spiritual narrative of Hester Ann Rogers, an eighteenth-century Methodist mystic whose writings represent three significant functions of rhetoric in early Methodism: spiritual self-rhetoric for the writer, moral argument defining "the good Christian woman," and material rhetoric on behalf of the post-Wesley Methodist establishment.

By the middle of the eighteenth century, the aftermath of the Protestant Reformation had effectively separated most English Christians from Catholicism and its mystical tradition. John Locke had exalted the primacy of empirical evidence in constructing knowledge. David Hume had proclaimed miracles "a Violation of the Laws of Nature," and Deists were quite comfortable with their remote clock-maker of a God. Even Roman Catholics like Alexander Pope had turned their focus from the ways of God to the ways of man.

But the mystic's light was not entirely absent from Enlightenment England, for at the heart of John Wesley's Methodist theology was a mystical core derived from his readings of Catholic patristic and mystical texts and based on his innate sense of wonder at the mysteries of the spiritual life.[4] From this mystical core he developed his doctrine of Christian perfection: through loving union with God, the individual can be cleansed of all outward and inward sin and endued with Christ-like virtues. Single-minded, steadfast love of God not only perfects but also permeates every aspect of the believer's life. Spiritual perfection is not the result of fulfilling the law through one's own efforts; rather it is a gift from God, the result of God's grace, available to the rare individual who is willing to open herself fully to union with God and completion by God's will.[5]

In his travels, John Wesley was always eager to meet Methodists who had had an extraordinary spiritual experience, so he was delighted and intrigued in April of 1776 when young Hester Roe of Macclesfield confessed to him in secret that she had experienced mystical union with God.[6] Unlike early Puritan conversion narratives in which the sinner typically finds salvation in a single, life-altering moment, Hester Rogers' story was a *jouissance* of sin/repentance/sin/repentance, on and on in cycles of rebellion followed by coming again to God. The mystic, says Evelyn Underhill, moves toward union with Christ in oscillations between pleasure and pain: *Gyrans gyrando vadit spiritus*, the spirit rushes in a circling spiral.[7] The cycle began with young Hester's decision at age thirteen to be confirmed, at which point she knew she became morally responsible for her acts. Examining her sinful soul, she resolved to lead a new life. But her repentance was selective: she resolved to give up anger, pride, and neglect of prayer, but not dancing, fashion, novels, or plays. When she could not keep these commitments even during the week between her confirmation and first communion, she despaired of her soul, but then experienced communion as a means of grace and forgiveness.

After a year of repeated commitment and backsliding, Hester, during a fevered illness, had a dream of her own damnation followed by the vision of "a cloud of uncommon brightness" and an angel clothed in white, who did not damn her but instead said, "The Lord Jesus Christ has forgiven all your sins, and washed you in his own blood, and I am come to bid you enter into the joy of your Lord, and to conduct you into his blissful presence!"[8] As is typical of the mystic's first stage, awakening to what Underhill calls the mystic's "consciousness of Divine Reality,"[9] Hester wrote that she experienced "joy unspeakable, love beyond compare" and "ecstacies unknown before."[10]

Her closeness to God did not hold. Over the next two years Hester read religious books and struggled with her own unholiness; at the same time she danced at assemblies until four in the morning. Like Catherine of Genoa,[11] Hester hated her own faults. One night after a particularly affecting sermon, Hester began acts of purgation intended to emphasize her own imperfection in contrast to Divinity and to embody her soul's distance from perfection. Hester wrote:

> I slept not that night: but arose early next morning, and without telling my mother, took all my finery, high-dressed caps, etc, and ripped them all up, so that I could wear them no more; then cut my hair short, that it might not be in my own power to have it dressed, and in the most solemn manner vowed never to dance again! I could do nothing now but bewail my own sinfulness, and cry for mercy. I could not eat, or sleep, or take any comfort.[12]

She searched for comfort by secretly attending Methodist meetings, only to be forbidden by her mother, the widow of an Anglican vicar, to associate with the sect on threat of being turned out of the family. Hester countered that if she were turned out of her mother's home, she would have to find a position as a servant; therefore, she should be allowed to be a servant in her mother's home. In return for her service, Hester maintained, she ought to be free to pursue her spiritual calling in Methodism. This act of manipulative abjection not only secured her place in the family but also furthered her sense of purgation through imitation of Christ's role as servant.[13]

After months of subjecting herself to bodily purgations[14] and the discipline of humble service, on the night of February 22, 1776, Hester Roe experienced intense and intimate union with God. She wrote:

> I come empty to be filled; deny me not . . . I take hold of thee as my fulness! Everything that I want, thou art. Thou art wisdom, strength, love, holiness: yes, and thou art mine! I am conquered and subdued by love. Thy love sinks me into nothing, it overflows my soul. Oh, my Jesus, thou art all in all! In thee I behold and feel all the fullness of the Godhead mine. I am now one with God; the intercourse is open; sin, inbred sin, no longer hinders the close communion; and God is all my own.[15]

At the climax of her union with God, it is not only God who possesses Hester, but Hester who possesses God. I am reminded of a mystical conversation between St. Teresa of Avila and Jesus, whom she called her Beloved. "Who are you?" her Beloved had asked her one afternoon. "I am Teresa of Jesus," she murmured, "and who are you?" He answered, "I am Jesus – of Teresa."[16]

Day by day Hester Roe carefully recorded her dealings with God. Although Hester does not say explicitly that she showed her journal to Wesley on that April day in 1776, it is likely that she did, for the literacy practice of keeping a spiritual journal was a central part of the method of Methodism. Wesley, himself an avid journal-keeper, urged the practice on his followers. Wesley saw spiritual value not only in the journal as spiritual record but also in journal-keeping as spiritual process. The actual writing of the journal entries constitutes a sort of self-rhetoric, a spiritual discipline that records the soul's journey and, in the act of recording, persuades the writer of her faith in and relationship with God – what we might call writing-to-believe. Hester's entries, for example, are not a mere tally sheet of sins and good works, but rather an organic exploration of her soul's relationship with God. Although the rhetorical tradition might resist calling persuasion of the self "rhetorical" because the audience is not in the public sphere, Wesley publicly encouraged this private literacy practice to deepen the faith of his flock. Of relevance here is James Kinneavy's observation that in the Greek New Testament the word for faith and the word for persuasion are the same, *Pistis*. To have faith is to be persuaded. Kinneavy observes: "That something like the partial congruence of the two concepts of persuasion and faith occurs in the New Testament is rather remarkable in view of the fact that no such structural congruence can be found for these concepts in the Old Testament."[17] In the case of Methodist journal writers like Hester Roe, the first audience open to persuasion was the writer herself.

Wesley believed his followers would also be persuaded in the faith by reading the experiences of other Christians. To this end, he published his own journals, abridged the spiritual autobiographies of numerous saints and holy figures, and published the accounts of ordinary Methodists in *The Arminian Magazine* and as separate tracts. Hester Rogers' journal was one of the texts published in this tradition.

Before his death, Wesley encouraged Hester Roe, now married to itinerant preacher James Rogers, to revise her journal for publication by the Methodist Press. In 1793, two years after Wesley's death, the first edition of *Account of the Experience of Mrs. H. A. Rogers* was published in London. Wesley's selection of Hester's journal for publication is not surprising because she held a privileged position in his theological system. Believing that she provided one of the few convincing proofs that union with God (spiritual perfection) was attainable in the midst of life as well as at the moment of death, Wesley urged Hester to testify publicly about her experience, first orally and later in writing. As Irigaray suggests, the mystic's narrative becomes a location of female rhetoric.

While exploration of her own soul was the purpose of Hester's original journal writing, implementing spiritual change in the audience is the primary goal of the published narrative. In the tradition of Paul, Augustine, and Thomas Aquinas, the testimony of private faith becomes public discourse so that others may also experience intimacy with God.

Because identification rather than logical persuasion is the primary method of convincing the audience in narrative rationality, Michael Osborn's notion of rhetorical depiction is useful here. Depiction is based on Longinus's notion that there is a "moment of rhetorical transport . . . 'when you think you see what you describe, and you place it before the eyes of your hearers.'"[18] Hester Rogers depicted the mystic's journey in such vivid language that readers could visualize and even feel in each "rhetorical moment" what it was like to seek and flee from God, to wilfully choose severe purgations, and ultimately to see and merge with the light from God's own being. Osborn calls depiction an "interactive metaphor" that can assist us in understanding how the rhetoric operates. By privileging the "symbolic moorings of human consciousness" over rationality, depiction seeks the rhetorical moments when listeners engage with "significant presentations of reality."[19] Indeed, depiction creates desire in the reader: desire to experience what has been described. In the case of Hester Rogers' readers, depiction creates desire for God.

The effectiveness of Hester Rogers' moral argument lies not only in her depiction of mystical perfection but also in her depiction of human imperfection. When Hester describes arguments with her mother, the attractions of worldly fun, and her seduction by Satan (whom she calls Reason), she increases the rhetorical effectiveness of her narrative and the weight of her moral argument because the reader, who is herself imperfect, can identify with Hester's failings. Although the text is a narrative of spiritual perfection, it is also the story of a woman who knows her own inner darkness – knows that she is prone to pride, anger, and a host of other sins. She confesses all in her text, calling herself a failure, a worm, and worse. Spiritual perfection is a gift of grace, not the triumph of Hester's will to be good. She allowed herself to be perfected, or to be fully made, by God, and in telling her story made a moral argument for the possibility of union with God.

Although Hester Rogers' account might seem the ideal text for promoting female piety and virtue among Methodists, it was, in fact, problematic. Hester's mysticism and focus on intimacy with God could destabilize certain cultural values that were central to eighteenth-century Methodism: filial loyalty and obedience, marriage, and motherhood. Hester devotes forty-eight pages to her spiritual life but covers six years of ministry in Ireland in four paragraphs. She devotes only two sentences to her marriage, two sentences to motherhood; and she never mentions her seven children by name. This text does not promote Methodist family values. She redefines certain spiritual values – faith, hope, love, good works – and de-emphasizes salient practices of evangelism in ways that could threaten the institutional church. If Hester Rogers' text might be ideologically problematic for the movement, why was it published? First, the Methodists needed a female exemplary text. To be sure, Hester's text was not the only female journal available, but most of the other prominent women journal-writers were even more problematic than Hester because they had dared to preach. Wesley had authorized certain women to preach, encouraged them, and protected their rhetorical space, but soon after Wesley's death, preaching was closed to women.[20] The Methodist hierarchy in Britain and America wanted their members to view women's preaching as an early aberration that had now been corrected by a return to patriarchal order. To this end they published the journal of Hester Rogers, portraying her as the good and holy woman who did not preach.

The publishers repackaged her mysticism into a more suitable female image through what I call the material rhetoric of accretion. At publication they appended male texts to her journal, texts that redefined who Hester was by ignoring her mysticism and emphasizing what a good wife and mother and Sunday School teacher she was. In the sermon preached at her funeral and later accreted to her journal, Thomas Coke praised Hester Rogers, emphasizing particularly that she never undertook any activity which might be seen as preaching.[21] Through the material rhetoric of accretion, the mystic was domesticated and *Account of the Experience of Mrs. H. A. Rogers* became the best-selling female text in a century of Methodism. Hester Rogers' account might awaken in female readers a desire for union with the godhead, but the accreted male texts reminded Methodist women that communion with God is only acceptable as long as dinner is on the table and the children say their prayers.

As Foucault suggests, we must always be aware of the institutional desire to control "the order of discourse," to decide who may speak and what may be said.[22] The Methodist hierarchy sensed that the mystic's discourse is dangerous and must be controlled. The mystic is dangerous because her discourse re-enacts the incarnation: the creative power of God becomes material in the life and text of the mystic and dwells among people through her words, all without clerical mediation. The Methodist publishing authority apparently believed that if the mystic is standing in the kitchen instead of the pulpit, if she is called Mrs. Rogers instead of Hester Ann, she can be kept in her rhetorical place.

Attending to the texts of Methodist mystic Hester Rogers makes several contributions to the history of rhetoric. First, it suggests a fresh historical site of rhetorical activity, a community where complex discourse practices developed outside the Rhetorical tradition. Second, it broadens the field of eighteenth-century rhetoric to include an interesting location of female discourse.[23] Finally, such study invites further exploration of a text's multiple rhetorical functions and provides a reminder that the uses of gendered spiritual discourse are often intertwined with gendered politics and institutional ideological agendas. Whether an institution's material moves can fully domesticate the dangerous discourse of a woman who has been one with God remains a question to be explored through further rhetorical study of *la mysterique* of Hester Ann Rogers and her spiritual sisters.

## *NOTES*

1. Luce Irigaray, *Speculum of the Other Woman*, trans. Gillian C. Gill (Ithaca, NY: Cornell University Press, 1985), 191.
2. Cheryl Glenn, "Author, Audience, and Autobiography: Rhetorical Technique in *The Book of Margery Kempe*," *College English* 53 (1992): 540–53.

3  Karma Locherie, "The Language of Transgression: Body, Flesh, and Word in Mystical Discourse," in *Speaking Two Languages: Traditional Disciplines and Contemporary Theory in Medieval Studies*, ed. Allen J. Frantzen (Albany, NY: SUNY Press, 1991), 115–40.

4  Robert G. Tuttle, Jr., offers a detailed study of Wesley's involvement with mysticism in *Mysticism in the Wesleyan Tradition* (Grand Rapids, MI: Francis Asbury Press, 1989).

5  John Wesley, *A Plain Account of Christian Perfection* (London: Epworth, 1952).

6  Hester Ann Rogers, *Account of the Experience of Hester Ann Rogers; and her Funeral Sermon, By Rev. T. Coke LL.D. To which is added Her Spiritual Letters* (New York: Mason and Lane, 1837), 50. All references to the text of Hester Ann Roe, later Hester Rogers, cite the 1837 edition of her account.

7  For Evelyn Underhill's version of the stages of the mystic's progress, see *Mysticism*, 12th ed. (London: Methuen, 1930), 168–72.

8  Rogers, *Account*, 8–11.

9  Underhill, *Mysticism*, 169.

10  Rogers, *Account*, 11.

11  Underhill, *Mysticism*, 182.

12  Rogers, *Account*, 22.

13  Ibid., 27. Hester Roe's experience is strikingly similar to that of Catherine of Siena, who had intense conflicts with her mother, cut off her hair, practiced acts of purgation, became ill (with pox) and subsequently withdrew from society, and practiced starvation and sleep deprivation. In the period following her withdrawal, Catherine, like Hester, acted as a household servant. However, Hester did not parallel Catherine's vision of Christ inviting her to drink the blood from his side nor did Hester follow Catherine's substituting the filth of disease (literally drinking pus from the wounds of the sick) for her own food. For a discussion of Catherine of Siena's purgations, see Caroline Walker Bynum, *Holy Feast and Holy Fast: The Religious Significance of Food to Medieval Women* (Berkeley: University of California Press, 1987), 167–70.

14  Joanna B. Gillespie's article "Angel's Food: A Case of Fasting in Eighteenth-Century England," in *Disorderly Eaters: Texts in Self-Empowerment*, ed. Lilian R. Furst and Peter W. Graham (University Park: Pennsylvania State University Press, 1992), suggests that Hester Roe's fasting constituted a life-threatening eating disorder.

15  Rogers, *Account*, 44.

16  Carol Lee Flinders, *Enduring Grace: Living Portraits of Seven Women Mystics* (San Francisco, CA: HarperSanFrancisco, 1993), 190.

17  James Kinneavy, *Greek Rhetorical Origins of Christian Faith: An Inquiry* (New York: Oxford University Press, 1987), 53. In the Old Testament, words other than *pistis* were used for faith, and the meaning was usually associated with trust in God rather than persuasion.

18 Michael Osborn, "Rhetorical Depiction," *Form, Genre, and the Study of Political Discourse* (Columbia, SC: University of South Carolina Press, 1986), 79.
19 Ibid., 97.
20 For a comprehensive history of women's preaching in eighteenth-century British Methodism, see Paul Chilcote's study, *John Wesley and the Women Preachers of Early Methodism* (Metuchen, NJ: American Theological Library Association and Scarecrow Press, 1991).
21 Thomas Coke, *The Character and Death of Mrs. Hester Ann Rogers: Set Forth in a Sermon, Preached on the Occasion in Spitalfields-Chapel, London, on Sunday, October 26, 1794*, in Rogers, *Account*, 118.
22 Michel Foucault, "The Order of Discourse," trans. Ian McLeod in *Untying the Text: A Post-Structuralist Reader*, ed. Robert Young (Boston, MA: Routledge, 1981), 52.
23 For a full discussion of women's rhetorical roles in eighteenth-century Methodism, see my article, "Walking in Light, Walking in Darkness: The Story of Women's Changing Rhetorical Space in Early Methodism," *Rhetoric Review* 14 (Spring 1996): 336–54.

# GROUP 3

# Participating in the Rhetorical Tradition

# Women and Latin Rhetoric From Hrotsvit to Hildegard

JOHN WARD

Women seem as yet to have barely entered the formal world of the "history of rhetoric in the Middle Ages." Real women, that is. Idealized women have long had an honorary place: the allegorical depiction (in both art and literature) of rhetoric as a well-adorned female is – as is well known – a long-standing one, and yet women seem entirely absent from J.J. Murphy's epochal *Rhetoric in the Middle Ages*[1] and present only in Brian Vickers' equally epochal *In Defence of Rhetoric* by way of secondary discussions of "rhetoric and the sister arts" and "rhetoric in the modern novel."[2] Is this picture a fair one? Do real women play so minimal a part in the evolution of medieval rhetoric? Did they in fact stand "outside the rhetorical situation"?[3] Is the paradox of allegorical women possessing the complete art and men being its only real practitioners during the Middle Ages accurate? What follows is an initial discussion of these questions.

It will be as well to define what we are in search of. The term 'rhetoric' must be taken in a fairly technical sense to indicate the formalized *scientia bene dicendi* of the ancient practitioners and their medieval successors. We are looking not so much for effective female persuaders in the broad and probably untutored sense, nor (simply) for women writers with some command of Latin: we are getting used to the idea that women may well, during the Middle Ages, have used Latin in a fairly normal way, with some – such as Hildegard of Bingen – acquiring considerable expository skill therein. What we are looking for is women who sat in the classes of the medieval rhetors, or women who taught the rhetorical art, or else women who practised it from a learned base. As the subject of the paper is Latin rhetoric, we can exclude women who displayed expertise in vernacular rhetoric (such as the female troubadours or Marie de France). Although there may be evidence of instruction in Latin rhetorical rules here, we must initially look elsewhere.

Abridging my search to suit the time available, we have only four initial points of reference: Hrotsvit of Gandersheim; the wife and daughters of the shadowy but legendary Manegold of Lautenbach; the female poetesses of Baudri of Bourgeuil's acquaintance; and Heloise, daughter of Hersindis. An optimistic approach might canvass the inclusion of Hildegard of Bingen, but the evidence suggests considerable manipulation of rather intuitive linguistic and visual techniques rather than reliance upon what the rhetors taught. Interestingly, the contrast between the simple, emotional, "incantatory" (self-taught?) prose of Hildegard[4] and the more mannered male style is apparent enough from a consideration of matching letters from lay ecclesiastics, with Hildegard's reply.[5] In her determination to secure a voice for her religious, prophetic, and reformist authority, Hildegard displayed considerable ability as a "persuader" or "disrupter," but, like Elizabeth of Schönau, her concern for *sermo humilis* and the concealment of art (manifesting itself in the twin "fiction" of prophetic inspiration and assistance from a male mentor) has succeeded in removing her from the frontier of the present enquiry.

Hrotsvit of Gandersheim is a frequently studied exception. Her autonomy of theme and expression mirrored the peculiar flexibility that surrounded her social origins, learning and working conditions.[6] Given the equivalence of the Roman *genus demonstrativum* and medieval epideictic poetry, we can only marvel at Hrotsvit's determined command of courtly discourse and poetic rhetoric. Consider – to choose a passage at random – her picture of the barefooted Queen Adelaide,[7] her body by day pressed against ripened ears of corn, or flattened into the furrows left by the plough, by night trying to find her way to some point of refuge from the agents of an aggressive, unwanted male. A high point of (leonine) hexametric ingenuity is attained in Hrotsvit's portrayal of the Queen lying panic-stricken but protected by welcoming earth and spreading corn, whilst in a neighbouring furrow, the unwanted male (the Italian King Berengar), in high (male) martial mode (lines 571–72), fails to find her "whom the grace of Christ kept hid," "however much the protecting fronds, to disjoin with all strength, by stretched-out spear he laboured." Such a translation, seeking to retain the Latin word order, can give no impression of the smooth flow of these lines (578–79), coloured as they are with their unobtrusive mid- and end-rhymes, let alone the striking association of images: Christ's grace, fecundity (earth / corn [Ceres]), vanquishing male steel and epic effort. The Latin rhetorical and poetic skills of Hrotsvit, which we cannot here examine further,[8] stand out as the high point of female absorption of the teachings of the schools, suggesting the observation that such skills must surely have been more widely evident in the centuries we are speaking of than the accidentally and imperfectly preserved manuscript tradition that has come down to us today would indicate. What survives today is, by and large, what male-dominated institutions chose or wished to preserve. The greatest casualty of such unbalanced selectivity must have been the testimonials of female eloquence.

An example of the vestigial survival of female eloquence is the poem addressed, by Baudri of Bourgueil, one of the most professional Latin poets of the Middle Ages, to a certain "Muriel."[9] From the poem we learn that Muriel was an accomplished conversationalist and poet[10] with whom Baudri himself was happy to "exchange songs." Her "eloquence" amazed both sexes and earned for her a prophetic mantle. She had, it seems, a "comely figure ... pleasing to men," nor was she "lacking in the nobility or powers of genius which of themselves are wont to hasten marriages." Yet Baudri is unskilled at exchanging verse with "virgins" (= women) and seems to feel that he should urge Muriel to "be strong in your virginity": a virgin's songs will comfort him "in exile." Now Baudry addressed ten verse epistles to other women, but of all his female addressees, a single reply from only one has been preserved (from a certain "Constance"[11]). The relationship between Anselm (of Canterbury) and Gunhild, to be mentioned shortly, provides another example of "women's silence."

Such a picture of gender-biased loss renders the few survivals doubly precious. A great deal of recent work has resurrected Heloise, daughter of Hersindis, as "a highly skilled writer who [was able to] appropriate the power of Latin culture but resist its totalising or essentializing force."[12] Discussion of Heloise has, of course, been long disturbed by the allegation that her surviving written work is not her own. Contrast with the situation of Gunhild and Anselm,[13] however, suggests the overwhelming uniqueness of Heloise's epistolary collection. Southern himself likens the case of Gunhild and Anselm to that of Abelard and Heloise, and Anselm's two extant letters are suggestive enough, and rhetorically powerful. Yet Gunhild, though she wrote Anselm "a letter full of sweetness," has been deprived of a voice to posterity because it was in no one's interests to preserve what she wrote. Twenty years on, and in a much more public context, we find Heloise, the abbess that Gunhild never became, credited with a collection of letters that posterity chose to keep track of (if exiguously). Although we are uncertain about the quasi-dictaminal or quasi-pastoral context that may have called forth the Abelard-Heloise collection as some kind of exemplary model, one suspects that a male forger, on the threshold of a new age in communications practice, a kind of Peter of Blois working for a primarily dictaminal market, or a Hildebert on the threshold of the courtly age, might have had (like Peter or Hildebert) a better idea of his market: at least seven manuscripts of Peter's letter collection from the twelfth century have survived, and forty-two from the thirteenth.[14] Yet the collection of Heloise and Abelard lay dormant until the inquisitive literary mind of Jean de Meun called it to account.[15] Though twelfth-century males who missed their market are to be found (for example Walter Map), the profile of survival for Heloise and Abelard's collection smacks of the sidelined and the marginalized, and nothing was so sidelined or marginalized in this period as the woman's voice. Heloise, indeed, whether we consider the beatings she received from Abelard[16] or the dead bat he played to her dictaminal virtuosity,[17] is a literary image of such subjection, sublimation, and repression that any actually surviving literary work must surely represent the vicissitudes of time and the determination of her learned personality rather than the gratuitous skills of a male forger.

There is no space here to recount the scholarship that has in recent times both deepened our understanding of Heloise's literary and intellectual achievements and placed a comprehension of it beyond a normal week's work.[18] Interesting questions are raised by consideration of Heloise's specifically rhetorical practices (*salutatio* theory and epistolary theory in general,[19] cursus theory[20]): from what persons/manuals did she imbibe them, how do we explain close coincidences with Abelard's practices, can we imagine a rough divide between what she learned from Abelard (logic, theology, philosophy, Biblical exegesis?) and what he imbibed from her (auctores,[21] certain rhetorical/dictaminal/stylistic practices?)[22] and what they learned together (shared reading of the auctores?)?[23] Heloise's skills as an exegete and theologian[24] tend to blur some aspects of such distinctions, and without much closer attention to rhetorical teaching in Paris around the time of her early education (after her return from Argenteuil), we cannot profitably advance an inquiry into "Heloissa rhetor." Dronke's researches, however, indicate that the more mobile clerical world of the eleventh and early twelfth centuries clearly brought literate (and therefore clerical/monastic) males and females together with unprecedented frequency, and this circumstance, coupled with the prominent role played by reading of the classical auctores, especially Ovid, in the humanism of the time, provided models and vocabulary for interestingly mannered exploration of the emotions of male-female love.[25] The Abelard-Heloise dialogue was by no means uninfluenced by this literature and the social phenomena that it accompanied. Nevertheless, the exact picture of women in the rhetorical classroom is still unclear, and it is difficult to know where to turn for evidence that might throw light on this problem. It is hard, indeed, to bring even the male rhetors of the day properly into focus, as my final illustration should indicate.

One of the major problems in charting the history of Latin rhetoric in the eleventh and twelfth centuries is the domination of two shadowy figures about whom little can be said with certainty. The eleventh century is dominated by the glosses (on the *De inventione* of Cicero and on the pseudo-Ciceronian *Rhetorica ad Herennium*) of a certain "Magister Menegaldus," while the twelfth is dominated by the glossing of a certain "Magister Alanus," who refers in his glosses to his predecessors as "seguaces Menegaldi."[26] There is no space here to elaborate this statement, but it is noteworthy that one of the major chronicle references to "Manegaldus" reads: "[I]n these days, there began to flourish in the Teutonic land Manegaldus the philosopher, who was learned in divine and secular letters beyond his contemporaries. His wife too, and his daughters were flourishing also in religion, and gained much attention from writers [or 'possessed considerable knowledge of the scriptures']. His daughters, indeed, used to teach their father's [or 'their own'] pupils."[27]

"Manegold" research is in its infancy,[28] but it should, in the future, make a place for this wife and these daughters, whether in the arts teaching that seems to have characterized Manegold's early teaching years,[29] or in the Biblical exegesis that seems to have filled his later years.[30] I find it more consonant with the implicit models we use for reconstructing events in this century to imagine that Manegold's "women" would have assisted him in his arts teaching rather than in his exegetical efforts. The flourishing reputation for piety ascribed by the chronicler to Manegold's wife and daughters is perhaps more a question of entitlement to the rank of intellectual in contemporary eyes than an indication that they concerned themselves with (his) Biblical teaching.

The key to the role played by Manegold's wife and daughters may, in fact, be provided by the recent suggestions of C. Stephen Jaeger.[31] He feels that the eleventh century was the last major age of oral teaching in the West. Leading figures enjoyed a charismatic oral authority, and early attempts to "capture" this personality in writing have left behind but a mass of puzzling fragments that make little sense when asked to yield information to our own age, with our thoroughly literate "written-culture" expectations. Jaeger argues that much of the humanist thought of the twelfth century must be explained by the idea that scholars of that age, conscious of losing the charisma of the great teachers of the immediate past, whose personalities were already dissolving in the emerging world of written culture, sought to embalm their memory of the past figures in the new literacy of the proto-university world. Twelfth-century humanism acquires in this way a distinctly nostalgic touch. Thus, a figure such as "Master Manegold"[32] becomes one of the "prolific and central players in the school of life" in the eleventh century (dominated as it was by oral charisma ill-recorded in the incipient written word of the day), and is remembered in a variety of contexts, his name surviving by way of attachment to a bewildering variety of documents that do not explain his biography as we now expect.

My feeling, as I work through the as yet ill-explored remnants of the rhetorical teaching attached in the surviving manuscripts to the name of "Magister Menegaldus" – and most of our evidence for eleventh-century rhetorical glossing is attached to his name – is that Manegold was a charismatic teacher in the arts, and especially rhetoric, at a critical time of expanding markets for persuasive instruction. It would seem that a shadowy group of lesser figures attended his schooling and quickly copied out his lectures in the new (for rhetoric) "catena" commentary form, reproducing them in other centres where new generations of ecclesiastics sought help in an increasingly competitive world in which mastery of words meant power and preferment. So rapid was the expansion of a market for his teaching that he made use of his (apparently) talented wife and daughters – much as, I suppose, Theon of Alexandria made use of his daughter Hypatia many years previously – and they, like the many wives who are thanked in learned academic monographs nowadays for typing, proofreading, providing feedback, coffee, understanding and similar services, left behind some curiously uncontroversial memory of their labours.

Such a reconstruction of events fits in with the role of women in early religious sectarian movements: from Robert of Arbrissel to Tanchelm and Henry of Le Mans,[33] the period c.1050–1125 was one in which women were permitted to play a role in religious creativity that later structuring and normalizing ruled out.[34] Is it too much to suppose that the norms of a later age, dominated by male ecclesiastical and written cultural paradigms, have obliterated the evidence for an active participation of women in the culture of the schools, some traces of which nowadays survive in the writings of Heloise and Hildegard, in the memory of Gunhild and Muriel, in the even dimmer memory of Manegold's wife and daughters? Are these fragments all that ever existed, or are they the tip of an iceberg that we shall never see in more than the most shadowy form? Further, how do we evaluate these fragments? Do they add up to a matter of women operating occasionally within a male discourse, or do they constitute genuine examples of "breaching" and "transgressing" this discourse, a rewritten and relativized "techne"?[35] How does the experience of the women mentioned in the present paper relate to that of their more numerous peers in the later Middle Ages? These are all challenges for future historians of rhetoric in the Middle Ages.

## NOTES

1 J.J. Murphy, *Rhetoric in the Middle Ages: A History of Rhetorical Theory from St.Augustine to the Renaissance* (Berkeley, Los Angeles, and London: University of California Press, 1974).
2 Chapters 7 and 8 of Brian Vickers, *In Defence of Rhetoric* (Oxford: Clarendon Press, 1988). I select the works of Vickers and Murphy (*Rhetoric in the Middle Ages*) for mention in the belief that they are, in this respect, typical of their genre.
3 Lisa Ede, Cheryl Glenn, and Andrea Lunsford "Border Crossings: Intersections of Rhetoric and Feminism," *Rhetorica* 13, no. 4 (1995): 412–41.
4 Hildegard's prose is often "musical," that is, marked by *repetitio, conplexio, exclamatio,* and especially *conpar (isocolon)* and *similiter cadens (homoeoptoton).* Curiously, the author of the *Ad Herennium* does not recommend repeated use of these forms of ornamentation, except "ad delectationem" (4.23.32). Such techniques are also, of course, evident in the rhymed poetry of the *goliardi* and in rhythmic lyric verse generally, set to some form of music as it often was. Composers of this last form of verse were, of course, usually also learned *clerici*, but in Hildegard's case, does not such "rhetoric" reflect more intuitive and oral – liturgical? – contexts rather than the schoolroom? Barbara Newman ("Hildegard of Bingen: Visions and Validation," *Church History* 54 [1985]: 170) speaks of Hildegard's "painful ignorance of grammar, rhetoric and dialectic."
5 For example, *PL* cols. 163–64, ep, XI "Arnoldi Coloniensis Archiepiscopi" and "responsum Hildegardis." The greater use of subordination is one contrast between the "male" and the "female" styles. Peter Dronke notes, however (*Women Writers of the Middle Ages: A Critical Study of Texts from Perpetua [d. 203] to Marguerite Porete [d.1310]* [Cambridge: Cambridge University Press, 1984], 194), how after Volmar, her secretary, had died in 1173, Hildegard in her mature epistolary style "acquired the power to construct complex, fluent and fluid sentences, apparently quite unaided." By contrast, Hildegard had hitherto relied "upon her scribes for grammatical advice and rhetorical flour-

ish" (Ann Clark Bartlett, "Miraculous Literacy and Textual Communities in Hildegard of Bingen's *Scivias*," *Mystics Quarterly* 18, no. 2 (1992): 45.
6  Karl J. Leyser, *Rule and Conflict in an Early Medieval Society: Ottonian Saxony* (Oxford: Blackwell, 1979; 1989); J.O. Ward, "After Rome: Medieval Epic," in *Roman Epic*, ed. A.J. Boyle (London and New York: Routledge, 1993), 285–93.
7  *plantis ... tenellis* Paul Winterfeld, ed., *Hrotsvithae Opera*, Scriptores Rerum Germanicarum in usum scholarum (Berlin: Apud Weidmannos, 1965), 220, line 549, translated in Boyd H. Hill, Jr., *Medieval Monarchy in Action: The German Empire From Henry I to Henry IV* (London: Allen and Unwin, 1972), 131, and Marcelle Thiébaux, ed., *The Writings of Medieval Women: An Anthology*, 2nd ed. (New York: Garland, 1994), 212.
8  See Katharina M. Wilson, "Antonomasia as a Means of Character-definition in the Works of Hrotsvit of Gandersheim," *Rhetorica* 2, no. 1 (1984): 45–53, and the same author's *Hrotsvit of Gandersheim: The Ethics of Authorial Stance*, Davis Medieval Texts and Studies 7 (Leiden: Brill, 1988), 135–42 and 154–56 ("it is quite obvious that she had a rigorous training in poetic and rhetorical exornations") for further analysis here. Also, Dronke, *Women Writers*, 56–57.
9  Dronke, *Women Writers*, 84–90.
10  Another verse epistle, from another accomplished male poet (Hildebert of Le Mans) seems addressed to the same Muriel, and refers (A.B. Scott, ed., *Hildeberti Cenomannensis Episcopi Carmina Minora* [Leipzig: Teubner, 1969], 17 #26 "Ad M[urielem] litteratam," lines 19–20) to the *pondera verborum, sensus gravis, ordo venustus* of her work: such terms are characteristic of work written in accordance with the rhetorical precepts of the *artes poetriae* and their predecessors. On the later twelfth-century treatises that professionalized the art of teaching Latin poetic composition according to rhetorical principles, see Douglas Kelly, *The Arts of Poetry and Prose*, Typologie des Sources du Moyen Age Occidental 59 (Turnhout, Belgium: Brepols, 1991).
11  Constance's reply is discussed by Dronke, *Women Writers*, 84*ff*. Constance's letter "is a deftly calculated histrionic performance, in which the personal expression is the sum of the incongruous conventions, Patristic and Ovidian, modifying one another" (ibid., 107). Dronke also discusses a few other survivals of female rhetorical poetasting from Baudri's day (ibid., 91–92), and an interesting collection of female love-letters in "profusely rhymed prose" (ibid., 93–97) that usefully rehearse some of the phrases to be picked up also in the Abelard-Heloise correspondence. Cf. also G.A. Bond, "*Iocus Amoris*: The Poetry of Baudri of Bourgueil, and the Formation of the Ovidian Subculture," *Traditio* 42 (1986): 168 and 189.
12  Martin Irvine, "Heloise and the Gendering of the Literate Subject," in *Criticism and Dissent in the Middle Ages*, ed., Rita Copeland (Cambridge: Cambridge University Press, 1996), 87.
13  Richard W. Southern, *Saint Anselm: A Portrait in a Landscape* (Cambridge: Cambridge University Press, 1990; 1991), 262–64), and Rhona Beare, "Anselm's

Letters to Gunhild, Daughter of King Harold," *Prudentia* 28, no. 2 (1996): 25–35.

14 Richard W. Southern, *Medieval Humanism and Other Studies* (Oxford: Blackwell, 1970), 105.

15 Fabrizio Beggiato, ed., *Le Lettere di Abelardo ed Eloisa nella traduzione di Jean de Meun*, I "Testo," (Modena: S.T.E.M.-Mucchi, 1977).

16 Abélard, *Historia Calamitatum*, ed. J. Monfrin (Paris: Vrin, 1967), 72.

17 J.F. Rhys, "Role-playing in the Letters of Heloise and Abelard: Readings of the Correspondence Between Heloise and Abelard," *Parergon* ns 11, no. 1 (1993): 53*ff.*

18 Peter Dronke, *Abelard and Heloise in Medieval Testimonies* (Glasgow: University of Glasgow Press, 1976); Linda Georgianna, "Any Corner of Heaven: Heloise's Critique of Monasticism," *Mediaeval Studies* 49 (1987): 211–53; David Luscombe, "From Paris to the Paraclete: The Correspondence of Abelard and Heloise," *Proceedings of the British Academy* 74 (1988): 247–83; Elizabeth Mary McNamer, *The Education of Heloise: Methods, Content and Purpose of Learning in the Twelfth Century* (with a translation of the *Problemata Heloissae*), Mediaeval Studies 8 (Lewiston, NY: Edward Mellen Press, 1991); Elizabeth Freeman, "The Public and Private Functions of Heloise's Letters," *Journal of Medieval History* 23, no. 1 (March 1997), 15–28 (I must thank Ms. Freeman for sending me an advance copy of her paper). Further details of Heloise's Latin rhetoric will be found in John O. Ward and Neville Chiavaroli, "The Young Heloise and Latin Rhetoric: Some Preliminary Comments on the 'Lost' Love-Letters and their Significance," in *Essays on Heloise*, ed. Bonnie Wheeler (New York: St. Martin's Press, forthcoming).

19 Ruys, "Role-playing"; Irvine, "Heloise and the Gendering of the Literate Subject," 90 and 103; 111–12. Also Freeman, "Public and Private Functions."

20 Tore Janson, "Schools of *Cursus* in the Twelfth Century and the Letters of Heloise and Abelard," *Retorica e Poetica tra i secoli XII e XIV (Atti...Trento e Roveretto, 1985)*, ed. C. Leonardi and E. Menestò (Perugia: Nuova Italia etc., 1988), 171–220; Dronke, *Women Writers*, 110–12.

21 Paul Archambault, "The Silencing of Cornelia: Heloïse, Abelard and Their Classics," *Papers on Language and Literature* 6 (1970): 3–17; Mews, "Un lecteur," 441; D.M. Stone, "Heloise: *la très sage Abbess* of the Paraclete," *Tjurunga* 37 (1989): 20; 24–28.

22 Dronke, *Women Writers*, 111–12. The musicality of the opening of Heloise's third letter (ed. J.T. Muckle, *Mediaeval Studies* 15 [1053]: 77, "miror, unice meus, quod praeter consuetudinem ... rerum dignitate") has often been commented upon. It makes uses of the same figures of speech that I have mentioned above, in connection with Hildegard's epistolary style. Frequent use of *exclamatio, repetitio*, and similar figures also mark the rest of this letter.

23 Andrea Nye, "A Woman's Thought or a Man's Discipline? The Letters of Abelard and Heloise," *Hypatia* 7, no. 3 (1992), reprinted in Linda Lopez

McAlister, ed., *Hypatia's Daughters: Fifteen Hundred Years of Women Philosophers* (Bloomington, IN: Indiana University Press, 1996), 41.

24 Eileen Kearney, "Heloise: Inquiry and the *Sacra Pagina,*" *Ambiguous Realities: Women in the Middle Ages and Renaissance* (Detroit, MI: Wayne State University Press, 1987), 66-81.

25 Dronke, *Women Writers,* chapter 4; Bond, "*Iocus amoris*" 158*ff,* 167*ff.*

26 The phrase occurs in MS Venice Marc. Lat. cl. XI, 23 (4686) fol. 27va in the course of a commentary on the *De inventione* (probably to be ascribed to the writer of the companion *Ad Herennium* gloss in the manuscript, which is dated "XII/XIII" or c. 1200 A. D., i.e. "Magister Alanus") 2.19.59: "aliter vero superiorem litteram leger[unt] antiqui, scilicet magister manegaldus et eius sequaces; dixerunt quod sic est illud intelligendum, nomen, i.e. ..."

27 "His temporibus florere coepit in Theutonica terra Manegaldus philosophus divinis et saecularibus litteris ultra coetaneos suos eruditus. Uxor quoque eius et filiae religione florentes multam in scripturis habuere notitiam, et discipulos proprios filiae eius praedictae docebant." Max Manitius, *Geschichte der lateinischen Literatur des Mittelalters* III (München: Beck'sche, 1931), 178. The (slightly fuller) original may be consulted in E. Martène and U. Durand, eds., *Veterum Scriptorum et Monumentorum Historicorum, Dogmaticorum, Moralium amplissima Collectio,* vol. 5 (Paris: apud Montalant, 1729), col. 1169. The original entry in the chronicle (cols. 1160-74, "Chronicon Richardi Pictavensis monachi Cluniacensis," covering the years 754-1153) seems to refer to the last three-quarters of the eleventh century.

28 I.S. Robinson, *Authority and Resistance in the Investiture Contest: The Polemical Literature of the Late Eleventh Century* (Manchester: Manchester University Press, 1978), 124*ff,* and n. 30 below.

29 Some early comments on Manegold as a "rhetor" will be found in Mary Dickey, "Some Commentaries on the *De inventione* and *Ad Herennium* of the Eleventh and Early Twelfth Centuries," *Mediaeval and Renaissance Studies* 6 (1968): 12*ff,* esp. p. 13: "Manegold's rhetorical commentary [Dickey knew of only one – incomplete – version] probably belongs to the earlier period of his life when he was teaching. This is the more certain because there is no evidence in the work itself of any interest in the reform movement. It is difficult to believe that, had it been written later, he could have avoided all reference to the questions uppermost in his mind."

30 I.S. Robinson, "The *Colores Rhetorici* in the Investiture Controversy," *Traditio* 32 (1976): 222*ff,* and "The Bible In The Investiture Contest: The South German Gregorian Circle," in *The Bible in The Medieval World: Essays in Memory of Beryl Smalley,* ed. K. Walsh and Diana Wood (Oxford: Blackwell, 1985), 83*ff.*

31 C. Stephen Jaeger, *The Envy of Angels: Cathedral Schools and Social Ideals in Medieval Europe 950-1200* (Philadelphia: University of Pennsylvania Press, 1994), 1-17.

32 Jaeger, *The Envy of Angels,* 16, 134-36.

33 R.I. Moore, ed., *The Birth of Popular Heresy* (London: Arnold, 1975), 27–38; B. Bolton, *The Medieval Reformation* (London: Arnold, 1983), chapter 5; J. Smith, "Robert of Arbrissel's Relations with Women," in *Medieval Women*, ed. Derek Baker (Oxford: Blackwell, 1978), 175–84; J. Dalarun, "Robert D'Arbrissel et les femmes," *Annales: Économies, Civilizations, Sociétés* 39 (1984): 1140–60, and the same author's *L'impossible sainteté: la vie retrouvée de Robert d'Arbrissel (1045–1116) fondateur de Fontevraud* (Paris: Cerf, 1985).

34 I have attempted to sketch some of the features of the "unstructured" or "liminal" age that preceded the death of Bernard of Clairvaux in "Rhetoric, Truth and Literacy in the Renaissance of the Twelfth Century," in *Oral and Written Communication: Historical Approaches,* Written Communication Annual 4, ed. R.L. Enos (Newbury Park, CA: Sage, 1990), 126–57, and "The First Crusade as Disaster: Apocalypticism and the Genesis of the Crusading Movement," in *Medieval Studies in Honour of Avrom Saltman,* Bar-Ilan Studies in History IV (Ramat-Gan: Bar-Ilan University Press, 1995), 253–92.

35 Barbara Biesecker, "Coming to Terms with Recent Attempts to Write Women into the History of Rhetoric," *Philosophy and Rhetoric* 25, no. 2 (1992): 155, 157.

# *Lady Mary Wroth's* Urania *and the Rhetoric of Female Abuse*

Victor Skretkowicz

By the time Lady Mary Wroth (*c.* 1587–*c.* 1653) published *The Countess of Montgomery's Urania* in 1621,[1] she had taken a conscious decision to enunciate publicly her adopted position as the foremost literary feminist of her epoch. In *Urania*, the first novel by a woman published in England, Wroth writes a skeptical exposé of pan-European patriarchal conventions that uphold chauvinistic abusive practices. Although she varies her rhetorical program within the novel, Wroth goes out of her way to establish the significance of stylistic plainness as fundamental to her rhetoric of female abuse.[2]

Wroth's choice of plainness reflects a kind of literary Puritanism that implies confrontation and opposition. The unornamented Attic style used by Plutarch in the first century, and by Longus in *Daphnis and Chloe* in the third century,[3] is adopted in English by late sixteenth-century Huguenot-inspired writers to convey stoic Protestant values that hearken back to the simple, unadorned, and uncorrupted beginnings of Christianity. At the leading edge of this movement is Wroth's aunt Mary Sidney, Countess of Pembroke, in her *Antonius*,[4] a translation of Robert Garnier's *Marc Antoine*,[5] published in 1592 in the same volume as her translation of her friend Philippe de Mornay's *Discours de la vie et de la mort*.[6] Mary Sidney's plainness in transforming Garnier's flamboyant alexandrine couplets into stark English blank verse identifies her with Mornay's Huguenot-inspired humanitarian liberalism, with Christian stoicism, and with a republicanism that advocates democracy and even king-killing as protection against tyranny.[7]

Plainness, within the Huguenot ethic adopted by the Sidney family, is the stylistic representation of naked Truth. Wroth understands its appropriateness to verify the credibility of her discourse. She therefore chooses a style dominated by plainness, itself emphasized by the lightness of the figuring, for her characterization of the Duke of Saxon, who describes how in the kingdom of Dacia female abuse has become the norm: "the country is a strict place, and a hard hand is held over the woemen, the men hauing an naturall knowing unworthines about them, wch procures too much hatefull Jealousy" (II, fol. 5v). In other words, superior Dacian men instinctively know that all women are unworthy. Their lack of trust produces such hateful jealousy that during national celebrations all women are obliged to accompany their husbands to court, where their behaviour is microscopically scrutinized. One hint of a self-conscious slip, and "itt shalbee for a perpetuall memorie sett up to continuall punnishment, soe as their libertie is butt the forerunner of a lastinger punishment, and perpetuall suffring" (II, fol. 5v). This plain expression of outrage over such immoral entrapment of women conveys Wroth's challenge to the Jacobean court. And she just as clearly prescribes her bold feminist antidote. Victimized wives, regarded as untrustworthy chattels, must grasp the solace of proffered human love whenever the opportunity presents itself.

Appropriating the genre of prose romance, successfully used to promote Protestant ethics and politics by her reformist uncle Sir Philip Sidney in *The Countess of Pembroke's Arcadia*,[8] Wroth in *Urania* turns the Greco-Roman literary and rhetorical traditions into the weaponry of a sophisticated anti-establishment iconoclast. As in Greco-Roman romance, and in particular Achilles Tatius's *Leukippe and Clitophon*,[9] illustrations of men engaging in tyranny and violence over women are woven into a multiplicity of parallel and digressive narrative strands. As often as not these episodes, more or less even in length and resembling a series of chapters, are entirely illustrative. Both principal and peripheral characters of both genders seem perpetually to be travelling, encountering one victim after another who is willing to reveal the emotional betrayal that forms the background of their misery and grief. But although these episodes remain largely inconsequential in terms of the action or development of the plot, their cumulative effect is to cast an undeviating mood of anxious despondency over the entire work.

When compared with the Greco-Roman novels, or even her uncle's *Arcadia*, Wroth's portrayal of misery, suffering, and pain seems to be far more reflective of first-hand knowledge. Wroth, the daughter of Sir Robert Sidney, first Earl of Leicester, like her many, many characters, lived in a world dominated by courtly society and politics. Unhappily married, she is acutely conscious of the vulnerability of women trapped in the isolation of great country houses and royal courts, and of their dependence on honourable behaviour by men during private social intercourse. One cannot, for this reason, ever feel confident that the examples of abuse illustrated in *Urania* are entirely idealized, rather than absolute representations of hard truth relocated into fictional settings.

This eerie aura of authenticity is very deliberately supported by the author's incorporating a strong but semi-transparent autobiographical element into her writing. In the introduction to her edition of *Urania*, Josephine Roberts emphasizes that the work is not a *roman à clef,* but "a highly complex fiction that provides for the intermittent shadowing of actual lives and events, often under multiple figures" (lxx). Tickling out some of these allusions, Roberts notes that Wroth represents herself "most prominently as Pamphilia, Bellamira, and Lindamira" (lxxi–lxxii). Her husband Sir Robert Wroth is Treborius, Charimellus, the Lord of the Forest Champion (or the Forest Lord), and Rodomandro the King of Tartaria. Wroth unashamedly makes her lover, her cousin William Herbert, Earl of Pembroke, the hero of the piece, portraying him briefly under the guise of Laurimello, but most extensively and flatteringly as Amphilanthus, the poet King of Naples who achieves international status as the King of the Romans, and then universal power as the elected Holy Roman Emperor.

Wroth relates the general aura of personal misery that pervades the work to the propensity of her characters, both male and female, to fall into unfulfillable love. She is particularly sensitive to the debilitating effects of deep and powerful emotions. Many of her female characters, of whom the most substantially discussed is Pamphilia (Wroth herself), experience the haunting impossibility of sacrificing their happiness in one-sided relationships. Their admiration for wealthy, powerful, personable, talented, demanding, and unfaithful chivalric kings such as Amphilanthus causes them freely to submit themselves to the vagaries and uncertainties of excruciatingly intense love. Many, locked into arranged marriages with incompatible husbands, as was Wroth herself, find themselves battling against the constraints of society's patriarchal dominance in order to embrace love, and even sexual fulfillment, however transitory.

The ambitious scope of her project provides Wroth with unlimited opportunities to use any Greco-Roman rhetorical schema that she feels suitable to convey her powerful theme of female abuse. In her story of Limena, the daughter of a Sicilian duke, Wroth consciously practises a rhythmic, clausally based style embellished, albeit with studied mannerist irregularity, with patterned repetition, alliteration, or assonance. Limena's father bestows her in an arranged marriage on a great but jealousy-prone lord symbolically named Philargus. Limena consents, "her tongue faintly delivering, what her heart so much detested; loathing almost it selfe, for consenting in shew to that which was most contrarie to it selfe" (5). During her marriage Limena carries on a clandestine but entirely chaste relationship with Perissus, nephew of the King of Sicily. Philargus's jealousy turns to possessive rage. Sword drawn, he corners Limena in her room, hurling threats at her in a sequence of tempestuous imperatives:

> Resolve instantly to die, or obey me, write a letter straight before mine eyes unto him, conjure him with those sweete charmes which have undone mine honour, and content to come unto you: Let me truely know his answere, and be secret, or I vow thou shalt not many minutes outlive the refusall. (12)

After her rescue she relates the horror of her marriage. There is no rhetorical ornament here to mitigate the cruelty of female abuse. She acknowledges Philargus's legal authority over her: "I know, as your wife, I am in your power to dispose of" (87). Deep in a dark forest, she submits to his degrading violence as he mutilates her breasts with his knife, the scene lit by the waiting fire (87). He isolates her on an island, where "once every day hee brought mee to this pillar where you found me, and in the like manner bound me, then whipt me, after washing the stripes and blisters with salt water" (88).

Through this portrait of her stoic heroine Limena, Wroth associates plainness in speech with equanimity of temperament. In the character Pamphilia this coupling of plainness and cool-headedness occurs as a family trait. Pamphilia's father, the King of Morea, has clearly never subjected her to the catastrophic tyranny practised by Limena's father. By contrast, when Pamphilia's father receives Leandrus's proposal of marriage, he invites discussion with her. Unlike Limena, whose guilt-ridden passivity reflects a recognizable posture of the chronically abused, Pamphilia has no qualms about refusing her father's choice of suitor. When she rejects Leandrus, her father sympathetically listens to her clear and unforced protest:

> "Not to Leandrus my Lord," said shee, "I beseech you, for I cannot love him; nor can I believe he loves in me ought besides my kingdome, and my honour in being your daughter; Antissia better fitteth him, who was appointed for him."
>
> The King knew she had reason for what she said, and so assuring her, that he would not force her to any thing against her mind, though he should be glad of the match, if it could content her, they fell into other discourse . . . (262–3)

The interplay between these two extremes of generosity and brutality in the treatment of daughters emphasizes the idealistic liberality of the one, the sadistic horror of the other, and the stark simplicity that divides kindness from abuse. The plainness of style and diction that Wroth chooses for the expression of complex issues is vital to the doctrinal strategy of her rhetorical program. Wroth, however, eschews the schematic balancing that these examples suggest. Where such personal misery prevails, the mere glimpses of optimism and slight glimmers of hope that sustain her characters through their continuous tribulations place her work squarely within the traditions of the Greco-Roman romance.

Repeated examples of brutality towards women (and if they are royal personages, towards their countries) identify the principal cause of this social pattern of abuse as the western European acceptance of the cultural dominance of the primitive warrior mentality. Nor is this aggressive dominance found only in men. In a revealing autobiographical narrative, where one of Wroth's personae speaks about another, Pamphilia tells how a manipulative woman's tattling about the married Lindamira's discreet love for the jealous Queen's favourite leads to Lindamira's disgrace at Court (499–505). The veracity of this tale, understood by the listener Dorolina to be "some thing more exactly related then a fixion" (505), is reinforced by being delivered in plain style.

Almost as soon as Pamphilia's story is finished an abrupt shift in the narrative describes how she too falls victim to a selfishly dominant personality. Pamphilia becomes just another in the succession of examples of abuse, as yet another male equates love, marriage, and possession with power:

> The young and proud King of Celicia, being her neighbour, her Wooer, and refused by her, would not as it seemd endure the scorne, or goe without her, wherefore he with an invincible Army, was come neare the confines of her Country, by force to win, what he could not by love, or faire meanes gaine. (505)

At this juncture Wroth embeds an aside within the narrative. She particularly emphasizes Pamphilia's uncompromising nature and her determination to stand up to intimidation. We know from her father's understanding response when she rejects Leandrus that he has nurtured Pamphilia carefully rather than broken her will, and we see the result of his care manifesting itself in her lack of fear in the face of intimidation by this King of Celicia:

> Force must not prevaile against such a spirit, if not to bring death for hate, but no affection or submission, threats can worke with her no more, then to command men to give resistance. (505)

Wroth's rhetorical strategy of interpolating moral reflections into her sequence of events imitates the modus operandi of the ancient historians. One might at this moment be reading a summary of Plutarch's reflections on Cleopatra. What particularly emphasizes this affinity with Plutarch is Wroth's clear preference for the undecorated stylistic purity and "plainness" of the Attic style. Her intention is to convince her reader of the historical truth of the events of her story, in particular of instances of female abuse, and in this instance of her persona Pamphilia's determination to resist intimidation.[10]

In other parts of *Urania*, several conventions of Greco-Roman rhetorical style operate in conjunction in a stylistic mixture calculated to emphasize their differences by contrast. The beginning of her novel and other passages that occupy themselves with the business of idealized romantic love demonstrate that Wroth is not averse to Greco-Roman ecphrastic and periphrastic adornment. Her rhythmic opening signals love and pastoral innocence:

> When the Spring began to appear like the welcome messenger of Summer, one sweet (and in that more sweet) morning, after Aurora had called all carefull eyes to attend the day, forth came the faire Shepherdesse Urania. (1)

While modeling her opening on her uncle Sir Philip Sidney's in his revised Arcadia,[11] Wroth immediately shifts the paradigm of love to one of sadness. Inverting the shock ending of Longus's *Daphnis and Chloe*, where the pastoral characters learn of their sophisticated origins, are reunited with their natural parents and marry, Wroth opens this heroic romance with her principal character Urania in a state of isolated devastation. She has just learned that she is a foundling, and has lost her identity. This knowledge of her royal birth, kidnapping, and theft are suspended till much further into the work. As Wroth's fair shepherdess begins to speak, the register changes. The loose meandering of the opening crystallizes into a rhetoric of studied clarity. An almost imperceptible shift moves the narrative from the lightly decorative Attic style, used by the Greek historian Appian and by the novelists Achilles Tatius and Heliodorus,[12] into a delicate style of cultured simplicity:

> "Alas Urania," said she, "(the true servant to misfortune); of any miserie that can befall woman, is not this the most and greatest which thou art falne into? Can there be any neare the unhappinesse of being ignorant, and that in the highest kind, not being certaine of mine owne estate or birth? Why was I not stil continued in the beleefe I was, as I appear, a Shepherdes, and Daughter to a Shepherd?" (1)

Thus, from the outset Wroth develops the expression of ultimate misery as essential to her rhetoric of female abuse. There can be no question that the rhetorical effect of the almost constant reiteration of the word "misery" fixes the prevailing tone of the novel at that end of human experience.

While plainness conveys the brutal reality of certain events, Wroth's many comments through her narrator and characters reveal her awareness of the effectiveness of variation in style. Perhaps the most explicitly rhetorically self-conscious of all the late Renaissance English writers, Wroth often provides explanations about why her characters choose to implement certain rhetorical postures, and describes how others react to them. She creates an episode in which Pamphilia, one of her most intelligent, literate and sensitive characters, and her principal persona, is rendered uncommunicative through sadness. Wroth confronts her with the boorish, self-centred Queen of Bulgaria, known as the Empress of Pride, who denounces Pamphilia as "the dullest shee ever saw." And though Musalina objects in Pamphilia's defence that "the world will doubt much of that judgement, that taxeth her for dulnesse," even when the Queen of Bulgaria hears Pamphilia speak she fails to understand her rhetorical sophistication. Pamphilia's story, "daintily and sharply ... related ... might have made the Queene see her error, but shee never went so farre as to weigh the excellency of the discourse, but heeded only the tale fitter for her capacity" (459–460). In uncompromisingly plain style, and perhaps as a caveat to the reader, Wroth's narrator describes how the Queen of Bulgaria's insensitive mind renders her unresponsive to the significance of rhetorical texture. Her rhetorically unsophisticated mind renders her receptive only to tales of adventure.

Wroth's narrator gives the reader a sharp reminder that the rhetorical program of the novel has been carefully thought through, and that it has a strong bearing on the interpretation of the matter it conveys. The most poignant moments, which another author might choose to embellish, are reduced through plainness as it were to first causes, as in the Queen of Naples' response to her long absent son Amphilanthus's return home with Pamphilia in tow. In order best to depict the maternal ecstacy of this highly charged scene, Wroth's narrator chooses "plaine relation":

> Shall I presume to express the Joye, the wellcome[,] the all, that rare Queene shoued, and felt, seeing her deerest son[n], and wt him her haulf self Pamphilia, Noe, I dare nott, nay I can nott, therfor I leaue itt to such (if any such ther bee) to relate itt, expresse itt I ame sure they can nott, therfor in plaine relation I say they mett, the Queen blessed them both, as truly hers ... (II, fol. 1)

The clearest indicator that "plaine relation" is Wroth's preferred style for the expression of reality and truth may well be enunciated through her fictional self-portraits. The lengthy scene between Wroth's persona, the widowed Lady of the Forest Champion, and two knights of contrasting character, the Duke of Florence and the irrepressible Talkative Knight, is dedicated to promoting this rhetorical preference. Wroth anticipates this scene with two parodic episodes involving both of these knights, in which she demonstrates by example her disapproval of certain exaggerated styles of speech. The first occurs when the Duke of Florence, newly arrived in Britain, tries to impress two ladies with the baroque mannerism of his excessive Petrarchan style:

> Wee are Travellers and strangers; yet more strangers to the sight of such beauty, as till this instant I never did behold; and which doth so amaze mee with content, as I am rapt into the cloudes of pleasure, not being able to express your excellencies but by my infinite admiration; beholding you like so many Sunnes contented to distribute your equall beames to let us be the abler to behold you: heere I see the excellentest excellency of the rarest perfections ... (628)

Not surprisingly, the Duke of Florence finds that he has an unsympathetic audience. This pair of sisters, renowned for their rudeness and vanity, cut him dead and walk away, "as who would say, by that time the Oration is done, wee will come againe" (629).

Incompatibility between speaker and spoken-to is emphasized by the derision heaped onto the Talkative Knight. The Talkative Knight, "who talk'd on, and regarded, or not, said Verses, spake Prose, and rime againe, no more heeding answers (so hee heard himself) then if he had rav'd or talk'd in his sleepe" (635), is a pathetic character who some people even believe suffers from a disease of the brain (631). Directly in contrast with the Duke of Florence's clichéd and overly figured style, this exhausting speaker blurts out a series of uncontrolled arrhythmic commonplaces:

> "Did you ever," said he, "see a sweet Lady so much changed as shee is? I knew her, and so did you, a faire, dainty, sweet woman, noble and freely disposed, a delicate Courtier, curious in her habites, danced, rid, did all things fit for a Court, as well as any brave Lady could doe? what can change her thus? they say shee is in love: would that man were hang'd would suffer such sweetnesse to decay by his curstnesse..." (631)

Wroth's capturing such a candid display of rhetorical naiveté emphasizes the intellectual control required to achieve plainness of speech. The facility with which she can write various styles of direct speech in character – Wroth is the author of the earliest English pastoral tragi-comedy by a woman, *Love's Victory* – inspires confidence in her judgement. As if setting herself up as a role model, the Florentine wooer of Wroth's persona

> admir'd her grave and yet courteous manner, the eloquence she spake such, as made him thinke she was the best spoken woman he had ever heard, and the greatest part of her eloquence was the plainness, but excellently well plac'd words she deliverd, her speech was as rare and winning, as the Knights troublesome, and most times idle. (635)

Wroth reiterates that plainness and plain words are her preferred vehicles for the expression of truth.

The cause of the Lady of the Forest Champion's misery is that she harbours a faithful but unenunciated love to an unreciprocating and unfaithful lover. Guided principally by arrogance, he misunderstands her modesty as rejection and peremptorily shuts her out of his life. Throughout *Urania* Wroth develops this plain expression of personal misery as a thematic motif. In this instance of excruciating psychological pain, a miniature of that experienced by her principal alter-ego Pamphilia, Wroth maintains the Lady's emotional control. When responding to the Talkative Knight's request "to hear your story," the Lady speaks in precisely this same measured plain style:

> "I have not," answered she, "ready, or perfect delivery of speech so well as you; therefore if it please you, especially of the Prince, I desire to be excused, since I can onely when I have said all, but conclude, I am, as you see me, the most unhappie, unfortunate, miserable, lost woman, that can be found breathing." (636)

Wroth emphasizes that, in contrast to the knight's studiously expansive style, this Lady's superb rhetorical command originates in the intelligent spontaneity of her discourse. She is a gifted speaker who condenses her emotion into a powerfully contrived crescendo of adjectives. It is the very simplicity of her declaration that defines Lady Mary Wroth's invention of a rhetoric of female abuse.

Mary Wroth's *Urania* represents the early English novel in one of the several experimental phases that it took during the seventeenth century. It is highly personal, grandiose in scale, and immensely ambitious — simultaneously wildly rhapsodic and closely thought through. Much of the burden of this thinking concentrates on the success of the representation of varying forms of female abuse, a challenge hitherto not undertaken by a woman writer of fiction in English. Wroth's appropriation for this purpose of "a plain kind of phrase," the rhetorical style understood by her uncle Philip Sidney "to make his speech the more credible,"[13] demonstrates the high priority that she gives to this subject. It is to fulfill the sensitive demands of her socially reformist aspirations that Wroth creates her rhetoric of female abuse out of the style most suited to elicit credibility.

## *NOTES*

1. Lady Mary Wroth, *The First Part of The Countess of Montgomery's Urania*, ed. Josephine A. Roberts (Binghamton, NY: Medieval and Renaissance Texts & Studies, 1995). Page references in the text are to this edition. References in the text prefixed by the roman numeral "II" are to the folio numbers in the unpublished manuscript continuation, "the first booke, of the secound part of the Countess of Mountgomeries Urania," Newberry Library, Chicago, Case Ms fY 1565. W 95.
2. Other uses of plainness are discussed by Kenneth J.E. Graham, *The Performance of Conviction: Plainness and Rhetoric in the Early English Renaissance* (Ithaca, NY: Cornell University Press, 1994).
3. Longus, *Daphnis and Chloe*, in *Collected Ancient Greek Novels*, ed. Bryan P. Reardon (Berkeley: University of California Press, 1989), 285–348.
4. See *The Collected Works of Mary Sidney Herbert, Countess of Pembroke*, ed. Margaret P. Hannay, Noel J. Kinnamon, and Michael G. Brennan (Oxford: Clarendon Press, 1998), 2 vol., i. 152–207.
5. Robert Garnier, *Two Tragedies: "Hippolyte" and "Marc Antoine"*, ed. Christine M. Hill and Mary G. Morrison (London: Athlone University Press, 1975).
6. See Mary Sidney Herbert, *A Discourse of Life and Death . . . Antonius, A Tragoedie*, in *The Early Modern Englishwoman: A Facsimile Library of Essential Works*, gen. eds. B.S. Travitsky and P. Cullen, 'Part 1: Printed Writings, 1500–1640,' vol. 6, introduction by Gary Waller (Aldershot: Scolar Press, 1996).
7. V. Skretkowicz, "Minced Words: Mary Sidney Herbert's *Antonius* and English Philhellenism," a paper presented at the 31st International Congress on Medieval Studies, University of Western Michigan, Kalamazoo, 1996; V. Skretkowicz, "Mary Sidney Herbert's Antonius, English Philhellenism and the Protestant Cause," forthcoming in *Women's Writing* 6. On the Sidney family connections with Huguenot thought, see Jonathan Scott, *Algernon Sidney and the English Republic, 1623–1677* (Cambridge: Cambridge University Press, 1988), 6, n. 17.
8. Sidney's novel exists in two versions, *The Countess of Pembroke's Arcadia (The Old Arcadia)*, ed. Jean Robertson (Oxford: Clarendon Press, 1973) and *The Countess of Pembroke's Arcadia (The New Arcadia)*, ed. Victor Skretkowicz (Oxford: Clarendon Press, 1987).
9. Achilles Tatius, *Clitophon and Leukippe*, in Reardon, *Collected Ancient Greek Novels*, 170–284.

10 Barbara Kiefer Lewalski, *Writing Women in Jacobean England* (Cambridge, MA: Harvard University Press, 1993), 126, 132, notes the extent to which Lady Ann Clifford (1589–1676), both in her 1616–19 *Diary* and in her 1653 memoirs of her parents writes "in the vein of Plutarch's moralized *Lives* but incorporating as well vignettes in the tradition of the literary 'character'."
11 *New Arcadia*, 3: "It was in the time that the earth begins to put on her new apparel against the approach of her lover, and that the sun, running a most even course, becomes an indifferent arbiter between the night and the day, when the hopeless shepherd Strephon was come to the sands which lie against the island of Cythera. . . ."
12 Heliodorus, *An Ethiopian Story*, in Reardon, *Collected Ancient Greek Novels*, 349–588. On the attic style of the ancient novels, see Tomas Hägg, *The Novel in Antiquity* (Oxford: Basil Blackwell, 1983), 104–7.
13 Sidney, *Old Arcadia*, 314.

# *Mary Astell's Rhetorical Theory: A Woman's Viewpoint*

ERIN HERBERG

The purpose of this paper is to evaluate Mary Astell's rhetoric – her theory as well as her own strategies – and to show that although her ideas are rooted in the classics they also reflect not only her own seventeenth-century philosophy but also her interest in the social and intellectual position of women. I have presented this interpretation of Astell's goal by addressing three of the major classical influences – Plato, Aristotle, and Cicero – and making them the starting point for what Astell says. I then touch on some of the dominant influences of the seventeenth century who to varying degrees and in varying ways affected Astell's ideas – figures such as Descartes, Bacon, and Locke.

It is the particular combination of these influences that makes Astell's rhetoric unique, not because it was the first written for women, but because it was the first that read these influences with women in mind – a major development considering the historical tendency of rhetoric to exclude females. However, to say Astell was developing a purely feminine rhetoric to stand in opposition to the male rhetoric of the day would be to misunderstand her. Although *A Serious Proposal* is addressed *to the Ladies*, it is not exclusively for women – it is developed and presented as a universal rhetorical theory, the way for men as well as women to engage in public discourse.

## Echoes of Plato

I begin the discussion of Astell with Plato, because much of Astell's philosophy has Platonic overtones and we cannot fully appreciate her view of logic and rhetoric without first understanding something of her philosophy. First, her Platonism was strongly coloured by the Cambridge Platonists, whose influences went back to St. Augustine and who were more Christian than Platonic. Not only was her tutor, her uncle Ralph Astell, a student of the Cambridge Platonists, but also a later correspondent, John Norris, was one of the last members of that philosophical school. Astell was a moral philosopher who adhered to a Platonic/Christian idealism. She believed in a world of spirituality and of ultimate truths that were discernable only by withdrawing from the material world and applying reason. We see in Astell's work a reverberation of Platonic ideas and images that were part of her own background, culturally embedded in her time.

In fact, we can see much of Plato in Astell's attitudes toward the subject of rhetoric itself. She shares some of the Platonic criticisms of rhetoric. She warns speakers and writers of babbling on subjects they know nothing about, of confusing and misinforming others,[1] and of using elaborate tropes and figures only to conceal their own lack of knowledge. However, instead of attacking rhetoric, as Plato does in the *Gorgias*, she discusses it as it should be practised, much as he does in his *Phaedrus*. She also differentiates between her rhetoric and disputation. Her theory of rhetoric shows a Platonic development along an Aristotelian line – it is the way to convince others, for their improvement, of what we have found true. Disputation, or sophistry, on the other hand, is to be avoided: its rules are meant to "Intangle [rather] than Clear a Question." She adds: "To be able to hold an Argument Right or Wrong may pass with some perhaps for the Character of a Good Disputant, which yet I think it is not, but [it] must by no means be allow'd to be that of a Rational Person" (Astell 12).

Astell, as much devoted to Christianity as to philosophy, believed the proper activity of all humans, male or female, was the search for truths about life through contemplative philosophy. Still, she recognized that one's success in this search depended on one's abilities, inclinations, and station in life; although everyone can *think*, not everyone can take the time to, or do so deeply.² However, this meditation on self and world that gives us control over the will and the passions or the "animal spirits" (Part II, 92) cannot be achieved without withdrawing from the materialism and vanity of the world. To keep our abilities in perspective, she admonishes us that compared to the "bright light of Divine reason," human reason is only a "short, faint ray" (Part II, 84); therefore we should always question what it is we think we know, lest like the jaundiced man who sees the world "tinged with yellow," we come to the conclusion that yellow is the true nature of the world (Part II, 99).

Astell strengthened and developed her philosophy to support and defend her most important convictions about the world and human existence. She believed in the existence of God and a world of spirituality that extended beyond human sensory perception. She also believed in the inherent right of women to be recognized as rational, intelligent beings who had both a right and a duty to acquire knowledge, including knowledge of philosophy, and to participate in the public sphere. Her perceived foes in this respect were the empiricists and specifically John Locke. Astell, however, was not at odds with everything Locke and the empiricists said. What concerned her was Locke's denial of what he called "innate principle" (Part I, 16) or "maxim" (Part I, 21) as opposed to knowledge based on proof through sensory perception. This was to be a topic of controversy for Astell for a number of years and supplied much of the content of her correspondence with Dr. John Norris and of her 1705 work, *The Christian Religion, as Profess'd by a Daughter of the Church of England*.³ It is through Astell's conflict with Lockean thought that we can see her articulation of her Platonist foundation and the development of her own philosophy. Although Locke certainly did not deny the existence of God, Astell felt he had at least diminished God's existence in a material world validated by quantifiable measurement. Unfortunately, her siding with the losers of this particular ancient versus modern battle has perhaps contributed to her historical obscurity.

Both Locke and Astell discussed the foundation of human knowledge: what Locke calls intuitive knowledge and Astell first principles. Locke's intuitive knowledge is gained from the senses about the physical world, and Astell's first principles are inherent ideas about the nature of existence. For Locke, human knowledge has limitations: "[I]t is evident, that the extent of our knowledge comes not only short of the reality of things, but even of the extent of our own ideas."[4] For Astell, Truths (with a Platonic capital *T*) may be difficult and elusive; still, she says that "[God] has so regularly connex'd one Truth with another, that, if we diligently Examine those Truths which we Know, they will clear the way to what we search after: For it seldom happens but that the Question it self directs us to some Idea that will serve for the Explanation or Proof of it" (Part II, 104). Whereas Astell takes the Platonic view that reasoning is an activity that involves the soul and the mind, Locke sees reasoning as only a mental activity.

Astell must also have recognized the more practical threat empiricism held for women, since by society's dictates the world they could experience and how they could experience it were limited. Empiricism, with its need for specialized knowledge and tools, could, in effect, re-erect the intellectual barriers that anti-scholasticism had supposedly demolished.

## *Echoes of Aristotle*

The philosophy that determined that truth and knowledge were acquired through a reasoning process fuels Astell's logical method. And because her logical method closely resembles a type of dialectic, we can begin to evaluate Astell's theories in terms of Aristotle. It is impossible and perhaps even irrelevant to trace a direct link between Astell and Aristotle, even though the first English version of Aristotle's *De Rhetorica* (Hobbes' *Aristotle's Rhetoric*) was first published in 1637,[5] and would have been available to Astell. However, her knowledge of Aristotelian concepts most likely was formed from her intellectual mentors. What is interesting is that while Astell may have been out of step with her own time regarding her theories of knowledge acquisition, her dialectic, which is essentially a dialogic or a personal monologic invention process, anticipated later centuries and particularly the Romantics' revolt against science.

The strongest argument for viewing her logical method as a type of dialectic is her discussion of the three modes of understanding: Science, Faith, and Opinion. Science, according to Astell, proceeds from premises that are so clear and evident that it is impossible for a rational creature to deny them, and thus end in a clear and undebatable conclusion. Faith can also reach undeniable conclusions, but faith's conclusions are based on proofs drawn from authority. Opinion begins with clear premises, as does science, but the proofs for its conclusion are questionable (Astell, Part II, 81). For all three, the difference lies not in the purpose, but in the type of question being asked. However, conclusions drawn on questions and proofs that combine science and faith result in moral certainty. Astell believes that science and faith can be complementary. This idea further distances her from Locke, who believes faith and opinion are inferior to [empirical] knowledge.

Bearing in mind Astell's definitions of science, faith, and opinion, we can see at least a loose corollary with Aristotle's methods of demonstration, dialectic, and rhetoric. For Aristotle, demonstration, dialectic, and rhetoric differ not in the logical method,[6] but in what the proofs are and how they are admitted, and the validity of the conclusions drawn. Astell also uses the same logical method for her three "modes of thinking." And Astell, like Aristotle, relies on the infallibility of language to reach her conclusions. Both phrase their propositions as questions and rely on syllogistic reasoning. Astell's method, however, differs from Aristotle's in that it does not require a respondent. In fact Astell says nothing of a respondent, offering a general method for reasoning that could be used for two or more people but one that seems intended for an individual (reflecting perhaps what Thomas Conley identifies as Descartes' need for self-persuasion[7] or Bacon's use of a type of dialectic as a solitary monologue of inquiry [Conley 164]).

Astell's own logical method represents her choice, as a moral philosopher, of a deductive method of inquiry as opposed to the empirical method that attempts to rid logic of the deficiencies associated with it since Descartes.[8] By the seventeenth century, dialectic was discounted as a way to discover knowledge and was considered, instead, as only a way to communicate ideas that were already known. What Descartes called for was a method of inquiry that did not incorporate a method of communication. Aristotelian dialectic method included communication; demonstration, dialectic, and rhetoric were distinguished by the type of conclusions drawn and by the participants in the process – philosophers, laypersons, or the masses.

We find the influence of Cartesian thinking in Astell's logical method in two ways. First, and perhaps most interesting, she detaches scholarly communication from logic and includes it within rhetoric. This is evident not only because she deals with writing more than speaking, but also because she advises us as writers or speakers to respond to our audience, changing or dropping our argument should we be proved wrong (Part II, 115). This type of communication is more like dialogue than traditional rhetoric. However, we find the Aristotelian definition of rhetoric as regards a rhetorical audience when Astell speaks of needing to be animating enough to excite "a stupid mind." She recognizes the necessity of "Florish and Rhetorick," if not for all audiences, at least for those with depraved palates who need "their medicines administered in a pleasing vehicle" (124).

She has two goals in reviving the reputation of the deductive method and she outlines six rules for doing so. Her first goal is to attempt to follow Descartes' call for a logical method that excludes communication theory.[9] Her second goal is to avoid the false reasoning attributed to the method by Descartes, Bacon and others. Bacon comments on the problems with dialectic in several of his works, including *The Advancement of Learning* (1605) and *Novum Organon* (1620). In both works, Bacon speaks of the "false appearances"[10] and "false idols"[11] of deduction and syllogistic reasoning; these relate to the flaws inherent in the human mind, the flaws inherent in an individual, the imperfection of language, and false dogmas. In the six rules she presents in her logical method Astell attempts to eradicate these faults, drawing upon the ideas of philosophers and scientists of her time. Four of her six rules come from Descartes (and Arnauld, who incorporated them into his work). These four have to do with reducing a subject under consideration to its purest form and proceeding then from evident truth (clear ideas, as Astell calls them – rule 2), reducing ideas from the general and simple to the specific and complex (rule 3), dividing the subject into as many parts as are required to understand it (rule 4), and closely observing the subject and the process at all times (rule 5).

Her other two rules seem to deal with language and the inadequacy of simple enumerative induction. Rule 6 appears to be addressed to this problem: "To judge no further than [you] Perceive, and not take anything for Truth which [you] do not evidently Know to be so" (Part II, 107). As for the problem of language, her first rule incorporates definition[12] and seems to follow Bacon's suggestion for reducing this problem, which he calls the most troublesome to reasoning. "Whence it comes to pass that the high and formal discussions of learned men end oftentimes in disputes about words and names.... [I]t would be more prudent to begin and so by means of definitions reduce them to order."[13]

Identifying Astell's logical method as dialectic, but modified by seventeenth-century criticism of that method, we can see that she was developing an approach influenced by other moral philosophers but not totally derivative. Astell's approach to such a syllogistic and deductive reasoning was not to replace it with scientific induction but to revitalize it. This was in fact the only choice she could make without abandoning her commitment to her theology and philosophy, and to women.

## *Echoes of Cicero*

When we speak of a rhetoric that is all communication and a logic that is all inquiry we cannot help thinking of the changes Ramus made to the Ciceronian rhetorical model of the Middle Ages and the Renaissance. And although Astell appears to believe that invention belongs to logic (seeming to refute Ciceronian rhetoric), there is actually a substantial amount of Ciceronianism in Astell, including a blurring of the distinction between logic and rhetoric in invention and arrangement. What makes reading *A Serious Proposal* difficult is that Astell often says she is doing or not doing something, only to do the opposite. Thus in her section on rhetoric, while she says she is speaking of style, she actually provides her most thorough discussion of arrangement and invention. She cannot discuss these topics under rhetoric, however, without also referring her reader back to her logical method: she believes the "method of thinking" is the "method to writing" (Part II, 118), since we cannot communicate upon a subject that we have not thought about.

Astell's sometimes contradictory approach to her subject matter may be read as a reflection of what the rhetoric historian Wilbur Howell[14] calls a Ciceronian revival that had a strong following in the seventeenth century. Two dominant figures in this revival are Charles Butler and Isaac Newton. At the end of the sixteenth century, Charles Butler was an adamant Ramist, producing a school text of *Taleus* that was well and widely received. However, thirty years into the seventeenth century he published his own work, entitled *Oratoriae Libri Duo* and dealing with speech making. What is notable about this work is that Butler includes invention and arrangement as elements of rhetoric. Although he does not totally reject Ramus and return to the Scholastic school, he acknowledges that invention and arrangement are not confined to logic, and despite the risk of breaking Ramus' Law of Justice (which dictated that propositions could belong to only one liberal art), Butler feels it necessary to discuss how the two affect rhetoric. Butler explained this breaching of Ramus by calling invention and rhetoric "extra-logical" (Howell 319). Newton also fell into the Neo-Ciceronian camp, which adhered to the Ciceronian five elements of rhetoric while admitting that invention and arrangement equally belonged with logic. It appears that Astell adhered to this school, a school that, according to Howell, had strong influences in the seventeenth century.

Perhaps Astell's Neo-Ciceronian take on rhetoric simply provides further proof that logic and rhetoric cannot be neatly divided. And although she says that her natural method of logic provides the material and order for presentation, much of her rhetoric deals not just with stylistics for presentations, but with reconfiguring that material in consideration of audience. She asserts that deep meditation will provide what we need to persuade others, but she also recognizes that we cannot express "all the Process our Mind goes thro . . ." as "this would spin out our Discourse to an unprofitable tediousness" (Part II, 118). Astell also acknowledges that although our meditations may bring us to conclusions about the world, simply restating them to others may not cause them to draw the same conclusions, since they have not thought about the subject as we have. Therefore, she implies, we must meditate on the best way to present our material so that it can be understood by others — which is the invention not of logic, but of rhetoric (Part II, 118). For Astell the fissure between rhetoric and logic seems artificial. Since we can recognize the conciliatory aspects of Neo-Ciceronianism — as logic and rhetoric share invention and arrangement — we could also see the division lines being erased entirely.

What Astell also shares with Cicero is that her *Serious Proposal,* much like his *De Oratore,* not only defines and presents rhetoric but defines what constitutes an orator (or, in her case, a writer). For both Astell and Cicero the ideal orator unites wisdom and eloquence. Wisdom for Astell consists of well-reasoned logic and personal integrity — or, as she says (borrowing the terms from Arnauld), probity, prudence, civility, and modesty. This is a combination of Cicero's ideal of wisdom or intellectualism with Quintilian's ideal of the good man. This ideal speaker met the cultural expectations of a century that believed in social and personal improvement and required individuals who spoke or wrote to be motivated by civic concern and responsibility. What must also be seen, however, is how the Ciceronian concepts of civic responsibility combined with a Christian idealism that recognized women's intellectual abilities. Thus it endorses a method that develops that intellect and then authorizes women to participate in the public life of a society. One can see how viewing civic responsibility in this light overrode the conflicting social expectation of silent modesty for women.

It is, of course, not surprising to find the rhetorical ideas of Plato, Aristotle, or Cicero in the rhetoric of Astell. Who, after all, can write about rhetoric without touching upon their observations and theories? However, the classical ideas advanced by these men provide an evaluative base on which to see how Astell responded to her own time and how she developed a logical and rhetorical method to support her philosophy about God, knowledge, and human existence. And although her rhetoric was uniquely pro-feminine, it was not exclusively so. She did not expect women to engage in a different rhetoric than men; she saw her rhetoric as the appropriate rhetoric for everyone.

## *NOTES*

1 Mary Astell, *A Serious Proposal to the Ladies Part I and II* (New York: Source Book Press, 1970), 117.
2 Specifically she says, "whoever has a Rational Soul ought surely to employ it about some Truth or other, to procure for it right ideas." She also says, ". . . yet all are not equally enlarg'd nor able to comprehend so much; and they whose Capacities and Circumstances of Living [re: the working class or the poor], lie not under that obligation of extending their which Persons of a larger reach and greater leisure do" (Astell, *A Serious Proposal to the Ladies Part II*, 84–85).
3 *Letters Concerning the Love of God, Between the Author of the Proposal to the Ladies and Mr. John Norris* was published in 1695. According to Ruth Perry, Norris, one of the last Cambridge Platonists, provided not so much Astell's philosophic approach but "the formal terminology – the philosophical arsenal – to defend [her] point of view." (For more on Astell's relationship with Norris, see Perry's *The Celebrated Mary Astell* [Chicago, IL: University of Chicago Press, 1986].)
4 John Locke, *An Essay Concerning Human Understanding*, ed. A.S. Pringle-Pattison (Oxford: Clarendon Press, 1947), 268.
5 Two later editions appeared in 1651 and 1681.
6 See Aristotle's *Topics: Posterior Analytics, Topica* VIII.I, Loeb Classical Library, ed. E.S. Forster (Cambridge, MA: Harvard University Press), 675.
7 See Thomas M. Conley, *Rhetoric in the European Tradition* (Chicago, IL: University of Chicago Press, 1990), 165.
8 As part of her self-improvement course, Astell recommends Descartes and his *Les Principles de la Philosophie* in the margins of her text. In fact, there are many marginal references and reading suggestions, including Lamy and Arnauld.
9 Astell states in the opening of her logical method section that purpose of reasoning is "either to deduce some Truth we are in search of . . . or to dispose our Thoughts and Reasonings in such a manner, as to be able to Convince others of those Truths which we our selves are Convinced of" (Part II, 97). But despite the fact that this statement implicates communication into her logic, for all practical purpose, she does not include rules or discussion to obtain this second goal. Instead she says under rhetoric that by following her natural logic, and when we are knowledgeable and enthusiastic about a subject, we will find the persuasive methods (121–2).

10  See Francis Bacon, *The Advancement of Learning*, Book II, ed. J.W. Kitchin (London: J.M. Dent and Sons, 1965).
11  See Francis Bacon's *Novum Organon* (New York: P.F. Collier & Sons, 1902).
12  "Acquaint [yourself] thoroughly with Terms [you] make use of. . ." (*A Serious Proposal Part II*, 105).
13  See Bacon's *Novum Organon*, 31–32. However, it is also important to note that Bacon goes on to say that definitions do not "cure the eveil in dealing with natural and material things" recognizing that definitions are themselves based on words, and thus the definition process can go on ad infinitum. An oft recognized problem in Aristotelian dialectic.
14  Wilbur Samuel Howell, *Logic and Rhetoric in England, 1500–1700* (New York: Russell and Russell, 1961).

# GROUP 4

# Emerging into the Rhetorical Tradition

# The Public Woman: Women Speakers Around the Turn of the Century in Sweden

BRIGITTE MRAL

TRANSLATED BY MALCOLM FORBES

In Sweden, as in other countries, research concerning rhetoric has been chiefly a male discipline. Except for the odd few cases,[1] women's rhetoric has been the subject neither of theoretical nor of empirical study. It goes without saying that there have been inspired and highly active women speakers in Sweden, too. Prominent examples from the past are Saint Bridget and Alva Myrdal, and from the present the politicians Mona Sahlin and Gudrun Schyman. Such women have influenced, and continue to influence, not only politics but also the language of the public sphere.

During the last hundred years, women in Sweden have been rhetorically active on a broad front during three historical periods: around the turn of the century, in the 1920s and 1930s, and during the past twenty years. In this paper I present some results of, and reflections on, a project concerning Swedish women's rhetoric around the turn of the century.

I shall refrain here from taking up the issue of the meaningfulness or otherwise of regarding, and thereby marginalizing, women speakers as isolated figures. Further, any discussion of questions concerning the specific interest, if any, of a "female rhetoric," if any, will have to wait until there is an empirical basis to start from. What we principally need to do, I think, is to rescue from obscurity the women who have in fact been active speakers, and to investigate their style. A great deal of empirical work is required; as Karlyn Kohrs Campbell puts it, "On the simplest level, one must begin somewhere . . ."[2]

Therefore I have chosen to devote attention to the women who were active in politics and cultural life around the turn of the century, roughly 1880 to 1910. During this period there was a first expansion of women's political activity and a rhetorical offensive not just restricted to cultivated upper-class women.

Though many women were involved (and many were the rhetorical strategies they employed), for the sake of cohesion I shall restrict myself in this brief essay to three key figures: Ellen Key, Kata Dalström, and Selma Lagerlöf. For the same reason I have chosen to base the presentation on an aspect I have found fruitful when it comes to grasping the specific nature of women's public speaking in Sweden, namely the speakers' personae. In simple terms, the Jungian concept of the persona can be defined as an external character that, in a complicated process, has to some extent been forced upon the person by society, but has also been chosen by the person. This character is a much-needed mask through which to speak. Hjalmar Sundén is of the opinion that "an author's persona appears in certain cases as being quite evidently a creation of the criticism to which the author has been subjected" (my translation, here and in the case of all other Swedish sources).[3]

It can be said that the personae of women speakers are formed in the same way, in this case deriving on the one hand from society, from social pressure concerning how a woman should be, and on the other hand from personal choice. Women in the public sphere have always been vulnerable to enormous criticism and have needed to take this into account. It has been necessary to choose a mask acceptable to an audience imprinted with contemporary norms concerning how women should conduct themselves. It would, of course, be a meaningless enterprise to attempt to discover "the true self" behind the mask.

What masks or roles, then, were adopted by women speakers around the turn of the century, and in response to what criticism on the part of society? That this was a question of socially acceptable roles rather than of individual characteristics is brought out by the fact that common tendencies are plainly discernible in how the women presented what they had to say, and also by the contemplation of what roles it was impossible for women to adopt at that time if they wanted to be heard. To the latter point I shall be returning.

What, then, was the political and rhetorical situation for women in Sweden? On the most general level it was considered in Sweden, as in other countries, that women who spoke in public lost their womanliness inasmuch as they adopted this male role. A woman in the public sphere was still regarded by many as a "public woman," and accusations of immorality were just around the corner. In the fiction of the time, women in general are portrayed as incapable children, as unreliable, emotional, babbling creatures. Politically active women, however, are portrayed as ugly, old and sterile, their political involvement being a sublimation of the unsatisfied sex instinct.[4] This twofold contempt, which on occasion descended into pure hatred, was a heavy burden for a woman wanting to put across a serious message.

But this misogynous attitude did not hold complete sway, and there was a vital struggle for positions in the gender debate. In respect of practical politics it needs above all to be remembered that a married woman was legally unentitled, and that it was only under certain narrow conditions that an unmarried woman could make her own decisions. Not until 1921 did women get the vote in Sweden. But ever since at least the 1880s there had been constant attempts to initiate discussion of women's rights. The increasingly strong advance of the so-called popular movements gave the decisive impetus to women's organizations and women's participation in the public sphere. Even though women exercised little practical influence in the Free Church movement, the temperance movement, or the labour movement, these movements did involve the idea of equality between men and women. Putting this idea into practice was up to the women in the different associations. In the rest of society, too, there was to some extent a liberally benevolent attitude to women's social involvement and women's rights. Though the sight of a woman on the rostrum was not customary, it could be accepted under certain circumstances. Thus women speakers were confronted with an attitude that was ambivalent but not wholly negative.

Women became involved in the public sphere in three principal ways: as speakers on temperance, as Social Democratic agitators for the organization of working-class women, and as speakers on women's suffrage. There were many women who for either a shorter or a longer period made their living by travelling around making speeches. What education did they have that prepared them for daring to stand on the rostrum? Many of the women were teachers and therefore had a certain amount of experience of speaking in front of groups. But with the limitations of the girls' schools of the time, none of these women had any training in rhetoric. Yet even though (in contrast with, for instance, the USA[5]) there was no formal rhetorical training whatsoever for women, the women's groups in themselves – and not least the discussion groups that emerged within the different organizations[6] and within the women's networks – did provide the opportunity for self-improvement. In these discussion groups the women educated one another. There was a great deal of reading and a broad range of lectures, while at the same time women were given the chance to learn to put forward their opinions and engage in discussion. There were exercises offering training to all who wanted – and dared – to speak in public. Women in general, and working-class women in particular, had by and large no other educational opportunities than those they made for themselves.

It seems to me that the special thing about Swedish women's activism is that, despite considerable differences of opinion, the women in the different associations had the determination, and to a large extent also the capacity, to collaborate across ideological borders. Which brings me to the woman who, as I see it, meant the most for the solidarity, and also strength, of the Swedish women activists: Ellen Key (1849–1926). She must surely be regarded as the most visible woman in the public sphere up to the turn of the century. Ellen Key had an upper-class, not to say aristocratic background. Her father Emil Key was a Liberal politician, and for many years Ellen acted as his secretary, which meant that she wrote out his articles and parliamentary speeches. Thereby she soon became accustomed to political discourse, and she took an active interest in social questions. During the latter part of the 1880s and throughout the 1890s she was in great demand as a lecturer, engaged by workers' associations, Good Templar lodges, women's clubs, and students' associations. In addition to subjects from cultural or literary history there were often topics of current interest, most of them concerning women's involvement in society. But Ellen Key's attitude to the woman question was far from straightforward, and she was regarded by many women as highly controversial. Principally in her *Missbrukad kvinnokraft* (*Women's Power Misused*, 1896) she elaborated on the idea that there are natural areas of work for men and women, respectively, and that the two areas should not be confused. Women should devote themselves only to things for which they had a natural predisposition. Ellen Key encapsulated her Utopian vision of the good society in the metaphor of woman as "mother to society."[7] Just as women build up happy homes for their own families, they should also be able to build up the good society for all, she thought. What women could contribute to society was motherliness, counterbalancing male aggressiveness and destructiveness. Many women were highly skeptical about this, interpreting it to mean that Key wished to banish women to the home. But what was perhaps most controversial of all, not least for the men in the audience, was her championing of free sexual love between free individuals.

Ellen Key was used to speaking and had the necessary education. But what impression did she make as a speaker, what sort of person did she seem to be? Certainly she was enormously valued as a lecturer, in spite of – or perhaps indeed thanks to – the provocative nature of the ideas that she expressed. Ellen Key was first and foremost a teacher, and as such she possessed an undisputed authority. This role was fully accepted for women (at least for unmarried ones – and Ellen Key never married). However, her choice of persona was not restricted to that of the teacher: she went a step further and quite deliberately adopted a woman's role deriving from classical antiquity, namely that of the prophetess or priestess. At any rate the audience regarded her as performing virtually a magic act:

> When she enters the hall, there is something of the priestess about her, and when she has taken up her position on the rostrum there is such a silence that one might think oneself alone, were it not that the sight of the packed hall shows that the silence is an expression of the reverence with which the speaker is received.[8]

Ellen Key's rhetorical problem was not that the audience distrusted her authority but that they might be morally prejudiced against her. But the almost sacred atmosphere that she sometimes was able to create around her when she spoke before an audience quelled all suspicion that there might be immorality in the message. The lofty, ethereal role was emphasized not least by what she chose to wear, as comes out in the following testimony:

> If there is anyone else alive who can recall her way of addressing an audience, he is sure to remember how she, dressed as a sibyl in white raiment and with a black shawl around her shoulders, spoke so quietly in a calm and reasoning tone.[9]

And despite the fact that her message was occasionally extremely provocative there is the following univocal judgment of her style as a speaker: "Moderate and considerate, she offended no one."[10] Moderation is a Swedish virtue, while large gestures and aggressiveness are regarded as offensive and un-Swedish, particularly if they come from women. She was well aware that she had more to gain from a soft, womanly image than from a sternly authoritative one. Nor would too intellectual an attitude have been wise. Ellen Key was well-educated and could have adopted a considerably more academic image than she did. By and large, however, she kept within the Swedish adult education tradition, conveying a great passion for culture through language fairly easy to understand.

As one of the first women speakers, Ellen Key of course played an important pattern-setting role – a role still not investigated.[11] But her influence was perhaps even greater in another respect, namely through her active building of networks. One of her pet concerns was the so-called Twelfths, an extremely loose organization of discussion groups in Stockholm. The idea was to bring together women from different social classes and let them benefit from one another's experiences by means of conversation. The Twelfths were a bridge between non-socialist and Social Democratic women, and this was important for the suffrage movement, the area in respect of which the two groups could best understand each other and collaborate.[12]

One who attended the meetings of the Twelfths was the Social Democrat Kata Dalström. She was not only the most well-known woman agitator in the Swedish labour movement but also the agitator who travelled round most of all, and for many years she supported herself full-time in this way.[13] At the same time she was so successful and popular that with the surplus from her lecturing she was able to boost the funds of the local Social Democratic associations. Kata Dalström had brought up seven children and become a widow before she seriously started agitating. Like Ellen Key, she had a solid upper-class background and a solid humanistic education. Also like Ellen Key, she wanted to bring art and beauty into the lives of the workers. First and foremost, however, she was a political agitator. She loved travelling all over the country, especially to the most remote parts. She was self-assured and had an air of authority deriving from her social position, even though she had to some extent left her own class. Her passion for justice and her political will gave weight to her words.

There is ample evidence that Kata Dalström was skilled at varying her manner and language in accordance with the composition of her audience. She too, however, always had to assume one of the roles considered acceptable for a woman. She alternated between such non-erotic roles as that of the teacher and that of the mother. She was fond of speaking of, and to, the Social Democrats who sat before her as "my boys." Sometimes – especially when her subject was cultural – she made the most of her bearing as a cultivated elderly lady of the upper class. But her words impress one as virile, not feminine – at any rate when she was addressing a mixed audience. When she was addressing groups consisting only of women, on the other hand, she toned down both the intellectual and the political/agitational sides. On these occasions she emphasized female solidarity, presented herself as the ordinary woman, literally or metaphorically put on an apron, and provided homemade buns.

Kata Dalström was divided in her attitude to women's suffrage. While she was of course in favour of equal rights for women, her sense of party loyalty dictated that priority should be given to obtaining universal and equal suffrage for men, which would automatically be followed by the same for women. On the other hand, one who called unconditionally for universal suffrage was Selma Lagerlöf. It may seem a little surprising to find this winner of the Nobel Prize for Literature occupying such a prominent position in political life. Naturally her principal medium was the book, and she did not wish to be a politician. But she has not, I think, been given sufficient credit in respect of the struggle for the right to vote, nor in respect of the creation of symbols within the women's movement. Of great importance was the speech entitled "Home and State" that she made at a suffrage congress in 1911.[14] Here Selma Lagerlöf has chosen the gently ironic mask of a deeply uncertain suffragette who considers a number of well-known arguments for women's suffrage – only to reject them as invalid. She uses, that is, a sort of self-opposing rhetoric. Apparently quite at a loss, she gropes after some way of justifying women's suffrage – and thereby happens to discover all the relevant arguments for it. The means that she employs here are rhetorical questions (which she hesitantly puts to herself), profound emotion, metaphor, and Biblical associations. Like Ellen Key, she uses the home as a metaphor – the home where women demonstrate their sense of responsibility and provide what is best for everyone. She portrays her utopia as a State performing the same humanitarian tasks as are already performed by women in the home. She concludes with a virtually religious confession of faith:

> We do not believe that the task will be done quickly, but we do believe that it would be a transgression and folly to reject our help. We believe that we are borne by the winds of heaven. The small masterpiece, the home, was our creation, with the aid of men. The large masterpiece, the good State, will be created by men when they seriously take women as their helpers.[15]

Thus in this speech Selma Lagerlöf plays with the mask of an uncertain woman, a woman trying to find her way – her attitude is non-aggressive and to all appearances non-threatening. But she thereby plays another role, that of the teller of tales. As the author of the tales of Nils Holgersson and Gösta Berling this of course came naturally to her, but it was also a role which it was perfectly acceptable for a woman speaker to adopt.

Three people with different though largely overlapping sets of socially acceptable masks – and all three chose that of the teacher. Furthermore, we find the motherly mask in the case of all three, most clearly in the case of Ellen Key. Her mask of prophetess and priestess is perhaps the most unusual, but it touches on deep layers in the collective memory, traceable back to the canonized female visionaries of the Middle Ages and to the accepted female roles of classical antiquity. Only Selma Lagerlöf dared to be the story-teller to the full, though both Ellen Key and Kata Dalström were also adept at story-telling.

Thus can one search for parallels between the ways the women acted – and run the risk of neglecting the differences that of course also existed. Regarding my emphasizing the persona aspect, furthermore, it might be objected that any good speaker will be careful to behave with proper decorum, will be careful to suit the address to the audience's expectations. Naturally a speaker must pay regard to decorum, to what is "proper," to the norms, conventions, and ideals that prevail in a particular society in respect of public speaking – this in order not to give offence, awaken animosity, and suffer a loss of public standing.[16]

What, though, if you know from the start that you are going to give offence and awaken animosity just by stepping onto the rostrum, and if you perhaps have precious little public standing anyway? The majority of women who ventured into the public sphere (not just in Sweden, of course) appear to have attempted to resolve this dilemma by speaking from behind a mask, by temporarily putting on a disguise in order to acquire scope for action.

The persona aspect becomes especially interesting if comparisons are made over time or between countries. For the moment, however, I can offer only some reflections, where many uncertainties remain. It is interesting, for example, to consider what mask would have been unfitting for a "public" woman in Sweden. Here one can make a comparison with the choices of persona made by women in the more distant past. The only role, for instance, that was available to a medieval woman politician such as St. Bridget was that of the mystic and visionary – but this role would by no means have served Ellen Key, Kata Dalström or Selma Lagerlöf. Less extreme contrasts appear if the comparison is between the Swedish women and prominent figures in the women's movements in other countries during the same period. The militant style of the British and American suffragettes was impossible in Sweden. Though there were tendencies toward, and attempts at, a more radical feminism in Sweden, they were quickly marginalized, not least by more moderate and pragmatic activists such as Kata Dalström.

Nor was it particularly fitting in Sweden to array oneself in a Biblical role as was done by a number of women speakers in the USA.[17] Sweden was already at that time more secularized than the USA, though other factors must have played a part, too. Nor would the intellectual attitude of the German activists such as Rosa Luxemburg and Klara Zetkin have served in Sweden. Though Ellen Key, Kata Dalström, and Selma Lagerlöf can be called intellectual women, their intellects were directed more toward non-academic adult education. The theorizing attitude to be found in Germany would have fallen flat in Sweden.

These are, of course, no more than loose suppositions. Somewhat sketchy as the comparisons may be, however, they do lend support to the thesis that on the one hand certain attitudes, certain masks, are to some extent forced upon women speakers, while on the other hand each individual speaker also chooses her own masks in accord with the national culture. Women speakers choose their strategies just as men do – but in the women's case this occurs from a different, and subordinate, position in a patriarchal society. Thus the role-playing of the woman speaker does not involve a denial of her own identity but more a choice as to which aspects of this identity to put to use and develop – resulting sometimes in virtuoso juggling with the prejudices of the audience.

## NOTES

1 Here can be mentioned Stina Hansson, *Salongsretorik. Beata Rosenhane (1638– 74), hennes övningsböcker och den klassiska retoriken* (Salon Rhetoric. Beata Rosenhane [1638–74], her books of exercises and classical rhetoric) (Gothenburg: Gothenburg University Press, 1993); Vivi Edström, "Selma Lagerlöf och kvinnans rösträtt" (Selma Lagerlöf and Women's Suffrage), in *Kvinnomystik och kvinnopolitik. Kvinnohistoriska studier*, ed. Gunnar Qvist (Gothenburg: Gothenburg University Press, 1974).

2 Karlyn Kohrs Campbell, ed., *Women Public Speakers in the United States, 1800– 1925: A Bio-critical Sourcebook* (Westport, CT: Greenwood Press, 1993), xvii.

3 Hjalmar Sundén, *persona och anima. En tillämpning av C.G. Jungs psykologi på sex författare: Karlfeldt, Strindberg, Camus, Lagerkvist, Heliga Birgitta, Mora-prosten Jacob Boëthius* (Persona and Anima. An application of Jung's psychology to six authors: Karlfeldt, Strindberg, Camus, Lagerkvist, St Bridget, Jacob Boëthius) (Stockholm: Proprius, 1981), 21.

4 On the portrayal in fiction of the emanicipation of women, see Bertil Björkenlid, *Kvinnokrav i manssamhälle. Rösträttskvinnorna och deras metoder som opinionsbildare och påtryckargrupp i Sverige 1902–21* (Women's Demands in Male-Dominated Society. The suffragettes and their methods as moulders of opinion and pressure group in Sweden 1902–21) (Uppsala: Uppsala University Press, 1982).

5 See, e.g., Joanne Wagner's survey of instruction in rhetoric at women's colleges in her study "'Intelligent Members or Restless Disturbers': Women's Rhetorical Styles, 1880–1920," in *Reclaiming Rhetorica. Women in the Rhetorical Tradition*, ed. Andrea A. Lunsford (Pittsburgh and London: University of Pittsburgh Press, 1995).

6 See Brigitte Mral, "'Någon annan än oss själva har vi inte att lita på'. Malmö kvinnliga diskussionsklubb 1900–1904" ("We have only ourselves to rely on." Malmö women's discussion club 1900–1904), in *Arbetarna tar ordet. Språk och kommunikation i tidig arbetarrörelse*, ed. Olle Josephson (Stockholm: Carlssons, 1996).

7 Concerning Ellen Key's notion of woman, see Ronny Ambjörnsson, *Samhällsmodern, Ellen Keys kvinnouppfattning t.o.m. 1896* (Mother to Society. Ellen Key's notion of woman up to and including 1896) (diss., Gothenburg, 1974).

8 Louise Hamilton, *Ellen Key, en livsbild* (Ellen Key, a Life Portrait) (Stockholm: Wahlstroem and Widstrand, 1987), 86.

9 Ernst Norlind, *Borgebyminnen* (Reminiscences of Borgbeby) (Lund: Gleerup, 1939), 224.

10 Hamilton, *Ellen Key*, 88.

11 See, however, Beata Losman, *Kampen för ett nytt kvinnoliv. Ellen Keys idéer och deras betydelse för sekelskiftets unga kvinnor* (The Struggle for a New Life for

Women. Ellen Key's ideas and their importance for young women at the turn of the century) (Stockholm: Liber, 1980).

12 On the Twelfths, see Birgit Persson's "Tolfterna – ett systerskap över klassgränserna" (The Twelfths – a sisterhood transcending class borders), *Arbetarhistoria* 56–57 (1990, no. 4 & 1991, no. 1).

13 On Kata Dalström's rhetoric and agitation, see Brigitte Mral, "Kata Dalström i talarstolen" (Kata Dalström on the Rostrum), in *Agitatorerna*, ed. Kurt Johannesson (Stockholm: Carlssons, 1996).

14 See Vivi Edström: "Selma Lagerlöf och kvinnans rösträtt" (Selma Lagerlöf and Women's Suffrage), in *Kvinnomystik och kvinnopolitik. Kvinnohistoriska studier*, ed. Gunnar Qvist (Gothenburg: Gothenburg University Press, 1974).

15 Selma Lagerlöf, "Hem och stat" (Home and State), in *Selma Lagerlöf, Troll och människor* (Stockholm: Bonnier, 1942).

16 See, e.g., Kurt Johannesson, *Retorik eller konsten att övertyga* (Rhetoric or the Art of Convincing) (Stockholm: Norstedt, 1990), 226.

17 See, e.g., Phyllis M. Japp, "Esther or Isaiah? The Abolitionist-Feminist Rhetoric of Angelina Grimké," in *Quarterly Journal of Speech* 71 (1985), 335–48.

# Flora MacDonald Denison and the Rhetoric of the Early Women's Suffrage Movement in Canada

ANDREA WILLIAMS

In exploring the rhetoric of Flora MacDonald Denison (1867–1921) I hope to bring the rhetorical practices of a particular Anglo-Canadian woman at the turn of the century into conversation with the rhetorical tradition. This project began in the fall of 1996 when I came across the ISHR's conference call for "Women and the Rhetorical Tradition." Having spent much of my graduate coursework exploring contemporary feminist issues in rhetoric and composition, I wished to make a contribution to the growing body of feminist scholarship in the history of rhetoric. Initially, I aspired to do for Canadian women what Karlyn Kohrs Campbell's work – and those who have built on and complicated Campbell's work – has done for American women; that is, I wanted to put a Canadian woman (or women) on the rhetorical map and help reconfigure the discipline in the process. Enter Flora MacDonald Denison.

Activist, reformer, dressmaker, mother, speaker, and columnist, Flora MacDonald Denison was engaged in a campaign to obtain the vote for Ontario women from 1906 to 1914. As leader of a national suffrage organization, the Canadian Women's Suffrage Association, Denison toured both North America and Europe, giving lectures on the subject of women's rights. In addition to undertaking a busy speaking schedule, Denison wrote a weekly column for the *Toronto World* from 1906 to 1913.[1] Born in Picton, Ontario, Denison left school at the age of fifteen, briefly working as a teacher before becoming a columnist for the *Toronto World*.[2] Unlike her more famous suffragist contemporaries, who included Nellie McClung, Denison was not middle class and made no attempt to soften her radical ideas for a moderate audience. Moreover, Denison was one of the first Canadian women to identify herself as a feminist.[3] Female, working-class, unpaid writer of editorials, Denison represents much of what has been overlooked or deprivileged in the field of rhetoric and composition. Nevertheless, Denison made a profound impact on the Canadian women's movement at the turn of the century. How was she able to do this? I will suggest that Denison's success was due to the following three rhetorical and political strategies – strategies that enrich and complicate our understanding of North American feminist rhetoric at the turn of the century:

1. using the editorial genre as a means of forging a more inclusive movement;
2. inviting women to see themselves not as lone individuals but as members of a transnational movement;
3. inviting women to locate themselves within a feminist tradition.

### *Forging a More Inclusive Movement Through the Editorial*

As I worked my way through "The Denison Papers," consisting of letters, scrapbooks, speeches, and editorials, I initially focused on Denison's speeches, but it was her editorials that I found most engaging. Working with distinctive anecdotal and statistical evidence, as well as private and public issues, Denison makes matters such as dress reform and meal preparation legitimate subjects of debate. Yet despite the complex rhetorical strategies of Denison's editorials, I initially wondered if they "counted" as rhetoric. Karlyn Kohrs Campbell's work established women's suffrage speeches as a legitimate subject for rhetorical inquiry, but editorials? Here I was guided by Jacqueline Jones Royster: her essay on the rhetoric of Ida B. Wells forges a place for activist rhetoric in general, and editorials in particular, within the rhetorical tradition.[4] Accordingly, rather than simply trying to fit Denison's work into the rhetorical tradition, I began to consider how Denison might alter the tradition. Denison's rhetoric stitches together personal and political subject matter, logical proofs and narrative; in a similar manner, I have stitched together available materials from journalism, history, women's studies, and philosophy in order to position Denison's work in relation to the history of rhetoric.

The structure of Denison's editorials is frequently recursive. She proceeds inductively, bringing together anecdotes culled from the everyday which she uses to forward her polemic; thus, she is both storyteller and debater. Denison often opens her editorials with vignettes and later moves to logical proofs, refuting suffrage opponents with airtight reasoning based on natural rights' philosophy: "The arguments of the [suffrage] pioneers are unanswerable. In this age of equality they ask by what right they are made to pay taxes without having a voice in their expenditure. They ask by what right they are obliged to obey the laws and rules without having a voice in framing them."[5] Moreover, although Denison's logic is impeccable, she emphasizes that logic alone is not the principal appeal of feminist social and political reform:

> That the women's movement of our day has not taken its origin from any mere process of theoretic argument; that it breaks out now here, now there, in forms divergent and at times almost irreconcilable; that the majority of those taking part in it are driven into action as a result of the immediate pressure of the conditions of life, and are not always able to logically state what propels them, or to point clearly to the results of their actions; so far from removing it from the category of the vast reorganizing movements of humanity places it in line with them, showing how vital, spontaneous, and wholly pragmatic and unartificial is its nature.[6]

Recognizing the complexity and heterogeneity of the movement, Denison frames conflict as a sign of the movement's strength.

Denison uses her editorials to make the feminist movement as inclusive as possible. Unlike many of her more famous suffragist colleagues, she makes no attempt to soften her radical ideas for a moderate audience. In fact, she repeatedly condemns the elitist tendencies of the suffragist movement, observing, "I have frequently known women to object to other women because, forsooth, they dressed badly, or because they spoke ungrammatically... If we cannot look behind an ungrammatical sentence, and see lack of opportunity, then we should not attempt public work in the suffrage movement."[7] Denison's efforts at inclusion are particularly noteworthy given the pervasive elitism of many members of the women's suffrage movement in turn-of-the-century Toronto. Conjoining the activities of women's daily lives with feminist principles of social justice, she writes of the lives of factory workers as well as those of society matrons, inviting women of every class to join the movement for women's equality: "I believe now that anyone is a credit to the cause, and that the cause is not good if it does not include all."[8] Denison's attempts to forge a feminist movement composed of women of all races as well as classes is evident in her praise of African-American rhetor and activist Sojourner Truth:

> We can recall the great suffrage meeting in Boston, when the poor slave woman, Sojourner Truth, made herself immortal by a never-to-be-forgotten speech. She lacked clothes and education, but she had the love of justice so deeply woven in every fiber of her being that, when impelled to speak, because no one had been able to rouse the audience to a sense of the real degradation of disenfranchisement, this slave woman, from the depths of her indignant soul told such compelling truths in her uncultured darky dialect, told them with such force and fire and conviction that her speech rose to the heights of sublime oratory and stands today as one of the most remarkable addresses in United States history.[9]

However, rather than seeing Denison's inclusive rhetoric and broad appeal as strengths, historian Deborah Gorham (whose groundbreaking work otherwise praises Denison's social and political activism) understands Denison's populism as adversely affecting the quality of her editorials. Gorham notes, "Denison was not an original thinker and the writing of popular pieces for a 'people's' journal encouraged her to blunt and simplify her thoughts rather than to refine and develop them. In spite of these limitations, she remained remarkably receptive to new and unusual ideas."[10]

But why see rhetoric aimed at a popular audience as inherently limited? After all, if effective democracy is contingent on an educated citizenry, then Denison's encouragement of broad civic participation through the promulgation of Nietzsche, Whitman, and Charlotte Perkins Gilman to a wide audience should make her contribution all the more notable. The many allusions Denison makes in her editorials to these and other writers suggest not only that she was widely read but also that she saw her own role as disseminator of complex ideas to a broader public. In the following passage Denison articulates her view of newspaper writing as a powerful means of educating citizens and thereby shaping the democratic process in order to effect political transformation:

> I am on the Press committee, and my advice is for the campaigners to do something different than has ever been done – not smash windows or destroy property – but give the newspapers news; something to tell their readers, something alive and vital, something that will make the voters curious to know more about the aims and ideals of the women who are spending their time and money and energy and ability for a reform they consider the most urgent in the world today.
>
> The ballot first, and then we have a weapon in our hands with which to mold social conditions – But the ballot first.[11]

In order to understand the rhetorical and political force of Denison's editorials, we need to reconsider the traditional privileging of so-called "original thinking." Denison is concerned with theory insofar as it relates to action, and the editorial is a particularly effective genre for broad-based calls to action. It is the very "bluntness" of Denison's style that makes her editorials so compelling for a wide audience. Directly addressing her readers, she asks them to put their money where their mouths are:

> We do believe that enfranchisement of women is the greatest and most urgent reform needed in the world today.
>
> Then what is our belief worth? Is it worth ten percent of our income? Is it worth giving up an hour of our time each day? Is it worth doing without a new dress, or hat, or coat?

> Many women in the United States are giving every hour of the day, their incomes and their ability. Many women in England are giving their all, even their lives . . . These women stand as the finest types the race has produced. I do not believe that the women of Canada, of Ontario, of Toronto, are lacking in those qualities of devotion to principle, and the willingness to sacrifice for a belief.[12]

## *Towards a Transnational Movement*

Closely related to Denison's forging of an inclusive feminist movement is her vision of the feminist movement as transnational. Denison repeatedly urges Canadian women to see their struggle as one that crosses national boundaries as she forges alliances with American suffragists and transcendentalists, along with British suffragettes, among others. Furthermore, Denison's frequently epideictic editorials regularly announce women's gains and setbacks in the international suffrage movement along with upcoming speeches and symposia being held both locally and internationally. The often blunt style of Denison's calls to action is countered in places by a more formal, high style that she uses to elevate the pioneers of the movement. Praising Pankhurst, Denison writes: "No queen ever made such a triumphal march through any country as she is making through the land of Lincoln and Walt Whitman."[13] Similarly, her eulogy of the Canadian, Dr. Emily Stowe, is written in the high style: "She fought the battle and had the satisfaction of seeing her own daughter the first to graduate in medicine in Canada, and a few years later, through her efforts, Toronto University opened its doors to women. This is the type of woman who led the suffrage movement in Canada and every woman from the Atlantic to the Pacific should uncover their heads and bless the name of Dr. Emily Stowe."[14] Through these "sketches" of local and international heroines Denison creates a transnational community of women:

> We are learning very much from the three great interpreters of the feminist movement, and the present social upheaval due to it. Olive Schiner [sic] who strikes such cutting blows on the parasitic class who are willing to gobble all

and give nothing – this class is a menace to society. Ellen Key does not survey the industrial question to the same extent, but rather runs the gamut of the psychology of superstitions and prejudices. While Mrs. Gilman, with keen practical insight, not only finds fault with conditions, but always and ever suggests a remedy, and her final word is that we should so work and live as to uplift and improve our social conditions, and so benefit every individual, young and old.[15]

Her editorials also feature obituaries of women suffragists from around the world, including one she wrote for Florence Nightingale that offers an alternative view to more politically conservative contemporary accounts of the event: "It was with great regret ... that I noticed few of the newspaper articles gave Florence Nightingale credit for being a pioneer suffragist as well as pioneer nurse."[16] Thus, Denison's editorials sought not only to mobilize readers but to educate them about some of the key figures and issues of the movement.

Despite the emphasis that these epideictic sketches place on individual women, Denison asserts that women's achievement is dependent not on exceptional individual accomplishment, but rather on favourable social conditions. In one editorial she observes, "It is often said that all great movements are but lengthened shadows of one person, rather, is it that the single person is but the focus of the great movement behind."[17] Unlike Elizabeth Cady Stanton whose "Solitude of Self" reflects the mainstream U.S. view of individualism and self-reliance, Denison attempts to forge a movement focused on the collective. Notably, she does not represent herself as an extraordinary individual, but rather frames her own actions as the product of a greater movement of which she is only a small part. Thus, Denison establishes her *ethos* through her membership in a tradition of collective activism – a collectivity that spans national boundaries.

## *Forging a Feminist Tradition*

In addition to fostering a transnational feminist movement, Denison's editorials invite women to see themselves as part of a movement that crosses historical boundaries as well. The creation of a distinctive women's history is among her most notable persuasive techniques. She writes of women being "caught by a great spiritual force, a force that has been gaining strength and growing from the minds of suppressed women for centuries past."[18] In order to underscore the importance of intergenerational connections, Denison chastises younger women for forgetting their debt to their foremothers: "The girls who accept all the advantages of to-day without being willing to shoulder the burden for the next generation are not worthy to walk the path that has been cleared for them."[19] Thus for Denison, history plays a crucial role in the cultivation of civic responsibility. Tellingly, Denison shows a keen awareness of the power of historical narratives when she observes, "The history of the Woman's Suffrage movement reads like some fascinating romance and its phenomenal worth and many successful stories places [sic] it without a parallel in the great reform movements of the world."[20] Moreover, Denison suggests that the artifacts available to historians are in part determined by social and political conditions that constrain or exclude the cultural production of traditionally disenfranchised groups such as women. Doubtless drawing on her own experience as a single parent, Denison protests the disabling double burden faced by many women, a burden that can interfere with, if not prevent, the production of privileged forms of discourse such as lengthy rhetorical treatises. Writing of a suffragist colleague, she observes: "You cannot burn the candle at both ends and expect it to last. Kit had it in her own hands to be an author of account as well as a journalist, we should have had a book from her pen – a vital telling, descriptive masterpiece, but it is impossible to answer myriads [sic] of letters and keep up-to-date on the latest fad in salads and other domestic problems and write books all at once."[21]

In short, Denison's language and activism are inseparable. Through her editorials, she invites a wide range of women to see themselves not as lone individuals but as members of a larger, heterogeneous women's movement and activist tradition that spans both national and historical borders. In doing so, Denison persuades her readers that they possess the power and the responsibility to actively shape events. Denison observes: "[I]t is good to be alive these days. We are too near events to give them their proper value, and we know not when an epoch-making speech or act will be added to our history; but we do know that social conditions and ideals are in a rapidly changing state and it is a great privilege to be in the fray."[22] Thus, Denison's work not only enriches and complicates both the history of North American feminism and rhetoric at the turn of the century, but also reminds us of our responsibility, as feminist rhetoricians, to act as well as to reflect. In order to learn from the lessons of radical reformers such as Denison, it is essential that we heed calls to revise the rhetorical tradition by looking beyond the traditional boundaries of our discipline.

## NOTES

1 According to Deborah Gorham, *The World* was a "people's paper" with a broad circulation ("Flora MacDonald Denison: Canadian Feminist" in *A Not Unreasonable Claim: Women and Reform in Canada: 1880's–1920's,* ed. Linda Kealey [Toronto: Women's Educational Press, 1979], 57).
2 Ibid., 50.
3 Ibid., 59.
4 Jacqueline Jones Royster, "To Call a Thing by Its True Name: The Rhetoric of Ida B. Wells," in *Reclaiming Rhetorica: Women in the Rhetorical Tradition,* ed. Andrea A. Lunsford (Pittsburgh, PA: Pittsburgh University Press, 1995) 167–184.
5 *Toronto Globe,* 23 November 1906, in "Newspaper Clipping Scrapbook" of the Flora MacDonald Denison Papers at the Thomas Fisher Library, University of Toronto. All subsequent citations of the *Toronto Globe* refer to this archive.
6 *Toronto World,* 28 May 1911, in "Newspaper Clipping Scrapbook" of the Flora MacDonald Denison Papers at the Thomas Fisher Library, University of Toronto. All subsequent citations of the *Toronto World* refer to this archive.
7 *Toronto World,* 7 December 1913.
8 *Toronto World,* 7 December 1913.
9 *Toronto World,* 7 December 1913.
10 Deborah Gorham, "Flora MacDonald Denison: Canadian Feminist," 62.
11 *Toronto World,* 30 November 1913.
12 *Toronto World,* 7 December 1913.
13 *Toronto Globe,* 23 November 1913.
14 Ibid.
15 *Toronto World,* 19 October 1913.
16 *Toronto World,* 28 August 1910.
17 *Toronto World,* 20 June 1909.

18 *Toronto World*, 19 October 1913.
19 *Toronto World*, 16 November 1913.
20 *Toronto World*, 28 February 1914.
21 *Toronto World*, 16 November 1913.
22 *Toronto World*, 30 November 1913.

# Resisting Decline Stories: Gertrude Buck's Democratic Theory of Rhetoric

Suzanne Bordelon

> The real advantage of society involves ultimately the advantage of the individual member of society. And, conversely, the real betterment of the individual must inevitably tend toward the betterment of society. The two are no more separable in practice than are faith and works, thought and feeling, capital and labor, or any of those delusive apparent dualisms whose unity is the life of each part.
> – Gertrude Buck[1]

A number of scholars have applied what Robert Connors labels the "Decline and Fall" narrative in detailing the history of rhetoric in the nineteenth century.[2] Although some scholars have recently challenged this narrative, more often historians have characterized the nineteenth century as virtually devoid of intellectual and social significance.[3] Typically, historians have portrayed the period as one of rhetorical regress – a lamentable lapse in the grand rhetorical tradition. Under this argument, traditional rhetoric declined in the nineteenth century, but was successfully revived in the twentieth century.[4] In my analysis, I resist such narratives in examining the work of Gertrude Buck, an English professor at Vassar College from 1897 until her death in 1922. I show the philosophical and particularly the social significance of Buck's work in order to challenge such reductive approaches to the history of rhetoric and composition. By doing so, I emphasize that Buck introduced a democratic ethics to rhetorical theory.

Specifically, I explore Buck's emphasis on a rhetoric of social justice. First, I examine the development of Buck's ethics, showing how her ideas converge with John Dewey's early "experimental idealism."[5] I argue that Buck's ethics is made up of a complex synthesis of social Christianity, functionalist psychology, and progressive idealism. I then examine how these ideas are reflected in Buck's early work and in her textbook, *A Course in Argumentative Writing* (1899). I contend that the central concepts in her work are grounded in democratic ideas and social ethics.

### The Influence of Dewey on Buck

To grasp Buck's ethics, it is necessary to trace the development of her ideas from Dewey, whose theories shaped her social philosophy. Buck came under the influence of Dewey during her years at the University of Michigan. Dewey was at Michigan from 1884 to 1894, minus a year at the University of Minnesota (1888–89). Buck received her bachelor's in 1894, her master's in 1895, and her doctorate in 1898, all at the University of Michigan. In two of her works, Buck acknowledges her deep gratitude to Dewey. In the introduction to her dissertation, *The Metaphor – A Study in the Psychology of Rhetoric* (1898), Buck says she is indebted to Dewey for "the fundamental philosophic conceptions embodied in it."[6] Similarly, in the preface to her book, *The Social Criticism of Literature* (1916), Buck says Dewey's "philosophy of society has directed all my thinking about literature."[7]

### Dewey's Social Ethics

Given Buck's connection to Dewey, it is useful to review Dewey's social ethics as a way of understanding Buck's ethics. In 1884, Dewey began as an absolute idealist who, as he describes it, "drifted away from Hegelianism in the next fifteen years: the term 'drifting' [expressing] the slow, and for a long time imperceptible character of the movement."[8] Dewey's "drift" gradually brought him to pragmatism or instrumentalism, which emphasizes thinking as a problem-solving instrument. Although there is substantial disagreement among scholars about exactly when Dewey rejected absolute idealism, recent scholarship associates his years at the University of Michigan with an evolving neo-Hegelian idealism.[9] After Darwin's theory of evolution brought the legitimacy of modern science behind the concept, neo-Hegelianism became what Steven C. Rockefeller calls "the most influential idea of the nineteenth century."[10] In Dewey's *The Study of Ethics: A Syllabus* (1894), he does not abandon his neo-Hegelianism, but he does appear to move away from its metaphysics and theology.[11] Written soon after William James's influential *Principles of Psychology* (1890), Dewey's textbook reflects a more functionalist approach to ethics.

I focus primarily on Dewey's *The Study of Ethics* because this was his major work of ethics written prior to the publication of Buck's textbook on argumentation in 1899. In *The Study of Ethics*, Dewey's evolving philosophy is evident in what he appropriately calls "experimental idealism," which reflects his belief that moral ideals should be rooted in experience and experimentally verifiable. Dewey had serious difficulty with the neo-Hegelian concept of the ideal self – eternal and cut off from reality. The problem for Dewey was that this concept created a duality between the moral ideal and everyday reality. For Dewey, ethics and the ideal should be continuous with experience.[12] Dewey's more progressive idealism is evident in his rejection of fixed separate ideals and traditional dualisms between the ideal and the everyday world, the self and activity; his emphasis on ideas that are experimentally verifiable and of practical use; and his opposition to faculty psychology in favor of a more functionalist approach to ethics. Dewey, for instance, no longer discusses human action in terms of the faculty of volition. Instead, he explains it in terms of interests and impulses. However, Dewey still seems strongly rooted in neo-Hegelian and Christian concepts. This grounding is evident in Dewey's belief that "truth" represents the absolute as reflected in a rationally and organically structured universe. It is also evident in his emphasis on the Hegelian notion of mediation or the impulse to idealize or unify experience.[13] Thus, in *The Study of Eth-*

*ics*, the goal is "the freeing of life reached through knowledge of its real nature and relations."[14]

In addition, Dewey still maintains his faith in Christian ideals, particularly Christian love. In *The Study of Ethics*, Dewey describes love as the "supreme virtue," and he adds that love

> is the complete identification of subject and object. . . . It is complete interest in, full attention to, the objects, the aims of life, and thus responsibility. It provides the channel which gives the fullest outlet to the self . . . and thus guarantees, or *is*, freedom, adequate self-expression.[15]

Dewey seems to be reconstructing his neo-Hegelian and Christian concepts in terms of Jamesian functionalist psychology. During this period, Dewey still had not come to view consciousness as constituted by nature and thus a natural process itself.[16]

## *Buck's Ethics*

Dewey's synthesis of social Christianity, functionalist psychology, and progressive idealism parallels ideas evident in Buck's writings in the 1890s. In the essay, "The Ethical Significance of *Coriolanus*" (1896), published in the student monthly literary magazine *The Inlander*, Buck's religious ideas seem to be evolving under the parallel influences of Dewey's social philosophy and functionalist psychology.[17] Buck argues that Shakespeare's tragedy shows "the organic inter-dependence of all individuals in society."[18] Her ideas about Christian love closely resemble Dewey's. At the conclusion of the article, Buck contends that when society recognizes

> that which in the New Testament phrase is called love, in our practical modern vernacular co-operation, as essentially the law of its life, then it may fairly be said in the psychological phrase, to have come to self-consciousness, to a sense of its own individual character, as a complex, highly differentiated, organic unity. (222)

Here, Buck describes the neo-Hegelian concept of self-realization in more psychological, natural terms as coming to self-consciousness. In addition, Buck's ethics reflects her attempts to reconstruct the Christian ideal of love in more everyday terms. She seems to be developing a socialized Christianity that harmonizes her theological and philosophical ideas, and her concept of Christianity and democracy. Buck's ideas are very much in step with the social Christianity of her age, which stressed social responsibility, sought to find Christian solutions to the challenges of the period, and aimed at realizing God's kingdom on earth.[19]

In addition, Buck's social emphasis seems to reflect her neo-Hegelian ideas. In "The Religious Experience of a Skeptic," a piece Buck wrote in her early college days, she discusses how her religious ideas moved from a "subjective – not to say selfish character" to a more social perspective through her association with "the so-called lower classes."[20] The next phase in her religious life is what Buck calls her "intellectual stage," where she saw the universe as a "single organism" (26). Buck's stages in religious development resemble Hegel's dialectic process. Buck describes the world in Hegelian terms as a dynamic organism, which interrelates all life through a staged dialectic process.

Similarly, Buck's neo-Hegelian emphasis on achieving unity through mediating differences is evident in her work in education. In *Organic Education: A Manual for Teachers in Primary and Grammar Grades* (1897) Buck and her co-author, Harriet M. Scott, say their book has been undertaken "as a contribution toward the solution of the problem on the practical side of child-study . . . ."[21] In chapter 3, the authors present their theory as resolving a conflict in education. Buck and Scott contend two theories of education are now in conflict: an "old institutional conception of education," where the individual exists for the institution, and a "newer theory of individualism," where the institution exists for the individual (18). However, Buck and Scott contend that out of the "clash" of these two battling theories, a new "truer" ideal – "social individualism," or the interrelation of the individual and society – is developing (18). The authors contend this ideal is reflected in the saying of Dewey, "Education is not preparation for life: it *is* life," and in that of Col. Francis W. Parker, a Chicago educator and innovator, "The common school is the central means for preserving and perpetuating the true democracy" (18–19). Buck and Scott's new approach reflects Hegel's dialectic process; the goal is to discover the ever-widening relationships or organic unity of life.

## A Course in Argumentative Writing

Buck's synthesis of social Christianity, functionalist psychology, and progressive idealism is evident in her *A Course in Argumentative Writing* (1899). In her textbook, Buck seems to apply an experimental approach to argumentation, and she similarly rejects faculty psychology in favor of a more functionalist approach, emphasizing human interests, the self, and thought. In her other works in rhetoric and education, Buck's neo-Hegelianism and Christian ideals are also evident. With her emphasis on the dialectic process and holism, Buck's ethics seems to represent her efforts to harmonize these different ideas and to introduce an ethics to rhetorical theory that is democratic.

In Buck's textbook a central concept is the idea that students should learn argumentation inductively from experience and practice, rather than starting deductively from principles of formal logic. According to Buck, such an approach is "at once more difficult and more stimulating" than the typical method.[22] This is because the student is "not asked simply to accept certain logical formulae on the authority of text-book or teacher; but to quarry out these formulae from his own writing and then use them for such modification of the writing as may seem necessary" (iii).

For Buck, the inductive method equates with the "laboratory" or experimental method of inquiry. Such a thought process, emphasizing personal responsibility and initiative rather than reliance on custom or principle, is also consistent with and necessary for a democratic society.

## A Focus on Student Interest

A second major tenet of Buck's approach to ethical argumentation is that the subject for argumentation should mirror the student's interests. This reflects Dewey's notion that without interest, an individual "has no heart for a course of conduct."[23] In a student this results in indifference. In "Recent Tendencies in the Teaching of English Composition" (1900), Buck contends that students have difficulty writing when the subject is remote from their interests.[24] Teachers, she believes, are often reminded that students have little to say about "'The vice of ambition' or 'Autumn thoughts.'"[25] However, she argues that all students have interests, which to them are worth communicating. Emphasizing student interest not only makes it easier for students to write, but also, by encouraging them to draw on their own interests, helps to break down barriers between academic work and life.

Buck's focus on interest and its relation to organic holism, or a cooperative, democratic society, is more fully discussed in *Organic Education* (1897). In the book, Buck and Scott characterize their educational approach as "the progressive organization of the child's interests" (16).

> Education is the widest and deepest living possible at any given moment. Or it is the most highly developed interrelation of life – on the one hand the life of the individual, on the other that of the social organism. And the relations of organism to individual are, from the standpoint of the individual, his interests, physical, economic, social, artistic, religious. Hence it is plain why education, which is, in the universe-sense, life itself, may be, from the practical side, defined as the progressive organization of individual interests. (16)

In other words, through widening individual interests, or concern for and interest in others, the individual extends and broadens the development of the self. Hence, because of a direct interest in others, the individual and the social good become interconnected.

## *Logic and Argumentation*

The third tenet of Buck's textbook on argumentation is the connection between the logical structure of argumentation and its substructure based in psychology. Buck contends that although the logical basis of argumentation is largely recognized, few recognize the psychology underlying logic. Buck argues that "cut off from its deepest roots, logic has come to seem rather like a dead tool than like a living expression of thought."[26] In her book, Buck emphasizes that the logical and psychological structure of each argument is revealed to the student, "so that the maxims and formulae, usually regarded by the learner as the malign inventions of Aristotle, represent to our students rather the ways in which real people think" (v).

Buck stresses the importance of logic in argumentation, emphasizing its practical benefits. She explains that she uses the "syllogistic brief" to analyze arguments because "it brings into clear relief the actual structure of an argument, which the ordinary brief so often allows to be forgotten" (v). Buck says the purpose of learning such methods of analysis is that "nothing is more indispensable than this to a mastery of argumentation as a practical art" (vi). For Buck, the syllogism provides a way to think through and to illuminate the basic structure of an argument. In this way, it has practical application to the everyday problematic situations of life. Buck's approach is significant, because traditional theories of knowledge and ethics, such as Kantian philosophy, located the object of knowledge in a transcendent realm of fixed absolutes removed from everyday life. Thus, logic tended to be formal and abstract, rather than informal and practical.

### *Critical Reasoning, Egalitarian Behaviour, and Sympathy*

In addition to Buck's three major tenets, her definition of argumentation reflects her democratic ethics. Buck's definition underscores her emphasis on the audience and its active thought process and critical reasoning ability. She also stresses that argument itself must be a cooperative, egalitarian activity. Buck defines argumentation as the "act of establishing in the mind of another person a conclusion which has become fixed in your own by means of setting up in the other person's mind the train of reasoning which has previously [*sic*] led you to this conclusion."[27] In Buck's interactionist approach, knowledge is something people do together. Argumentative knowledge must engage the mind of the hearer in a reasoning process; in other words, the hearer needs to identify with the speaker's thought process. For Buck, argumentation is not something a speaker does to the passive mind of the hearer. Instead, it is a more egalitarian process involving a speaker and an active, thinking auditor. Buck's egalitarian emphasis is particularly evident in her article, "The Present Status of Rhetorical Theory" (1900). Buck synthesizes two competing rhetorical theories to reconstruct a new democratic theory of rhetoric aimed at promoting equality and cooperation. She justifies the synthesis by arguing that all "true" social functions are egalitarian in action, "leveling conditions" between speaker and hearer.[28] Hence, the goal is not the persuasion or coercion of the hearer to the speaker's position. The hearer must first re-enact the "train of reasoning" of the speaker and then make his or her own decision on the matter in question.

Buck's more cooperative, interactive idea of argumentation is also evident in her view of how people think through arguments. According to Buck, in complex arguments a sympathetic imagination may be required. Sometimes an individual may refuse to accept "the train of reasoning" of the other person. In this instance, the individual "must put himself imaginatively in the place of the person he addresses, and then come, by any way he logically can, to the conclusions he desires to establish."[29] For Buck, sympathy, or the ability to put oneself in the place of another, is key to resolving difficult situations. Furthermore, by using imagination an individual can experimentally test out different options before applying them in the real world.

In the appendix of her textbook on argumentation, Buck contends that argumentation has typically been devoted to persuasion, rather than her more social or cooperative view of argumentation. She characterizes the bibliography of argumentation as "meager."[30] In addition, Buck contends that much of Aristotle's and Quintilian's work in rhetoric was "devoted to 'persuasion,' in which argumentation was regarded as a factor of varying importance" (204). She adds that George Campbell and Richard Whately had a similar emphasis and that "modern rhetoricians" have devoted "scant space, or none at all, to argumentation, and those who consider it have thrown little light upon its problems" (204). In *A Course in Argumentative Writing*, it is evident that Buck is introducing a new approach to argumentation. Her goal is to move away from persuasion to a more socially cooperative method emphasizing informal reasoning.

## *Conclusion*

Buck's approach to argumentation and ethics reflects her attempts to synthesize her ethical beliefs in social Christianity, functionalist psychology, and progressive idealism. Buck's synthesis is evident in her early writings at the University of Michigan, in her textbook on education, and in the central ideas underlying her textbook on argumentation. With her social Christianity, Buck reconstructs Christian love or cooperation in everyday terms. With her functionalist approach, Buck focuses on explaining conduct in terms of individual interests and impulses. And finally, with her neo-Hegelian focus, Buck views life as a dynamic organism and uses a dialectic process to mediate difference to achieve a harmonious whole.

At the center of Buck's synthesis is her belief that the ethical ideal in rhetorical theory must be synonymous with democracy. The ideal of democracy for Buck seems to be summed up in the values of cooperation, freedom of inquiry, and equality. These values are evident in her belief that cooperation or love is "essentially the law" of life itself.[31] They are also evident in her emphasis on free inquiry or the inductive method of argumentation so that students can learn to think for themselves rather than to simply accept the ideas of others. The student's individual intellectual growth then is viewed in terms of gaining a deeper understanding of the interrelated nature of life. Finally, these values are evident in her emphasis on equality, where she tries to encourage communication on an equal basis. These three ideals reflect Buck's commitment to social reconstruction; ultimately, she wants society to become more democratic.

In exploring Buck's ethics, I have emphasized the philosophical and particularly the social significance of her work to challenge more simplistic "Decline and Fall" narratives. As John C. Brereton points out, viewing the history of composition as the loss of rhetoric in the nineteenth century, and the last two decades as the period of triumphant revival, not only represents a limited perspective, but it "explicitly devalues almost a century of teaching and learning" (xiii).[32] In my analysis, I have contextualized Buck's ideas within the intellectual currents of her time to show the complex interplay of ideas that form her democratic ethics. Such an analysis is significant because it shows how studying Buck's work can add depth and dimension to our often-simplistic, one-dimensional nineteenth-century narratives. Furthermore, by studying Buck's work we can see the inadequacy of the traditional narrative and the need to look more closely at the historical context of rhetoric and composition. By doing so, we may better understand the situated and multilayered nature of our historical past, and therefore better understand our present situation.

## *NOTES*

1 The excerpt is taken from *Organic Education: A Manual for Teachers in Primary and Grammar Grades* (Boston, MA: D.C. Heath & Co., 1897), 19–20. Buck coauthored the book with Harriet M. Scott.

2 Robert Connors, "Writing the History of Our Discipline," in *An Introduction to Composition Studies*, ed. Erika Lindemann and Gary Tate (New York: Oxford University Press, 1991), 64–65. One of the first historians to point out the decline of rhetoric in the nineteenth century was A.R. Kitzhaber in his influential 1953 dissertation, which was published in book form in 1990. See *Rhetoric in American Colleges, 1850–1900* (Dallas: Southern Methodist University Press, 1990).

3 For a recent challenge to the "Decline and Fall" narrative, see Nan Johnson, *Nineteenth-Century Rhetoric in North America* (Carbondale: Southern Illinois University Press, 1991).

4 John C. Brereton, preface to *The Origins of Composition Studies in the American College, 1875–1925* (Pittsburgh, PA: University of Pittsburgh Press, 1995), xii–xiii.

5 Buck seems to define ethics as Dewey does in the 1890s: "Ethics, rightly conceived, is the statement of human relationships in action. In any right study of ethics, then, the pupil is not studying hard and fixed rules for conduct; he is studying the ways in which men are bound together in the complex relations of their interactions." Dewey, "Teaching Ethics in the High School" (1893), *John Dewey: The Early Works, 1893–1898*, vol. 4: 1893–94, ed. Jo Ann Boydston (Carbondale: Southern Illinois University Press, 1971), 56.

6 Gertrude Buck, *The Metaphor – A Study in the Psychology of Rhetoric* (Ph.D. dissertation, University of Michigan, 1898; reprint, *Contributions to Rhetorical Theory* 5, ed. F.N. Scott, Ann Arbor, MI: Inland Press, 1899), iii.
7 Gertrude Buck, *The Social Criticism of Literature* (New Haven, CT: Yale University Press, 1916), vi.
8 John Dewey, "From Absolutism to Experimentalism" (1930), *John Dewey: The Later Works, 1925–1953,* vol. 5, ed. J. Boydston (Carbondale: Southern Illinois University Press, 1984), 154.
9 See Steven C. Rockefeller, *John Dewey: Religious Faith and Democratic Humanism* (New York: Columbia University Press, 1991), 198–99; Robert B. Westbrook, *John Dewey and American Democracy* (Ithaca, NY: Cornell University Press, 1991), 60; and Jennifer Welchman, *Dewey's Ethical Thought* (Ithaca, NY: Cornell University Press, 1995), chapters 4 and 5. There are many examples of scholarly disagreement over when Dewey rejected absolute idealism. The following authors represent a few examples. In "The Influence of William James on John Dewey's Early Work," *Journal of the History of Ideas* 45 (1984): 451–63, Michael Buxton argues that Dewey's change from an absolute idealist to a functionalist position was more sudden and without the degree of difficulty usually suggested. However, in the introduction to *John Dewey: The Early Works, 1893–1898,* vol. 4: 1893–94, xiv, Wayne A.R. Leys argues that Dewey didn't proceed in "one jump" to ethical naturalism, and that in 1894 Dewey was still in the process of rejecting idealist doctrine. Similarly, in *Dewey's Ethical Thought,* Jennifer Welchman argues that the transition from absolute idealism to a functionalist and pragmatic position followed a slow transition in the period 1894–1903.
10 Rockefeller, *John Dewey: Religious Faith,* 15.
11 Ibid., 198.
12 Ibid., 199.
13 Leys, introduction to *John Dewey: The Early Works,* vol. 4, xii.
14 Boydston, ed., *John Dewey: The Early Works,* vol. 4, 226.
15 Ibid., 361.
16 Welchman, *Dewey's Ethical Thought,* 115.
17 For Buck, functionalist psychology meant studying the mind or consciousness as a part of nature, focusing on how it helped the human organism live in its environment. Hence, she rejected the faculty theories of the Scottish realists and the relational approach of the British associationists. Instead, she focused on habit, the self, and perception as the basis of her approach to rhetoric.
18 Gertrude Buck, "The Ethical Significance of *Coriolanus,*" *Inlander* 6 (1896): 217.
19 Buck's Christian beliefs reflect the ideas of the Social Gospel movement, which exerted a powerful influence on American thought during this period. For more information on the Social Gospel movement, see Henry R. May, *Prot-*

*estant Churches and Industrial America* (1949; reprint, New York: Octagon Books, 1963).
20  Gertrude Buck, "The Religious Experience of a Skeptic," special Gertrude Buck issue of *Vassar Miscellany Monthly* (February 1923): 25.
21  Buck and Scott, *Organic Education*, 9.
22  Gertrude Buck, *A Course in Argumentative Writing* (New York: Henry Holt and Co., 1899), iii.
23  John Dewey and James H. Tufts, *Ethics*, revised ed. (New York: Henry Holt and Co., 1959), 321.
24  Gertrude Buck, "Recent Tendencies in the Teaching of English Composition," *Educational Review* 22 (1901): 371–82.
25  Buck points out that these specific subjects "have actually been assigned to college preparatory students during the past year, by schools otherwise respectable. . . ." See 373, n. 4.
26  Buck, *A Course in Argumentative Writing*, v.
27  Ibid., 3.
28  Gertrude Buck, "The Present Status of Rhetoric Theory," *Modern Language Notes* 15, no. 3 (1900): 85.
29  Buck, *A Course in Argumentative Writing*, 7.
30  Ibid., 204.
31  Buck, "Ethical Significance of *Coriolanus*," 222.
32  Brereton, Preface, *The Origins of Composition Studies*, xii–xiii.

# GROUP 5

# Engaging the Rhetorical Tradition

# Re-inventing Rhetorical Epistemology: Donna Haraway's and Nicole Brossard's Embodied Visions

PHILIPPA SPOEL

Recent discussions in the feminist historiography of rhetoric call not only for a recuperation of the lost or neglected voices of women within the rhetorical tradition, but also for a critical reading of the gendered nature of the discipline's canonical history.[1] When combined, these approaches can create spaces "for redefining the whole notion of rhetoric" from female and/or feminist perspectives, thus avoiding the problem of simply including women within the rhetorical tradition according to established masculinist theories and criteria.[2] The project of redefining rhetorical theory and practice makes feminist approaches to the history of rhetoric, necessarily, both backward- and forward-looking. As Susan Jarratt explains, the question is "How can feminist practices in the history of rhetoric become an active source of inspiration for the future?"[3]

In the following discussion, I adopt primarily a "forward"-looking orientation that addresses future possibilities for the rhetorical tradition conceived in feminist terms. Specifically, I want to look at how the work of two contemporary feminist scholars from outside the discipline of rhetoric could help us to reformulate the epistemological role and status of the body in rhetorical theory and practice. The writers to whom I turn for this preliminary exploration are Donna Haraway, American feminist theorist of science and technology, and Nicole Brossard, Québécoise lesbian poet, novelist, and essayist. The particular texts on which I will draw are

Haraway's article "Situated Knowledges: The Science Question in Feminism and the Privilege of Partial Perspective"[4] and Brossard's theoretical-poetic essay, "The Aerial Letter."[5] Although my discussion does not look backward into history in the sense of attending to the voices of women from the past, it is strongly prompted by the dominant Western cultural tradition of denigrating the power and significance of bodies in opposition to the validated function of the rational mind which ostensibly transcends and controls the base sensual practices of bodies. This mind-body dualism, as feminist scholars have pointed out, operates according to a gendered hierarchy in which the higher domain of the mind and reason is masculinized while the lower domain of the body and its sensual, emotional behaviours are conceived as feminine.[6] One of my objectives, then, is to participate in the general disruption by feminist scholars across disciplines of this historical-cultural legacy by revalidating and reformulating the body's role in the generation – not only the communication or delivery – of rhetorical knowledge.

Unlike the dominant Western philosophical tradition, rhetoric has always acknowledged and on occasion even celebrated the role of the body in persuasion. Typically, this bodily aspect of rhetoric has been treated under the canon of delivery, the fifth of the five divisions of oratory established in classical rhetoric. This acknowledgement of the body's role has, however, been highly ambivalent. Aristotle, for example, grudgingly grants that delivery "affects the success of a speech greatly" but he characterizes it as an "unworthy" subject, especially when compared to the more elevated question of "how persuasion can be produced from the facts themselves."[7] Citing Cicero, Quintilian offers a more positive representation of bodily persuasion, characterizing powerful delivery as a passionate "fire" through which "all emotion reaches the soul."[8] But this strong association of bodily rhetoric with pathos also makes its nature problematic, at least according to Western mind-body, reason-emotion hierarchies. As Edward Corbett has recently reminded us, "There is something undignified about a rational creature being precipitated into action through the stimulus of aroused passions."[9] One episode in the rhetorical tradition that seems to elevate the subject of bodily persuasion to a new level of respectability is the elocutionary movement, which made this fifth canon virtually the whole focus of its attention. Yet even the elocutionary texts, which initially seem "to rescue the body from neglect or disrepute," nonetheless draw on standard hierarchies to legitimate their attention to delivery.[10] For example, Gilbert Austin's *Chironomia, or A Treatise on Rhetorical Delivery* employs an inner-outer hierarchy to represent the relationship between delivery and the other divisions of oratory: bodily rhetoric is the "external" or surface division of oratory, as opposed to the four divisions of invention, arrangement, style, and memory, which relate to the more elevated internal mind or "understanding."[11]

My purpose in recounting this very brief and highly selective review of the representation of delivery in the rhetorical tradition is to highlight the recurringly problematic status of the body within past theories and practices of rhetoric, a problematic status which I argue reflects and perpetuates an entrenched gendered hierarchy of the masculinized rational mind over the feminized emotional body. In looking forward to future possibilities for bodily or embodied rhetorics, I do not wish simply to reformulate the canon of delivery as an integral, valuable component of rhetoric.[12] Rather, I am interested in exploring – via Haraway's and Brossard's passionate situated thinking on this subject – ways in which we might conceive of the body as itself integral to rhetorical processes of knowledge-generation, or of invention. Traditionally, the canon of invention has been associated with the discovery of logical or rational arguments and with the formulation of reasons based, as Aristotle claims, "on the facts themselves." In this framework, logic, reason, and the realm of invention are hierarchically dissociated from the necessary but less worthy question of the body's pathos, or its sensual and emotional persuasion.

By contrast with this traditional configuration, my main argument is that a feminist approach to embodied rhetorics opens up possibilities for re-integrating bodily, emotional ways of knowing into the process of invention; that is, into the process through which rhetors and audiences generate together socially and historically situated knowledges.[13] The point is not to validate a kind of irrational, illogical form of rhetorical invention and knowledge in opposition to a purely rational, logical method. Instead, reintegrating the body's situated, sensual, and emotional realities into rhetorical invention necessarily asks us to redefine the whole notion of "reason." As feminist epistemologists such as Susan Hekman and Janet Sayers point out, the conception of objective, disembodied, dispassionate rationality which informs dominant Western epistemologies is a misconception that supports the knower's power over the object of knowledge.[14] In reality, however, the epistemological distinction of reason from emotion and the body "overlooks the fact that reason is intertwined with emotion and passion"[15] and that the creation as well as the communication of knowledge is a situated, embodied process.

Haraway describes the myth of transcendent, disembodied knowledge that underlies modern science as "the god trick of seeing everything from nowhere," "the conquering gaze" that "distances the knowing subject from everybody and everything in the interests of unfettered power."[16] Brossard similarly critiques a patriarchal epistemology "in which presumably eternal truths and disembodied ideas lend themselves to the violent abuse of power."[17] This epistemology excludes women and other dominated groups from the realm of knowledge by situating them as objects rather than subjects of knowledge, thus disqualifying their perceptions of what is real. Both Haraway and Brossard, in their different fashions, make cases for a radically reformulated conception of reason, knowledge, and objectivity that, as Brossard says, "calls into question the very notion of what we call intelligence; which, taken from its strictest dictionary sense, is 'the set of mental functions having as its object conceptual and rational knowledge (as opposed to sensation and intuition).'"[18] For both, recognition and articulation of the embodied, sensual dimensions of knowledge and reason are essential to the feminist project of envisioning "a more just future."[19]

In the remainder of this discussion, I will foreground a few features of Haraway's and Brossard's conceptions of bodily knowledge(s) and make preliminary suggestions about the possible significance of their views to a feminist reformulation of the body's epistemological role and status in rhetoric. Specifically, I want to look at their re-appropriation of the sense of vision for a feminist epistemology, a sense that, as Haraway notes, has been much maligned in feminist discourse.[20] The embodied vision that informs Haraway's and Brossard's differing, yet inter-connected, theories of knowledge disrupts the traditional opposition of knower from known or subject from object by emphasizing the wholly engaged, affective process of knowing. This process does not alienate or subjugate the 'Other' – the object of knowledge – beneath a dominating gaze, but instead inclines toward the other in a reciprocal, caring relationship which itself generates "a previously unheard of knowledge."[21]

By contrast with the "god trick of seeing everything from nowhere," Haraway proposes a feminist theory of objective vision which always acknowledges its situated or embodied nature. "I would like," she explains, "to insist on the embodied nature of all vision and so reclaim the sensory system that has been used to signify a leap out of the marked body and into a conquering gaze from nowhere." Reversing the traditional myth that scientific objectivity provides infinite and transcendent knowledge, Haraway argues that "objectivity turns out to be about particular and specific embodiment and definitely not about the false vision promising transcendence of all limits and responsibilities." By privileging the partiality of all perspectives, of all eyes, Haraway makes a case for a theory of feminist objectivity characterized by "limited location and situated knowledge," not "transcendence and splitting of subject and object."[22] Perhaps most importantly, such a theory makes the knower accountable or responsible for the knowledge that she claims to see or to have discovered because the knower, as much as the known, is situated within her particular social and historical context and within her material body. Further, the recognition of the local and partial – and therefore "real"[23] – nature of all knowledge-generating perspectives makes the building of meanings dependent on the sharing and translation of embodied knowledges across and among communities. This is simultaneously a political process of solidarity and an epistemological process of "shared conversations," both of which counter "totalizing versions of claims to scientific authority."[24]

Brossard's theory of *écriture au féminin*, as elaborated in her essay "The Aerial Letter," likewise explores the metaphor of sight for a feminist approach to the creation of "previously unheard-of knowledge" through this material, bodily writing. She contrasts the rapacious, objectifying gaze of patriarchy with the different visions of reality spoken by female-lesbian bodies, whose knowledges and realities have been dismissed for centuries by patriarchal culture as mere fictions. These different visions are displaced visions which see the world "otherwise," against the dominant representations of reality inscribed by masculine culture:

> I am talking here about a certain angle of vision. To get there, I had to get up and move, in order that the opaque body of the patriarchy no longer obstruct my vision. Displaced, I am. . . . Displacement of sense, not to be confused with disorder of the senses.[25]

Brossard's specification of vision occurring from an "angle" foregrounds its partiality and situatedness, not its universality or transcendence. Rather, the rich texture of this displaced vision unleashed beyond the boundaries of dominant culture emerges from its wondrous capacity for mobility and synthesis. Brossard imagines a "sixth sense . . . at work in the life of women . . . which offers reality from diverse mobile angles." It is because this aerial, utopian vision – this "sixth sense" – "never freezes its gaze on any one thing that it becomes possible to see the state of reality with incalculable precision."[26] Embracing paradox, refusing the dualism of mind and body, or of imagination and material reality, the aerial vision that sees the world in ways that make sense to women is also a sensual and embodied vision, grounded in the reality and vitality of "the living breathing body" and in the political-historical contexts that these bodies inhabit.[27] Likewise, the aerial vision embraces both past and future: in a utopian manner, it foresees new possibilities for women's lives and knowledges, but these interventions and projections emerge from the history and memories of each woman's body. These "infinite individual memories," writes Brossard, create a "thinking body," they give the body "its reasons."[28]

Haraway's and Brossard's different articulations of embodied vision as the basis for a new feminist epistemology offer, I believe, potential for a specifically feminist approach to the construction or invention of rhetorical knowledge. Indeed, rhetoric's emphasis on the situatedness of communicative acts already makes it an obvious candidate for such an approach. But more than the act of communicating or conveying knowledge to others, Haraway's and Brossard's views stress the act of inventing or generating knowledge as always situated and embodied.[29] This stress places the body at the centre rather than the margins of rational, persuasive discourse. It makes the knower's or speaker's body into a legitimate source of evidence and reasons. And it affirms a strong interconnection between the canons of invention and (bodily) memory, an interconnection which Lisa Ede, Cheryl Glenn, and Andrea Lundsford see as integral to feminist re-thinkings of the rhetorical tradition.[30] At the same time, emphasizing the rhetor's embodied positionality ensures that her vision or knowledge claims only an authority appropriate to its location and partiality, not a universal or transcendent authority. This limited kind of authority, rather than being in agonistic opposition to other authoritative claims, depends on and grows through "a web of connections" with other embodied and perhaps contradictory perspectives, with other angles of seeing and knowing the world that emerge from the perceptions and memories of diverse bodies. It opens up the possibility for rhetorics motivated less by the desire for "power-over" than the desire for "power-with,"[31] for working with other women and feminists to create a more just society.

The socio-political imperative that underlies such an approach directs our attention to the ethical issues at the heart of a feminist rhetorical epistemology. In particular, Haraway's conception of the knower's accountability within a feminist theory of objectivity foregrounds the inextricability of ethical and epistemological questions.[32] In other words, how the viewer or speaker "knows" as well as what she claims to know is not simply a logical or rational issue, but also a question of ethos and of pathos. As Jarratt and Reynolds explain in their article on the ethics of ethos,

> Haraway grounds ethical knowledge ... in a rationality through partiality. This is decidedly not a logos divorced from pathos. Rather, it is a passionate detachment which

> sees and respects difference and leaps toward an imagined web of connections among those differently positioned subjects.[33]

Only by fully acknowledging the centrality of the knower's or speaker's embodiment to how and what she knows can we reformulate a rhetorical epistemology that makes ethics and emotions, along with the body's cultural-historical memories, crucial dimensions in the invention of rational or logical arguments.

The emotional or affective dimension of embodied knowledges figures prominently in Haraway's and Brossard's theories. This emphasis on the "emotion of thought" or the "thought of emotion"[34] draws our attention to the intimate relationship between the knower and the known, between the subject and object of knowledge that Haraway and Brossard envision. To play on the meaning of one of Haraway's key terms, we could say that feminist objectivity is "partial" not only in the sense of limited and located, but also in the sense of being partial toward the 'object' that it seeks to know. Feminist objectivity does not dispassionately distance itself from the objects of knowledge that it studies, but instead approaches the other with affection and "loving care."[35] Far from being the source of distorting bias, this partiality, this affection, allows the knower to become engaged and intimate with the worlds she studies. Her vulnerability to the 'Other' is a source of strength and richness, not a weakness, in the "passionate construction"[36] of new knowledges. This reconfiguration of the knower as vulnerable and caring necessitates a similar reconfiguration of the nature of the object of knowledge. As Haraway explains, "[s]ituated knowledges require that the object of knowledge be pictured as an actor and agent, not as a screen or ground or resource" to be exploited and dominated by the authoritarian knower. This reconfiguration of the nature of both the knower and the known, or the subject and the object, leads Haraway to argue that scientific accounts of "reality" depend not on the logic of "discovery" but instead "on a power-charged social relation of 'conversation'."[37] Literally, the ideal feminist knower converses, respectfully and caringly, with the active, embodied world she seeks to know but does not control.

Even more than Haraway, Brossard stresses the emotional and bodily aspects of thinking and knowing. Women who write the aerial vision of new worlds and realities use "a sensual and cerebral capacity" in which "words/knowledge/emotion" occur simultaneously.[38] As with Haraway, Brossard's specification of the emotional or affective dimensions of thought implies not only the writer's or knower's attunement to her own feelings and sensations but also her awareness of and openness to the emotional thoughts and realities of other women. The writer's ability to articulate "previously unheard-of knowledge" depends on her intimate, loving relationships with other women similarly committed to "taking on reality in order that an aerial vision of all realities arises from the body and emotion of thought."[39] Brossard's description of the scene of writing shows the reciprocal, non-dominating nature of the relationship between the writer-knower and the 'Other' for whom and about whom she writes:

> I see that when I write, I do it in struggle and for my survival. See very well what in my gaze sends me alarmed toward other women and solidarity. No hidden reef: I don't want to possess anything or anyone, text or persons, unless it's by mutual pleasure.... How do I write? with a woman's gaze resting on me. Or with the body inclined toward her.... I do not submit to a woman's gaze...[40]

Reversing the roles of knower and known, of writer and reader, Brossard places herself – the writer, the inscriber of knowledge – in the position of the one who is viewed or read by "a woman's gaze." But this gaze, unlike the threatening, dominating gaze of patriarchy, gently rests on the writer from a physically proximate and equitable position. This non-threatening, empowering gaze does not force the feminist writer to reproduce a version of reality that conforms to the patriarchal tradition, but instead spurs her on "to a relentless exploration of sense."[41]

For rhetoric, Haraway's and Brossard's emphasis on the emotional dimension of the knowing process helps to re-legitimate the role of pathos in both the invention and communication of embodied knowledges. In other words, pathos is not simply an appeal that the "rational" speaker or rhetor makes in order to manipulate his emotionally susceptible audience, but is a valid and significant part of how the rhetor herself comes to know or invent her discourse. By contrast with the commonplace view expressed in Corbett's Aristotelian representation of rhetoric, a feminist approach to rhetorical invention that stresses the affective and sensual dimensions of knowing sees nothing "undignified about a rational creature being stimulated into action by the stimulus of aroused passions."[42] Further, the embodied pathos of feminist knowing, as Haraway and Brossard see it, gives us a framework for reconceiving the relationship between speaker and audience as one of intimacy, reciprocity, and conversation. Again, such a reconception counters the traditional Aristotelian view that the main reason the speaker needs to venture beyond "the bare facts" to be persuasive is "owing to the defects of our hearers."[43] The feminist view that I am proposing instead perceives emotions and physical senses as the ground for the creation of shared knowledges, knowledges that emerge out of our diverse but interconnected bodily histories and memories.

Haraway's preferred metaphor of "conversation" rather than "discovery" for the process of feminist epistemology lends itself aptly to the possibilities for future theories and practices of rhetorical invention. In foregrounding this metaphor of conversation, I am extending a concept that already figures quite prominently in several historical approaches to women's rhetorical modes.[44] Conversation, in an ideal form, suggests the possibility of a more equitable and reciprocal interaction between participants in a rhetorical situation than the classical "conquest" model of persuasion[45] in which the speaker's objective is to win, or gain control, over the audience (Haraway, though, never naively presupposes absolute equality of power, stressing always the power differentiations between and within communities of knowers[46]). In an idealized conception of shared knowledge produced through a conversational mode of rhetoric, all participants in the situation act as both rhetors and audience members, as both the producers and receivers of knowledge. And this knowledge consists not in "the bare facts" only, but in the vital, rich knowledges located in our physical and emotional perceptions of reality. As I strive to learn – or, rather, to acknowledge

– this bodily and emotional way of thinking, I hope that the perspectives I have begun to explore here will engage you in conversations that help us move beyond traditional, masculinist views of rhetoric by together "remembering forward into the open."⁴⁷

## NOTES

1. See, for example, Susan Jarratt, "Speaking to the Past: Feminist Historiography in Rhetoric," *Pre/Text* 11, no. 3-4 (1990): 190-205; Jarratt, "Performing Feminisms, Histories, Rhetorics," *Rhetoric Society Quarterly* 22, no. 1 (1992): 1-6; and Barbara Biesecker, "Coming to Terms with Recent Attempts to Write Women into the History of Rhetoric," in *Rethinking the History of Rhetoric*, ed. T. Poulakos (Boulder, CO: Westview Press, 1993), 169-71. Miriam Brody's *Manly Writing: Gender, Rhetoric, and the Rise of Composition* (Carbondale: Southern Illinois University Press, 1993) provides one example of a gendered re-reading of the traditional association of good style with the category of 'manliness' that informs the rhetorical canon, an association which, she argues, is still privileged in contemporary composition studies.
2. Patricia Bizzell, "Opportunities for Feminist Research in the History of Rhetoric," *Rhetoric Review* 11, no. 1 (1992), 51. See also Sonja Foss, Karen Foss, and Robert Trapp, "Challenges to the Rhetorical Tradition" in *Contemporary Perspectives on Rhetoric*, 2nd ed. (Prospect Heights, IL: Waveland, 1991), 284-87; Biesecker, "Coming to Terms," 156; Lisa Ede, Cheryl Glenn, and Andrea Lundsford, "Border Crossings: Intersections of Rhetoric and Feminism," *Rhetorica* 13, no. 4 (1995): 440-41.
3. Jarratt, "Speaking to the Past," 191. Biesecker similarly notes the future orientation of re-reading the canon of rhetorical history from a feminist perspective: "For what is beginning to emerge there under the guise of information retrieval is the cathected story of what it is that we wish to become" ("Coming to Terms," 170).
4. Published in *Feminist Studies* 14, no. 3 (1988): 575-99. I am grateful to Susan Jarratt for first introducing me to Haraway and this particular article through a pre-publication copy of her and Nedra Reynolds' article "The Splitting Image: Contemporary Feminisms and the Ethics of *êthos*," in *Ethos: New Essays in Rhetorical and Critical Theory*, ed. J.S. Baumlin and T.F. Baumlin (Dallas: Southern Methodist University Press, 1994), 37-64.
5. I am working with Marlene Wildeman's translation of this essay in the collection *The Aerial Letter* (Toronto: Women's Press, 1988), 67-90. [*La lettre aerienne* (Montréal: Remue-Ménage, 1985)]
6. For discussions of Aristotle's influential association of masculinity with rationality and active form, and of femininity with irrationality and passive matter, see Patricia Parker, *Literary Fat Ladies: Rhetoric, Gender, Property* (London:

Methuen, 1987), 181–82; Lorraine Code, "Feminist Theory," in *Changing Patterns: Women in Canada*, ed. L. Code, S. Burt, and L. Dorney (Toronto: McClelland & Stewart, 1990), 21–23. For discussions of Enlightenment interpretations and reinforcements of this classical dualism, particularly in Descartes' work, see Genevieve Lloyd, "The Man of Reason," in *Women, Knowledge, and Reality*, ed. A. Garry and M. Pearsall (Boston: Unwin Hyman, 1989), 111–28; Susan Bordo, "The Cartesian Masculinization of Thought," *Signs* 11, no. 3 (1986): 439–56; Susan Hekman, "The Feminization of Epistemology: Gender and the Social Sciences," *Women and Politics* 7, no. 3 (1987): 65–83.

7   Aristotle, *Rhetoric*, trans. W. Rhys Roberts (New York: Modern Library, 1954), III.1403b–1404a.
8   Quintilian, *Institutio Oratoria*, trans. H.E. Butler, 4 vols. (1920; reprint London: Heinemann, 1961), 11.3.2, 11.3.14.
9   Edward J. Corbett, *Classical Rhetoric for the Modern Student*, 3rd ed. (New York: Oxford University Press, 1990), 86.
10  Roy Porter, "History of the Body," in *New Perspectives on Historical Writing*, ed. Burke (University Park, PA: Pennsylvania State University Press, 1992), 206.
11  Gilbert Austin, *Chironomia or A Treatise on Rhetorical Delivery* (London: T. Cadell and W. Davies, 1806; facsimile reprint Carbondale: Southern Illinois University Press, 1966), 1.
12  For an interesting discussion of how intersections between feminism and rhetoric might contribute to a reformulation of the canon of delivery, see Ede, Glenn, and Lundsford, "Border Crossings," 428–37.
13  Ede, Glenn, and Lundsford note how the traditional view of invention presupposes a masculine, rational rhetor whose ideas and arguments are untainted by emotional instabilities. Feminist perspectives, by contrast, seek to expand both who counts as knowledgeable and what counts as knowledge. This includes revalidating "the intuitive and paralogical, the thinking body, as valuable sources of knowing, as sites of invention" ("Border Crossings," 412–13).
14  Hekman, "The Feminization of Epistemology," 69–74; Janet Sayers, "Feminism and Science: Reason and Passion," *Women's Studies International Forum* 10, no. 2 (1987): 171–79.
15  Sayers, "Feminism and Science," 176.
16  Haraway, "Situated Knowledges," 581.
17  Louise Forsyth, "Errant and Air-Born in the City," in *The Aerial Letter*, 14.
18  Brossard, "The Aerial Letter," 75.
19  Jarratt, "Speaking to the Past," 191.
20  Haraway, "Situated Knowledges," 581.
21  Brossard, "The Aerial Letter," 76.
22  Haraway, "Situated Knowledges," 581, 582, 583.
23  Ibid., 579.

24  Ibid., 584.
25  Brossard, "The Aerial Letter," 79.
26  Ibid., 85.
27  Ibid., 78. Brossard's appreciation of the cultural and historical constructedness of bodily realities and reasons is apparent in her explanation of her own situatedness: "But the body has its reasons, mine, its lesbian skin, its place in a historical context, its particular environment and its political content" (77–78).
28  Ibid., 77. Brossard elsewhere comments that "What is learned at the expense of one's body is never forgotten" ("Turning Platform," in *The Aerial Letter*, 48). For many women, she notes, bodily memories are memories of "torture": "My body's plural memory also tells me that 'women's memory is torrential when it has to do with torture' – systematic torture which, as Mary Daly shows in *Gyn/ecology*, has been camouflaged in the name of value systems and customs: Chinese foot-binding, the custom of suttee in India, clitoridectomy, gynecology, and contemporary psychiatry" (78).
29  I recognize that this distinction between the communication and creation of knowledge or ideas, though it may have been assumed in classical rhetorics, is one that much contemporary rhetorical theory calls into question. Nonetheless, as Ede, Glenn, and Lundsford note, Corbett's fairly recent conventional discussion of style demonstrates an ambiguity about its epistemological role and status, denying that it constitutes merely the "dress of thought" yet explaining that verbal style acts as the "medium of communication" for the speaker's arguments which are "discovered, selected, and arranged" *before* being put into words ("Border Crossings," 421). Clearly, this conventional logic can be extended to commonplace notions about the role of the body in delivering or presenting, but not inventing, the speaker's message.
30  Ede, Glenn, and Lundsford, "Border Crossings," 409–14.
31  See Sonja K. Foss and Cindy L. Griffin, "A Feminist Perspective on Rhetorical Theory: Toward a Clarification of Boundaries," *Western Journal of Communication* 56 (1992): 334–36, for an explanation of the feminist writer Starhawk's conceptions of "power-with" and "power-over."
32  Feminist philosopher Lorraine Code likewise makes the question of the knower's responsibility or accountability a central theme in her epistemological theories ("Experience, Knowledge, and Responsibility," in *Women, Knowledge, and Reality*, 157–72). Ede, Glenn, and Lundsford, for their part, note how bringing feminism and rhetoric into dialogue foregrounds "the need to develop an ethics of communication" in which the subject or theorist of knowledge acknowledges the "interestedness and situatedness" of her discourse ("Border Crossings," 439–40).
33  Jarratt and Reynolds, "The Splitting Image: Contemporary Feminisms and the Ethics of *êthos*," 55.
34  Brossard, "The Aerial Letter," 76.

35 Haraway, "Situated Knowledges," 583.
36 Ibid., 585.
37 Ibid., 592–93.
38 Brossard, "The Aerial Letter," 85,82.
39 Ibid., 68.
40 Brossard, "Turning Platform," 44.
41 Brossard, "The Aerial Letter," 81.
42 Corbett, *Classical Rhetoric*, 86.
43 Aristotle, *Rhetoric*, III.1404a.
44 See, for example, Annette Kolodny, "Inventing a Feminist Discourse: Rhetoric and Resistance in Margaret Fuller's *Woman in the Nineteenth Century*," in *Reclaiming Rhetorica*, ed. Andrea Lundsford (Pittsburgh: University of Pittsburgh Press, 1995), 137–66; Christine Sutherland, "Mary Astell: Reclaiming Rhetorica in the Seventeenth Century," in *Reclaiming Rhetorica*, 111–12; Andrea Lundsford, "On Reclaiming Rhetorica" and "Afterword," in *Reclaiming Rhetorica*, 6–7, 319.
45 Sally Miller Gearhart, "The Womanization of Rhetoric," *Women's Studies International Quarterly* 2 (1979): 195.
46 Haraway, "Situated Knowledges," 580. Similarly, I wish to stress my awareness that what I am describing is an *ideal*, not necessarily an empirical representation of what actually occurs when women converse together. Just as the socially inscribed power-differentiations between men and women will affect styles of conversation that take place in mixed gender groups, so too the power-differences among diverse women (e.g., differences relating to race, class, age, education, as well as the vast range of more contextually derived variables such as workplace, family, and other social positions) will affect the mode of conversation in any particular situation. Nonetheless, the feminist *desire* to promote a more equitable, caring style of interaction between participants in a rhetorical situation that depends on sensitivity to power-differentiations can, I believe, effect some real changes in both our theories and practices of rhetorical communication.
47 Brossard, "Turning Platform," 46. In her introduction, translator M. Wildeman thanks Jeffner Allen for permission to use this expression (31).

# *Feminist Epistemologies, Rhetorical Traditions and the* Ad Hominem

MARIANNE JANACK AND JOHN ADAMS

The shadowy arena between rhetoric and philosophy is home to an enemy common to both. Its name is Fallacy. It circles back and forth, around and around, calling both to err. It wears a human face.

And what is Fallacy if it isn't an instance of being wrong – of being called to account for what one has done – of being found guilty of being amiss? In the commission of a fallacy one's character is implicated, as deeds are signs of character and committing a fallacy is indeed a deed – people perform them – they are acts or signs of acts – they are speech acts. Fallacy, then, is *ad hominem par excellence*, when being wrong in making a point is being somebody being impugned, or corrected, or both simultaneously – being put back on the path of right(eous)ness for his or her name's sake, so that one will not be wrong, but right, and thereby maintain one's right to make a point. But if being wrong is blameworthy in making a point, one would think that being right is praiseworthy ("Brilliant!") and that the lustre gained by such a feat is a part of the feat's feat – and that so-being when titled positively is just the flip side of the *ad hominem* coin – the side with the smiling face on it that gains one fame and affects people's positive perceptions of one's credibility. After all, outside of the texts of the logicians' and the rhetoricians' lore, *ad hominem* does not carry a negative (or a positive) charge – as if one can only be a bad logician or rhetorician by saying *bad* things about people's point-making, and saying *good* things is not bad – in both cases the deflection (or defection) 'to the man' as an index of judging her or his point-making rings a conclusive bell for good or for ill that adds to, or detracts from, the import of a person's point. The *ad hominem* (which may be Fallacy's first name), has until recently had a very uncheckered past: the consensus was strong on its place – one could recognize its face easily among the crowd of fallacies inhabiting logic and rhetoric (or public speaking or writing/composition) textbooks.

In Patrick J. Hurley's *A Concise Introduction to Logic*, a text from which one of us learned our logic as an undergraduate, we get the following example of the *ad hominem*:

> Economist Milton Friedman has argued in favor of reducing federal income taxes. But Friedman's argument should be discounted. Friedman is a millionaire who would benefit greatly from a reduction in taxes. Also, Friedman has no need for the government programs that higher taxes provide for.[1]

In his explanation of why this is a fallacy, Hurley says that the author of this argument does not pay attention to the substance of Friedman's argument. "Merely because a person happens to be affected by certain circumstances is not sufficient reason to think that the person is incapable of arguing logically. Any attempt to discredit such an argument in this way therefore involves a fallacy" (107).

This understanding of the *ad hominem* and the sin it embodies – the sin of irrelevance – has recently come under examination by philosophers and scholars in the discipline of speech communication. The *ad hominem* and its presumed invalidity has also been an issue for feminist epistemological projects, either directly or indirectly. We will begin with a discussion of the relationship between feminist epistemological projects and the *ad hominem*, and then move to a discussion of the argument against understanding the *ad hominem* as a fallacy in all cases, presented by Douglas Walton in *A Pragmatic Theory of Fallacy*. We will then orchestrate a conversation between Lorraine Code and Douglas Walton to examine where Code's feminist project overlaps with Walton's project and where they part company, and conclude with some remarks on how these projects differ from other social epistemological projects.

## Feminist Standpoint Epistemologies, Situated Knowers, and the "Argument Against the Man"

Feminist standpoint epistemologies represent probably the most direct attack on the notion of the *ad hominem* argument as a fallacy. Although these epistemological projects differ somewhat in their articulations, they share some common presuppositions. The first presupposition which feminist standpoint theorists agree on is that who does the theorizing – whose presuppositions, models, and methods are used – is of the utmost importance in deciding whether a social scientific theory (as in the Friedman example quoted above) should be accepted. The second premise shared by feminist standpoint theorists is that one's social position will influence one's theorizing. So, for example, upper-middle-class white men, like Milton Friedman, have a certain perspective on the social world that makes some aspects of that world invisible. But, as Sandra Harding points out, they can come to see aspects of that social world which in the normal course of events would remain hidden from them by starting their thought out from the perspective of marginalized lives. Hegel was not a slave, she argues, and Marx and Engels were not members of the proletariat, but these upper-middle-class white men were able to shift the centre of their theoretical focus from the lives they themselves led and the interests embodied in those lives to the lives of the marginalized.[2] It was this shift in solidarity and the concomitant identification of interests which were alien and even competitors with their own class interests that allowed Hegel, Marx, and Engels to see new aspects of the social world.

According to feminist standpoint theory, marginalized lives often put the lie to social theories or conventional wisdom. So, for instance, the understanding of the relationship between the capitalist and the worker as one based on a freely chosen contract in which the worker sells his or her labour power to the capitalist for a salary is dismantled by shifting one's attention to the standpoint of the worker. From this perspective, the contract appears to be less freely chosen, as the worker must often choose between this contract and destitution and starvation (so Marx and Engels argued); this is hardly a "free" choice – or it is free only insofar as the choice you make to hand over your wallet is free when a gun is held to your head and you are given the choice, "Your money or your life."

The relationship between the *ad hominem* and standpoint theories can be best seen by attending to the example cited in Hurley. It seems reasonably clear that a standpoint theorist would reject Friedman's theory, not on exactly the grounds put forward in the example, but on fairly similar ones. The standpoint theorist would indeed attack the argument by attacking the man, not on the basis of his presumed simple self-interest, but on the basis of his sociopolitical situation and what it allows him to "see."

For the feminist standpoint theorist, then, the question is not whether Friedman can argue logically. Rather, the question is whether Friedman has all the facts. And his social position and interests militate against his access to the facts.

### *Lorraine Code, Epistemic Responsibility, and Epistemic Authority*

Although Lorraine Code does not consider her project to be a feminist epistemological project, her account of epistemic responsibility has many affinities with such projects. Like many of those projects, hers emphasizes the interested nature of all attempts to know, as well as the fact of epistemic dependence which she claims has been overlooked by most traditional epistemologies. The conclusion that she reaches is that the question of 'Who knows' — a question common to projects that wish to examine the politics of knowledge — cannot readily be addressed within a traditional philosophical model.

> When philosophy presents itself as a disinterested and universal/impartial pursuit of truth — indeed of the underlying and overarching truth of all truths — or as a quasi-scientific inquiry, the assumption is that the philosopher-as-thinker is a neutral vehicle through whom truth passes.[3]

Traditional epistemological accounts extend this conception of the philosopher to that of the knower, Code claims, presuming that would-be knowers are interchangeable epistemic agents. What that means, practically, is that it is assumed by these accounts that knowledge properly so-called, and epistemic agency worth its name, are the same across the board – that variations according to gender/race/class and social position either do not occur or should not occur.

Code recognizes the democratic urge behind this. Ideally, it seems, all of us should have equal epistemic authority, and these "arbitrary" facts about ourselves should not be factors in determining how our statements will be taken. It seems as if our claims ought to stand on their own.

But Code also recognizes that the mythology which says that claims are taken on their own mystifies the real practice. This real practice, she claims, confers credibility differentially. So, Code argues, "the rhetorical spaces that a society legitimates generate presumptions of credibility and trust that attach differentially according to how speakers and interpreters are positioned within them. Philosophical assumptions about the veracity of first-person privileged access and automatic up-take bypass these everyday occurrences, which are shaping forces in the ongoing construction of subjectivity and agency, especially in places of unequal power and authority."[4] It is because of this, Code claims, that any politics of knowledge must begin with a re-examination of the *ad hominem*.

Unlike the account given by standpoint theorists, Code's emphasizes the fact that a shift in philosophical attention from the end-product of knowledge-seeking – that is, beliefs and propositions – to the cognitive practices out of which our everyday beliefs arise is what occasions this re-examination. It is not that the socially and economically privileged occupy a position from which they may not be able to "see" parts of the social world. Rather, it is the fact that we must and do rely on our judgments of people's character and interests in our decisions about whether we ought to believe what they say. Paradigmatic examples of knowledge claims in traditional coherentist and foundationalist accounts are "I see a tree" or "I see a red book." Such examples, taken as paradigms of knowledge, obscure the fact that very few of our everyday beliefs exemplify this sort of epistemic self-sufficiency. Most of what we know, Code argues, comes from what we learn from other people. Most of our beliefs and what we claim to know come to us from "testimony," not from first-hand observation. Because of this, the issue of trust becomes paramount. Once the pervasiveness of common ability is recognized, the question "Is John believable?" becomes as pertinent as "Is p believable?"[5]

A re-examination of the *ad hominem* circumstantial is called for, on Code's account, because (1) as a matter of epistemic practice, credibility attaches differently to different speakers depending on where they are positioned within sanctioned rhetorical spaces in society, and (2) so much of our knowledge comes from others that we must be able to determine who is a trustworthy source and who is not.

These two reasons seem to be in conflict with each other. After all, if it is a problem that credibility attaches differentially to speakers and interpreters, then it also seems to be a troubling aspect of the human situation that we must attribute different levels of trust to different speakers. The solution, one might object, is simply to focus on the content of the argument and ignore the content of the arguer's character.

Code wants to find some middle ground (in true Aristotelian fashion) between claiming that we should not attach different levels of credibility to speakers and that we should attend very carefully to the epistemic character of that speaker. What Code objects to is not that we judge different speakers to be more or less reliable sources of knowledge, but the fact that we try to ignore the fact that we do make such judgements. In her discussion of the Anita Hill/Clarence Thomas hearings, Code claims:

> The hearings were presented to the North American public as inquiries conducted according to positivist-empiricist principles which ensured that everyone would say what she or he had to say, and that all the statements would be weighed fairly, equivalently, and openly. This presentational format produced the possibility of exploiting the resources of a power structure that obscured its own power behind a mask of monologic epistemic neutrality. Hence the very idea that who was believed and who met merely with incredulity had anything to do with who – specifically – they were could be represented as preposterous.[6]

Her examination of Toni Morrison's *Race-ing Justice, Engendering Power*, and Patricia Williams' *The Alchemy of Race and Rights* confirms for Code the claims made by critics of the Enlightenment and feminists that no such democracy of epistemic authority holds across the epistemic terrain. We may all enjoy equal epistemic authority in some (fairly small) arena of knowledge claims, Code asserts, but in most areas of discourse

> hearing is believing expectations tend to attach differentially according to the credibility of testifiers and their solidarity with or differences from their interlocutors, rather than according to the simple 'strength of the evidence.' And credibility is by no means conferred only on the basis of a good epistemic record. Epistemologically, these issues are as much about subjectivity as they are about knowledge, and questions about who is speaking figure centrally in their analysis.[7]

Code's main objection to the unconditional condemnation of the *ad hominem* as fallacious is that such condemnation ignores the fact that we do – and must – rely on judgements of character in our evaluation of knowledge claims. By condemning such argumentation universally, such philosophical approaches to argumentation close off possibilities for evaluating what types of "arguments against the man" are reasonable and which are not. Further, it reinforces an epistemological story of disinterested and neutral observers who come to know monologically rather than dialogically, obscuring the ways in which argumentation is central to epistemology.

### *Douglas Walton's Pragmatic Theory of Fallacy*

Douglas Walton claims that logicians have paid scant attention to informal fallacies in general and the *ad hominem* particularly for much the same reasons. According to Walton, "informal logic is identified with strategies of persuasion where two parties reason together. To Western logicians this identification has seemed to come uncomfortably close to rhetoric and salesmanship."[8] Western logic's preference for formalism, coupled with its monolectical and monotonic presumptions, has resulted in a view (which, Walton claims, would have been foreign to Aristotle) of informal fallacies as "failures of validity" with unfortunate psychological appeal. In the view of traditional canons of Western logic, informal fallacies are invalid arguments that "seem" to be valid – another rhetorical trick set up to ensnare the tenderfoot reasoner.

Walton recognizes the *ad hominem* as a certain sort of move by one party in a two-party dialogue, and its fallacious uses are those in which it is (1) used to trick or deceive a partner in dialogue or (2) a paralogism. We cannot judge whether a certain use of an *ad hominem* argument is fallacious, however, without looking very closely at the dialogic context. We must judge, contextually, whether a particular *ad hominem* argument tends to block or interfere with constructive discussion. In Walton's words: "How harmful irrelevance is, in a particular dialogue, depends on the purpose and setting of the dialogue and on practical constraints. If each side has an allotted time to present its side of an issue then a side that wastes its time on irrelevant arguments is simply weakening its own arguments . . ." (190). In order to judge whether an *ad hominem* is dialectically relevant, according to Walton, six kinds of factors need to be considered: (1) type of dialogue; (2) stage of dialogue; (3) goal of dialogue; (4) argumentation scheme; (5) prior sequence of argumentation; and (6) speech event (given institutional setting or particular speech event, e.g., legal trial, committee meeting). The primary ways in which an *ad hominem* is used fallaciously, according to Walton, are the following: (1) when the imputation of bad character is seriously under-supported, such as when innuendo is used; (2) when the arguer shifts from weak refutation to strong refutation; or (3) when the argument is irrelevant in some serious way. The one version of the *ad hominem* which Walton claims is almost never non-fallacious is what he calls the "poisoning the well" version, which is an extension of the bias version of the *ad hominem.* The "poisoning the well" argument claims that the person attacked can never change – thus blocking any attempt at critical discussion of the point at hand.

## Code, Walton and the Ad Hominem Argument

We are now in a position to evaluate the different approaches to the *ad hominem* presented by Code and Walton. Code and Walton agree on the dialogic nature of reasoning, but whereas Walton stresses the importance of the goals of critical discussion, Code emphasizes the epistemological priority of testimony. Walton's attempt to pick out fallacious uses of *ad hominem* arguments is generally confined to those arenas in which the institutional setting of the dialogue requires that irrelevant "quarreling" not be allowed to interfere with the goals of the argument (e.g., in timed debates over legislation). Code is more concerned with everyday occurrences in which we must determine whether to trust the testimony of another in our attempts to gather information. It seems reasonable to conclude, given Walton's outline of when *ad hominem* arguments constitute fallacies, that he would conclude that such common everyday uses of negative and ethotic argument and bias arguments would not constitute fallacies. The only uses of the *ad hominem* which Walton seems inclined to consider fallacious in these informal exchanges of information are the "poisoning the well" uses of the *ad hominem.*

Code, we think, would agree with this, as her main objection to the differential allotment of epistemic authority is that it is a systematic undercutting of the claims of some categories of subjects. Code's more serious concern is that these systematic presumptions or epistemic vices operate, not in public argument, but as suppressed (and unsayable) premises.

For both Code and Walton, then, the question of whether a particular version of the *ad hominem* argument is fallacious depends on the context of the claim: on who is involved in the dialogue and on the purpose of the dialogue. The main difference between Walton and Code seems to be a difference in approach. Code sees the discussion of *ad hominem* arguments, and argumentation generally, as an epistemological concern, whereas Walton's concern is more narrowly circumscribed to the discipline of argumentation and logic. The relationship between Code and Walton can be most uncontroversially described as a difference between a broad approach and a special case. Code, we might say, is concerned with broad implications for epistemology of our reconsideration of the *ad hominem*. Walton, on the other hand, is concerned with argumentation, and is trying to develop rules for argumentation in institutional settings which must have some discretionary power in admitting or banning certain types of argumentation.

If this were all of the story, however, the story would be a dull one. But it is not, really, all that dull. In fact, the differences between Code and Walton point to an issue of great importance: the need to examine the boundaries between logic, epistemology, ethics, and political theory. Along with the need to question the value of drawing these boundaries also comes the need to question that most vigilantly guarded boundary: the boundary between philosophy and rhetoric.

While Walton's discussion is fairly narrowly targeted toward argumentation and logic, it is easy to see that Walton's theory could be used to fill out Code's discussion of the differential allotment of epistemic authority. But part of what that means is allowing logic, epistemology, and political theory to overspill their boundaries, to allow them to inform each other. And what that implies is that rhetorical theory, with its overt interest in persuasion practices and the construction of ethos, is a necessary component of developing an epistemology which is meant, not simply for rarefied discussions in science, law, or politics, but for helping us to lead better lives. Because part of living good lives involves trusting the right people and developing epistemically responsible practices, a discussion of the role of *ad hominem* arguments must recognize that we do operate with premises about whom we ought to believe and who is not a credible testifier. But as theorists like Code have pointed out, such premises are not developed in a social vacuum. They are developed in social contexts marked by the particularity of persons and social structures. In North America, part of that social structure involves deep-seated racism and sexism and a hierarchy: not only a socio-economic hierarchy, but also a hierarchy of epistemic authority. The effects of this hierarchy are not limited to the political sphere. In fact, if they were limited to that sphere, they would probably be less pernicious than they are. The fact that this hierarchy operates, unexposed, in our everyday epistemology, in our constructions of ethos, and in our decisions about whom we should trust has primarily been ignored (or denied) by traditional philosophical approaches to epistemology and argumentation. The arena in which ethos, argumentation, and epistemology are entwined is also the arena in which the space between rhetoric and philosophy can be explored and mapped – the shadowy arena between rhetoric and philosophy where Fallacy is what they have in common – where the indices of error are reflected backwards in the precepts of what counts as right, correct, proper, appropriate. *Ad hominem* has two faces: what is "to the man" is not always "against the man." It can promote mistrust *or* it can lend a lustre, inducing belief. People make points, and there is something of the person, for good or ill, entwined in any statement. What is '*ad hominem*' – pro or con – should be a criterion of judgement brought to discussion in the evaluation of any argument in any field at any time. In principle, it is *never* inappropriate to do so.

Whether in the formal key of a syllogism in Barbara or in a city council meeting at Santa Barbara, people may err in making or judging a point. But the other "face" of *ad hominem* is "*for* the man" and it may face toward the fallacy of *ad vericundiam*. In questions of trust, too much and not enough may be equally pernicious in casting and receiving arguments. Moreover, in the late twentieth century, queries into the source(s) and persuasive slant(s) of a speaker's/writer's ethos (for better or for worse) are further complicated by the insights/arguments of anti-essentialism, reader-response criticism, and deconstruction's endless semiosis – where finally deciding anything at all about anything at all may require the reader/hearer to affect an aporia-breaking époche and cast a judgement anyway – where one's ethos is always contingent.

Now that the very idea of character is *ad hoc* we are back to Aristotle's intimation in the *Rhetoric* that tokens of character are occasional and accomplished through one's speech.[9] So, in the late twentieth century, what is *ad hominem* is *ad hoc*, but one's character (imputed or avowed) still matters even if it is a fiction concocted and accepted for purposes of identification and the formation of floating communities: for creating timely sites to help us cope with and accomplish what we can not do or feel on our own.

## *NOTES*

1 Patrick J. Hurley, *A Concise Introduction to Logic*, 2nd ed. (Belmont, CA: Wadsworth, 1985), 107.
2 See Sandra Harding, "Rethinking Standpoint Epistemology: 'What is Strong Objectivity'?" in *Feminist Epistemologies*, eds. Linda Alcoff and Elizabeth Potter (New York: Routledge, 1993), 49–82.
3 Lorraine Code, *Rhetorical Spaces* (New York: Routledge, 1995), 69.
4 Ibid., 60.
5 Lorraine Code, *Epistemic Responsibility* (Hanover, NH: University Press of New England, 1987), 173.
6 Code, *Rhetorical Spaces*, 68.
7 Ibid., 69.
8 Douglas N. Walton, *A Pragmatic Theory of Fallacy* (Tuscaloosa, AL: University of Alabama Press, 1995), 4.
9 See Aristotle, *The "Art" of Rhetoric*, trans. John Henry Freese (Cambridge, MA: Harvard University Press, 1975), Bk. I, ch. 2, I35a.

# *Voice and the Inevitability of Ethos*
## ROBERT L. KING

In 1990 *Critical Inquiry* articles, Cheryl Walker and Marilynn Desmond both point out that feminist criticism does not accept the death of the author as a critical given. Walker's view is qualified:

> Though the postmodern feminist critic is almost certain to practise her trade in defiance of authority, often proceeding polyvocally herself and rarely claiming that a unified, coherent, and transcendental subjectivity lies behind the text, nevertheless the author has never quite disappeared from our practice.[1]

Desmond is more categorical:

> Resistant and skeptical though it may be to the concept of authorship, feminist scholarship generally remains bound to the historical identity and gender of the author.

Desmond goes on to question the priorities of critics in her field:

> A feminist poetics must acknowledge the medieval attitudes toward authority and authorship that allow the medievalist to privilege the voice of the text over the historical author or implied author.[2]

This distinction, common enough in literary and composition theory, forecloses any consideration of rhetorical ethos as a useful critical concept and gives authority to voice, an often slippery and impressionistic one. Yet women who advocate social change in the public arena inevitably establish their moral character. To praise them for finding or having a voice ignores a fundamental component of their rhetorical strategy and, as an ironic consequence, reduces their stature as agents for meaningful reform.

In his introduction to *Landmark Essays on Voice and Writing*, Peter Elbow argues metaphorically to explain the appeal of the voice metaphor and rejects terms more closely associated with ethos:

> We see why voice has been such a tempting metaphor. That is, the physical voice is more resonant when it can get more of the body resonating behind it or underneath it. "Resonant" seems a more helpful word than "authentic," and it is more to the point than "sincerity," because it connotes the "resounding" or "sounding-again" that is involved when distinct parts can echo each other.[3]

Elbow readily admits that his central term raises fundamental problems. When he asks himself for "examples of resonant voice," he replies, "We are in the dicey business of pointing to the relation of textual features to an inferred person behind the text." One of the contributors to Elbow's collection finds another of his terms at least as dicey: "Authentic voice is, for most of those who advocate it, somehow natural, innate, magical, unavailable for empirical verification or rational explanation."[4]

Ethos, too, can have various meanings. Elbow summarizes the "traditional debate in rhetoric" between "ethos as real virtue in the real person and ethos as the appearance of virtue," and he distinguishes that debate from the "modern" one that opposes "voice as self" to "voice as role" (xv–xx). Nan Johnson points out first that "the status of ethos in the hierarchy of rhetorical principles has fluctuated as rhetoricians in different eras have tended to define rhetoric in terms of either idealistic aims or pragmatic skills," and later adds that "in treating the principle of ethos, today's rhetorical education offers a range of alternatives narrower than that typically relayed to students in earlier periods."[5] Our range has surely narrowed, but we cannot shake ethos as a theoretical standard no matter how automatic, frequent, and seductive the use of voice has become. Elbow, for example, surely judges D.H. Lawrence's character, his ethos, as more than "sound" and "voice" when he writes, "Lawrence's dramatic voice here is vivid: the sound of a brash, opinionated person who likes to show off and even shock" (xxix). Likewise, Elbow invokes the related principle of decorum without identifying it: "We may feel just as natural and like ourselves in slangy talk with sporting pals and highly formal professional talk at conferences. . . . [W]e can try to use the dramatic voice or persona that seems most appropriate for the audience" (xliii). This passage lacks a couple of key parts of Cicero's formulation but is remarkably close to it otherwise: "The universal rule, in oratory and in life, is to consider propriety. This depends on the subject under discussion, and on the character of both the speaker and the audience."[6]

One eminently defensible use of voice subordinates "the subject under discussion" when political and social structures have denied the means of self-expression to the unjustly silenced. These people have often been denied a forum precisely because they have something to say; their message can be anticipated, with the result that content is subordinated to tone or voice in the first stages of movements for emancipation. At first, anger, outrage and pain need to be voiced, often by a spokesperson; later, when specific issues are addressed – when voting rights becomes voter registration, for example – the character of the speaker is more likely to be developed. Catharine MacKinnon provides evidence of abuse of women and credits "the women's movement" with making "this information available, in the absence of the words of sexually abused women."[7]

Other speakers who voice the unquestioned pain of others or their own often feel no need to establish a credible ethos, but the shortcut can lead to a rhetorical and political dead end. Tobin Seibers quotes Jean Elshtain's "Feminist Discourse and Its Discontents": "The presumption is that the victim speaks in a pure voice: I suffer therefore I have moral purity and none can question what I say."[8] In a critique of Carol Gilligan's *In A Different Voice*, Linda Kerber raises a similar objection; she sees the potential to antagonize an audience: "What, then, are the risks of relying on women's allegedly 'different voice'? One danger, I think, is a familiar variety of feminine self-righteousness."[9] Responding directly to Gilligan in a public "conversation," Catharine MacKinnon found much to praise in her famous study of voice but also found one basic deficiency:

> What is infuriating about it ... and this is a political infuriation, is that it neglects the explanatory level. Why do women become these people, more than men, who represent these values? ... The answer is the subordination of women. ... I am troubled by the possibility of women identifying with what is a positively valued feminine stereotype [of woman as victim].[10]

Further, it can be argued that when the voice of the victim monopolizes discourse, the prospects for political change diminish. In a 1983 interview entitled "Of Holy Writing & Priestly Voices," Esther Broner yoked a change in voice to political action:

> My sense of change is of women getting stronger. ... We have to become sure ... of our voices; we can no longer have highpitched, giddy voices – we have to be very deep-voiced, loud. ... We must raise tender men and strong women, women who will be political warriors as well.[11]

A decade later, bell hooks, speaking with the authority of a black feminist, sees pure voice as a potential obstacle to effective political speech:

> In the United States ... the idea of finding a voice risks being trivialized or romanticized in the rhetoric of those who advocate a shallow feminist politic that privileges acts of speaking over the content of speech.[12]

Likewise, MacKinnon would channel her energies into effecting social change; distinguishing her work from Gilligan's, she said: "I am trying to work out how to change that system, not just how to make people be more fully human within it" (74). In her preface to the latest edition of *In a Different Voice* (1993), Gilligan herself identifies a more socially responsible voice; she objects to the "psychological seclusion of girls from the public world" because it "sets the stage for a kind of privatization of women's experience and impedes the development of women's political voice and presence in the public world."[13] If to go from the private to the public is to be political, some corollaries seem inevitable: one must have something to say about "experience"; that something – the content – precedes "the development of . . . political voice," and that voice, basing a political position on individual experiences, must be both personal and general. In the first stages of raising political awareness or social consciousness, voice legitimately gains an audience in its call for recognition of a problem or injustice. In later stages when change is advocated or promoted, mere voice, abstracted from a speaker, a point of view, or an argument, is, to borrow hooks's term, "shallow."

In the consciousness-raising programs of contemporary feminism, in MacKinnon's preliminaries to her attacks on pornography, and in Nadine Gordimer's fiction, a fundamental assertion is implied: Oppression exists. To support this claim, one must establish matters of fact – the "Is it?" of stasis theory – and of value – the "What is it worth?" Statistics on salary inequities and on limited opportunities for women in the business world and academe are readily available now. MacKinnon opens the first of her Christian Gauss lectures with graphic descriptions of sexual exploitation.[14] In the oppressive circumstances that apartheid created, Gordimer insists upon for herself "the integrity Chekhov demanded: 'to describe a situation so truthfully . . . that the reader can no longer evade it.'" [15] Directing a reader's choice so deliberately is both a rhetorical and a moral act, for descriptions of oppression and discrimination inevitably carry values for a sensitive audience. Even those who want to perpetuate themselves in positions of power are unlikely to say for the record that separate pay scales for the same work are good, that the traumas endured by unwilling participants in the porno industry are a reasonable price to pay for free speech, or that the multiple injustices imposed on all blacks and some whites in South Africa simply preserve public order.

When one gives "voice" to the fact of oppression, then, she is speaking ethically, for she has chosen a moral point of view and has committed herself to the need for a change in the status quo. Like a rhetorical narration, the matters of fact lead to propositions of policy, most clearly in MacKinnon's argument for new legal protections. That is to say, in the public arena persuasive strategy prohibits sharply distinct roles for voice and ethos. Indeed, C. Jan Swearingen's syntax yokes the two concepts:

> Classical and subsequent treatments of ethos provide ample and engaging attention to the formation of voice and [my emphasis] *character*, treatments that are far more complex and interesting than those provided in today's textbook definitions.[16]

Making a complementary point, Susan C. Jarratt and Nedra Reynolds see a "crucial" connection between the social and the moral:

> Unlike poststructuralism, classical rhetoric cannot be charged with removing the subject – the speaker or writer – from political and ethical reality. In fact, those political and ethical realities are crucial to classical ethos.[17]

Catharine MacKinnon's *Only Words* retains appropriate characteristics of oral delivery; the book is a somewhat revised version of her 1992 Christian Gauss Lectures at Princeton. In a direct, oral style, MacKinnon can make a legal distinction: "Pornography is not restricted here because of what it says. It is restricted through what it does. Neither is it protected because it says something, given what it does."[18] She frequently distinguishes issues as well as verbal implications; she gives examples of obscene films and acts with a remarkable blend of personal involvement in the subject and professional detachment from it as a legal matter. Her learning is relegated to her footnotes; her intelligence comes through clearly on every page. In television interviews, her delivery – her voice – conveys commitment and confidence. In sum, she establishes her ethos as knowledgeable lawyer and committed feminist. No wonder, then, that she gives credibility priority over voice in analyzing racial and sexual harassment. MacKinnon argues that when Anita Hill testified in the Clarence Thomas confirmation hearing, "the language of sexual abuse collided with the language of public discourse." When Hill cloaked her charges against Thomas in abstract terms, she was "more credible" than when she was obliged to be specific. "The real language of sexual abuse" (65) had a literal effect on Hill's voice:

> The speakable words were "[he] told me graphically of his own sexual prowess." We then heard the long breath of the woman passing the point of no return in what can now be

done to her preceding, "He also spoke on some occasions of the pleasures he had given to women," then the pause, the drop in her voice, before speaking even the clinical words "with oral sex" (65).

The "real language" was unacceptable to many in the forum created by the Senate, in the circumstances beyond Hill's control. Even when "given a voice," she was not believable. In MacKinnon's analysis, the words, allegedly Thomas's, attached to Hill for using them; she was held responsible for a radio commentator "left feeling dirty somehow" and for President Bush feeling "unclean watching" (66). As a real victim of sexual harassment, in MacKinnon's view, Hill needed only to "speak the abuser's words" to lose credibility; as a result, her "voice" was "used against [her]" (68).

As one who values a speaker's credibility and as a lawyer who argues that pornography has damaging personal and social effects, MacKinnon has no patience with postmodern indeterminacy. To her, the language of the First Amendment guaranteeing freedom of speech has had too sweeping an effect, and the Fourteenth, guaranteeing equal protection under the law for everyone, too narrow a one. The law as it deals with pornography gives her book its title, and the promise of equality in the Fourteenth Amendment has not been fulfilled. Words matter; they have consequences. Her style and tone enclose the other voices; MacKinnon presents a case or argument, and Thomas's words as supplied and paraphrased by Hill are part of her evidence. Neither she nor her reader questions whose voice is being heard.

In her constant, almost relentless, reasoning about justice, MacKinnon's voice "speaks about equality, reciprocity, fairness, rights," the topics that characterize the masculine voice in Gilligan's construction.[19] Besides the many distinctions in *Only Words*, its overall rhetorical strategy incorporates other elements of the courtroom or debating chamber. To supply a few of the many instances, she argues from causality throughout; she refutes a circular argument (88) and subjects a court opinion to a logical *reductio* (92). Although she risks shocking or antagonizing some members of her audience with obscene diction from court cases and with slang terms of her own, she expresses them in a direct style that can also accommodate "sui generis," "coterminous," and other formal terms. She further develops her ethical proof through detailed arguments from comparisons that reveal her concern for racist treatment of blacks and Jews.

Despite MacKinnon's being "infuriated" by Gilligan's *In A Different Voice*, however, and despite a pointed exchange between them (74–75), their positions can be reconciled without wrenching them out of recognizable shape. Gilligan says that "most people, both men and women (the percentages were not different) represent both voices [i.e., of justice reasoning and care reasoning] in defining moral problems" (47). Earlier, she says that "as women began to talk about their decision [about pregnancy and possible abortions] I picked up moral language. Spontaneously, words appeared like 'should,' 'ought,' 'right,' 'wrong,' 'good,' and 'bad'" (37). Moral concerns seem like a natural reflex in "defining" the problem. Gilligan does not – apparently by design – consider which voice is appropriate in recommending to a public how one tries to address or resolve "the problem." She does, though, identify the boundaries of her theory:

> I was ... talking about a voice literally different from the voice represented in psychology, from the voice represented in moral philosophy ... and from the voice that was represented in the legal system (39).

The last voice is no doubt MacKinnon's, a voice necessarily rising out of the ethical proof because it must earn credibility and authority before advocating a proposition of public policy.

A more demanding critical challenge to ethos as inevitable is presented by fictions in which the author's voice is filtered through a persona or is heard more objectively in the third person. A politically committed writer, Nadine Gordimer puts great distance between her personal life and her work. She consciously sets out to create distinctive voices, and is indifferent to readers' complaints about the ensuing difficulty, but will not abdicate her responsibility to an indeterminate text:

> I think a great failure in Hemingway's short stories is the omnipresence of Hemingway's voice. People do not speak for themselves, in their own thought patterns; they speak as Hemingway does. The "he said," "she said" of

Hemingway's work. I've cut these attributions out of my novels, long ago. Some people complain that this makes my novels difficult to read. But I don't care. . . . [I]f I can't make readers know who's speaking from the tone of voice, the turns of phrase, well, then I've failed. And there's nothing anyone can do about it.[20]

In *July's People*, Gordimer's style conveys "thought patterns" independently of individual styles; her "turns of phrase" are the narrator's and subtly establish a controlling voice, or ethos. Gordimer, in short, honors decorum personae. The first words of the novel are those of the black servant, July: "You like to have some cup of tea?" The paradoxical appositive that appears after his name some dozen lines below, "their servant, their host,"[21] signals the more complex and challenging point of view of the narrator. Her style can absorb conventional, deceptive ones:

> At home, after weeks of rioting out of sight in Soweto, a march on Johannesburg of (variously estimated) fifteen thousand blacks had been stopped at the edge of the business center at the cost of a (variously estimated) number of lives, black and white. The bank account for whom Bam had designed a house tipped off that if the situation in the city showed no signs of being contained (his phrase) the banks would have to declare a moratorium. (7)

At the opening of one section, Gordimer is referring to Bam and Maureen Smales, but she puts herself into the woman's "thought patterns," mixing her voice with Maureen's silent one: "she could no longer stay in the hut while the blond man fiddled with the radio"; as she runs at the novel's end, Maureen hears "the man's voice and the voices of children speaking English somewhere to the left" and her separation from her family is complete.

After the narrator has alerted us to ambiguities, we hear them in many of July's otherwise simple statements. To rely only on his authentic voice would be critically reductive:

> I'm work for you fifteen years. That you satisfy with me. (98)

> Everybody he's like money. (110)
> You, master, your children. All is going. (101)

The narrator has a distinctive mode of expression, aware of clashing registers and uneasy juxtapositions. Her "turns of phrase" include the "male chivalry of the suburbs" (104), native dancers on a "turntable of dust" (34), "Children hung together and moved like the comet's tail of bees she had seen roll out of the sky the other day" (66), "Her victory burned in her as a flame blackens within a hollow tree" (73). Throughout, we are reminded that the styles of place and race jar against each other – we are invited to see hers as the controlling one, as in this sentence from the final section:

> At this moment in its span, its seasons, the village coincides with the generic moment of the photographer's village, seen from afar, its circles encircled by the landscape, held in the pantheistic hand, the single community of man-and-nature-in-Africa reproduced by skilled photogravure processes in Holland or Switzerland. (156)

Although she cannot be said to argue a case in her novels, Gordimer's fictional views of South Africa have been perceived as political enough to be banned there. A single sentence about black writers in her country could apply to herself; she wants more from an author than a distinctive voice:

> The black writer's revolutionary responsibility may be posited for him as the discovery, in his own words, of the revolutionary spirit that rescues for the present – and for the post-revolutionary future – that nobility in ordinary men and women to be found only among their doubts, culpabilities, shortcomings: their courage-in-spite-of.[22]

The emphasis on responsibility and discovery in an uncertain world recalls rhetorical guidelines, and her hyphenated noun ("courage-in-spite-of") could derive from the ideas and voice of Kenneth Burke.

Like MacKinnon, Gordimer speaks for the oppressed and knows that words have consequences:

> This is the kind of demand that responsibility for the social significance of being a writer exacts: a double demand, the first from the oppressed to act as spokesperson for them, the second, from the state, to take punishment for that act. (287)

Her agenda is remarkably similar to MacKinnon's, and the lawyer would no doubt endorse the writer's imagery:

> Writers who accept a professional responsibility in the transformation of society are always ... asking of themselves means that will plunge like a drill to release the great primal spout of creativity, drench the censors, cleanse the statute books of the pornography of racist and sexist laws. (297–98)

Gordimer flatly asserts that "all writers are androgynous beings" (113). Her career may well combine the masculine and feminine voices that Gilligan describes, for Gordimer identifies an "urge to move towards blacks, not alone as a matter of justice, but as a human imperative,"[23] a remark that honors both equity and caring concern.

To apply "voice" as a critical standard to MacKinnon or Gordimer would, to invoke hooks once more, render them "shallow." Some early feminists, notably Mary Wollstonecraft, achieve ethos through style and through the strategies that MacKinnon employs: distinguishing the question and logical analysis. To say that she found her voice would reduce her achievement. The danger of emphasizing voice in composition and feminist theory is that simple self-expression or forceful delivery may become the governing principle. People who earn a credible ethos in discovering arguments that investigate issues of public policy are more likely to become citizens with voices that can address questions of injustice in society.

## NOTES

1 Cheryl Walker, "Feminist Literary Criticism and the Author," *Critical Inquiry* 16 (1990): 554.
2 Marilynn Desmond, "The Voice of Exile: Feminist Literary History and the Anonymous Anglo-Saxon Elegy," *Critical Inquiry* 16 (1990): 577, 577–78.

3 Peter Elbow, "Introduction: About Voice and Writing," in *Landmark Essays on Voice and Writing*, ed. Peter Elbow (Davis: Hermagoras Press, 1994), p. xxxvi. Further references to this essay will be made in the text.
4 Randall R. Freisinger, "Voicing the Self: Toward a Pedagogy of Resistance in a Postmodern Age," in *Landmark Essays*, 193–94.
5 Nan Johnson, "Ethos and the Aims of Rhetoric," in *Essays on Classical Rhetoric and Modern Discourse*, ed. Robert J. Connors, Lisa S. Ede, and Andrea A. Lunsford (Carbondale: Southern Illinois University Press, 1984), 105, 114.
6 *Orator*, in *Brutus & The Orator* (Cambridge, MA: Harvard University Press, 1971), xxi, 72.
7 Catherine MacKinnon, *Only Words* (Cambridge, MA: Harvard University Press, 1993), 8.
8 Tobin Seibers, *The Ethics of Criticism* (Ithaca: Cornell University Press, 1988), 195.
9 Linda Kerber, "Some Cautionary Words for Historians," in "On In a Different Voice: An Interdisciplinary Forum," *Signs* 11 (1986): 307.
10 Catherine MacKinnon, "Feminist Discourse, Moral Values, and the Law – A Conversation," *Buffalo Law Review* 34 (1985): 73–74. Emphases in original. Further references to this forum will appear in the text.
11 Esther Broner, *The Massachusetts Review* 24 (1983): 263.
12 bell hooks, "When I Was a Young Soldier for the Revolution: coming to Voice," in Elbow, *Landmark Essays*, 55.
13 Carol Gilligan, "Letter to Readers, 1993," in Elbow, *Landmark Essays*, 182.
14 MacKinnon, *Only Words*, 3.
15 Nadine Gordimer, "The Essential Gesture, " in *The Essential Gesture: Writing, Politics and Places*, ed. Stephen Clingman (New York: Knopf, 1988), 299.
16 C. Jan Swearingen, "Ethos: Imitation, Impersonation, and Voice," in *Ethos: New Essays in Rhetorical and Critical Theory*, ed. James S. and Tita French Baumlin (Dallas: Southern Methodist University Press, 1994), 135.
17 Susan C. Jarratt and Nedra Reynolds, "The Splitting Image: Contemporary Feminisms and the Ethics of Ethos," in Baumlin & Baumlin, *Ethos*, 39.
18 MacKinnon, *Only Words*, 23. Further references are made in the text.
19 MacKinnon, "Feminist Discourse," 44. Further references are made in the text.
20 Nadine Gordimer, "The Art of Fiction, LXXVII: Nadine Gordimer," *The Paris Review* (1983): 108–9.
21 Nadine Gordimer, *July's People* (New York: Penguin Books, 1982), 1. Further references are made in the text.
22 Gordimer, "Essential Gesture," 293. Further references are made in the text.
23 Nadine Gordimer, "That Other World that was the World," in *Writing and Being* (Cambridge, MA: Harvard University Press, 1995), 127.

# *Feminist Thoughts on Rhetoric*

LYNETTE HUNTER

Standpoint theory has conducted its critiques largely by way of a repositioning of epistemology, but there has been no similarly intensive critique for aesthetics that might reposition textuality. The result is a gesture toward the arts in general that indicates a hiatus in standpoint approaches. With Alison Jaggar I would suggest that feelings are often unauthorized modes of knowing, that the rational is an authorized feeling;[1] in other words, that aesthetics and epistemology are closely intertwined. However, to arrive at a place that could make sense of this suggestion requires a shift in the conceptualization not only of knowledge but also of beauty; it requires an understanding of the idea of partial and situated textuality to complement that of partial and situated knowledge. Knowledge remains tacit until articulated, so the situatedness of knowledge is bound to the situatedness of the textuality that communicates it.

Standpoint theory argues that knowledge articulated from the standpoint of those excluded from ruling relations of power is particularly important, first because it is usually unheard since it is denied access to dissemination, and second because it is quite different from the standards and discursive systems of a society and its culture precisely due to that denial: hence it can be a place for change, assessment, and renewal. Standpoint is concerned with situated knowledge which is necessarily partial;[2] it is concerned with retaining a concept of the real as a critical realism rather than a naive realism;[3] and with re-defining the individual to account for people who are not subjects[4] – or to account for the not-subjected of people's lives. One of the primary contributions of standpoint theory is to delineate an area of social, political, economic, and domestic relations that lies at a considerable distance from the ruling relations that govern the relationship between ideology and the subject.

The position of those excluded from ruling power has been derived from contemporary political critiques of western liberal democracies,[5] particularly the work of Carol Pateman and of Dorothy Smith.[6] From these two very different writers one can delineate three areas for the elaboration of power. The first is the predominant field of ruling government relations mediated by ideology via the representations it allows to the subject: the ideology-subject axis.[7] The second is the intensely contradictory discrete systems of discourse where subjects, in other words the five to twenty percent of enfranchised citizens, contest those representations on the edges of government and in civic spaces closely related to capitalism. These discourse systems are often nodes along the ideology-subject axis, and are especially connected to the analyses and critiques of psychoanalysis.[8] The third area is that of the non-ruling civic and domestic relations of power simultaneously negotiated among and between individuals and groups. This third area of non-ruling civic and domestic relations of power argues that the subject is not only governed by ideology, and inflected by the contradictions of systematization that analyzed by discourse, but is also constituted by local daily communications, discussions and negotiations.

The areas of government, capital, and civic and domestic, of ruling relations, discourse and non-ruling relations, establish a pattern that has been taken up by standpoint theorists to focus on the last term in each and produce a series of feminist critiques: a feminist critique of objectivity in science that asks about the exclusion of women's knowledge;[9] a feminist critique of politics that questions the curious simultaneity of the autonomous yet universalist man in which the isolation of the individual obscures their situatedness;[10] a feminist critique of philosophy that notes the denial of history in the value-free assumptions of both empiricism and idealism;[11] and a feminist critique of sociology centred in the debate between quantitative and qualitative methodology, which argues that enumeration, verisimilitude, and repeatability (as distinct from the broader and more various repetition) evades the contextual. In each case the obscured, evaded, denied, excluded situated knowledge is without authority and often, if not usually, without words.

The critiques delineate tacit knowledges of various kinds, and all recognise the need to work on words to bring those tacit knowledges into communication. In nearly every case the pathway out toward agency is through story, or narrative, or poetics.[12] However, there is no analogous critique of aesthetics, of art and/or criticism. Even Lorraine Code takes narrative as a "good thing" in itself and as a result finds the arguments pushed to a defence of relativism because there is no vocabulary for talking about any textuality that works between relativism and the absolute.[13] It is as if, textually, standpoint operates in awareness of this third place, but without any idea of how to discuss it; hence it turns toward the arts, and gestures toward strategies that seem to articulate situatedness. Several years ago, in an unselfconsciously rhetorical turn, Rita Felski described the hiatus that this leads to, saying that no technique or strategy or genre is in itself a good thing.[14] Yet in that understanding and with an acute sense of the growing importance of autobiography studies, Felski moves aesthetic value to the recipient. In a contemporaneous move, Janet Wolff moves the aesthetic focus to the institution.[15] Yet without a vocabulary to discuss the situated textuality of the arts that lies analogous to and embedded within situated knowledge, an element central to contemporary western aesthetics, the critical notion of language as (in)adequate to representation, which underwrites the absolute/relativist divide in the arts, goes without critique. I would propose that the history of rhetoric offers an appropriate vocabulary for such a critique.

In the post-Cartesian world of seventeenth-century politics and linguistics one finds a concept of language as inadequate to full communication. Despite indications that what writers and readers actually do may not much change, that many elements of poetics and rhetoric appear to retain their activity in more or less historically appropriate ways from the Renaissance to the modern European worlds, critical language becomes either a second-order code overtly inadequate, or a first-order medium continually to be transgressed or transcended. The canonical writing around which criticism has developed has largely been written by propertied people affluent enough to find time to write, and by definition citizens and subject to the state. The vocabulary for appreciation is an embodiment of the liberal social contract: the isolated genius speaking nevertheless on behalf of others, conveying absolute truth, through pure beauty. It is a vocabulary for the subject, and not for the individual writer who appears from, say, the diaries and letters of the Romantic poets to have operated on quite different relations in non-ruling areas of civic and domestic life where they impinged on the activity of writing.

There have been attempts to critique the isolated genius, for example Barthes or Foucault on the "author,"[16] but these are often treated as an erasure of the "individual." Similarly there have been attempts to critique pure truth, particularly in the work of Derrida, although his critique along with other moral stances, is usually dismissed as caught in an essentialist/relativist dichotomy. Yet there is no recent critique of beauty as something wrested from ideological obscuring into cultural articulation at the moment it loses its power within ruling relations,[17] no analysis of the extraordinary joy it offers at that moment when it still fits so precisely into the structures of social representation, and no critique of the ensuing pleasure and the conditions of its continuance or dissipation. Most of all, there is no critique of why it is so hard to value aesthetic production from those not in the five to twenty percent, from valued domestic and civic places that raise issues of class, gender and age, and those of race and ability imbricated particularly deeply with class. This material tends to be called 'popular' but is not analyzed as a different aesthetic, taking into account different writers, audiences, media. It is often subjected to the same critical analysis as canonical art, and held to fail. This is a tautological move, since non-canonical work is by definition not represented, and hence always appears to be inadequate to representation. The material is dismissed, as is the entire field of craft work: it is skilled, and grounded in tacit knowledge, but since it is not transgressive or transcendent it is not immediately relevant, nor can it be appreciated.

Why is there no critique? Of many reasons, I offer here only three. First, the critics (who make critiques) have conventionally over the past 300 years been part of the represented populace by class or education or gender. Hence they recognize that the key elements of post-Renaissance art – transgression and transcendence – do offer important possibilities for dealing with the inexorably inadequate representations of ideology/subject axis. For them transgression, defamiliarization, alienation, and "art" in general are to be valued for this activity. Second, and more complex, the arts are where men, powerful in terms of ruling relations, go to be female. There is the insistent imagery of the muse as the reproductive body temporarily brought to life by the male poet – recalling Pygmalion and Galatea. The image is the true pair to Nature as woman-to-be-conquered in science, to be brought to death. The arts are where rational isolated people go to be emotive, dialogical, feeling, and feminine. Third, and even more complicated, concerns the art that works with the limitations of a medium, which I understand as the focus of poetics. When that art is studied in detail it often enacts precisely the negotiations and communication within a group that is attempting to arrive at decisions that will articulate value and instigate action and agency. This, after all, is the purpose of poetics. For example, again, the Romantic poets: I have no problem with what they were doing with their poetics. They were addressing profound issues of identity, truth, and perception; they were rewriting the possibilities of representation by going out with the (in)adequate concept of language to an engagement with the limitations of language. They wrote a poetics that took people over a hundred years to understand, significantly becoming popular with the institution of working-class education; it is a poetics from which I have learned much in my own attempts to speak about women's experience. But of course groups such as the Romantic poets are also working within a political system of privilege quite different from our own, and dealing with issues and representations appropriate to their positions of class privilege and with agency for themselves. From a standpoint position, the poetics is engaged, and the moral and ethical interrelation with discourse is ignored. Yet the rhetoric of that poetics, its interrelation with ruling relations of government and other non-ruling relations of power, needs to be understood.

If we take the vocabulary of transgression/transcendence, dialogism, and agency, which is used by feminist standpoint theory to critique science, politics, philosophy, and so on, we find that it is at the centre of western aesthetics and appears to justify arts' strategies in general. What is not done is a broader analysis within historical context, that looks across partial knowledge to the relation of partial knowledge to the rest of society. Standpoint theorists would never analyze science without looking at the institutional structure that supports it, partly because it is so difficult to do science without an institution. Yet the arts are not perceived to be institutionally based, and so they escape any of this analysis. There is little analysis of the imbrication of the arts with state, national, and capital interests, and little assessment of the complexity of poetics with regard to the attendant rhetorical context of moral and ethical issues in society. This is another way of saying that beauty is political, that aesthetics is inexorably concerned with morality and ethics, that partial textuality can, like partial knowledge, be dealing with systems or with the messier interactions with reality, with adequacy, or with the necessary limitations of materiality.

The evasion of the ethics of aesthetics is the problem that needs to be addressed. What this paper proposes is that current work in the history of rhetoric is well placed to conduct such a critique. I would like to combine feminist standpoint theory with issues in the history of rhetoric that bring together textualities, society, and politics. Rhetoric offers, among other things, a history of the swing between the autocratic and the communal or social, and while conducting an acute analysis of the pros and cons of each, is also concerned with the complexity of ongoing negotiations in daily life, and articulates at least one vocabulary for the non-ruling relations of power through the elaboration of the consensus and the corporate. Classical rhetoric is concerned with social context, and distinguishes between the situated and the negotiated on the one hand, and the enclosed and systematic on the other, as different kinds of context. In Aristotle, the distinction is between the rhetorics of dialectic and science or philosophy, and in Plato, between the rhetorics of philosophy and success. Classical rhetoric is also concerned with truth, and distinguishes among the certain, the probable, and the plausible: the certain and the plausible are the domain of the autocrat or demagogue, whereas the probable is the domain of the orator who is engaged with the audience in working out probably-the-best set of grounds for action. This is truth determined through moral responsiveness and employed within social ethics. And classical rhetoric is concerned with notions of the individual and the group as wielders of power, with the difference between negotiated and represented power: the monarch and the tyrant, the aristocrat and the oligarchy, the constitutional democracy and the popular or populist democracy. Rhetoric always included the position of the audience or recipient, technically under the terms ethos, pathos, and stance. It recognizes that if ethos and pathos are separate then an unequal power distribution can occur, and that stance includes the rhetor, audience, and text. Ethos and pathos are the positions of the citizens, perhaps the seedbed for representations of the subject; whereas stance is the engaged interactive work of rhetor and audience in the textuality of a particular history.

Classical rhetoric is not set up to deal with any political or social activity as a fixed end. Hence its classical form had little effect on ideology in the post-Renaissance world. Ideology technically has the structure of Aristotle's science: it is enclosed, systematic, self-evident and self-justifying. If you enter it as a subject, you assent to the rules. Aristotle called such rhetoric inappropriate for social locations and denounced it as demagoguery. In the classical period it would have been difficult to maintain such a structure for very long, but, with the increasingly normalized and extensive media communications of current technology, it became very effective in western liberal democracies. However, if Aristotle's critique of science is applied to ideology, a highly acute account of political representation can be realized, which is one reason why so many political theorists get excited by the idea of science as "best case" politics.[18] If that critique by rhetoric of ideology is extended to aesthetics, we can derive a workable vocabulary for distinguishing between the subject and the individual in terms of ethos and stance, between objectivity/subjectivity with the logic of rational ordering that it has supported in the post-Renaissance period, and other positions for argumentation with rather different dialectical ordering, and between the essentialist/relativist dichotomy and the negotiated in terms of the certain/plausible dichotomy and the probable. Agency and dialogism can be understood not only as transgression and transcendence, but as engagements of moral and ethical negotiation.

What feminist historians of rhetoric have done over the last ten to fifteen years is implicitly take a standpoint position and look at those excluded from citizenship in order to test the applicability of rhetoric to relations of non-ruling power. They have looked at rhetorical strategies and stances within specific historical, socio-political contexts from Aspasia in the pre-Platonic period[19] to the many post-Renaissance studies. Accounts have been provided of women such as Mary Astell[20] attempting to work within the rhetorically privileged fields of, for example, rational logic; of women as icons, for example, from Queen Elizabeth I through to Elizabeth II,[21] accessing state power through the representations of ideology; of women like Jane Austen, living lives under ideological constraint;[22] and of those women attempting to live lives in areas of non-ruling relations evidenced in their letter-writing and diaries.[23]

With these studies in mind, it is possible to suggest that a rhetorical analysis from the standpoint of women as effectively disenfranchised and excluded from ruling relations of power would take the 'death of the author' argument, made explicitly through rhetoric by Barthes, and insist that it is not the death of the individual, only the subject. This is something auto(bio)graphy studies do.[24] Within those studies, standpoint first insists on personal materiality and the reality of individual experience and existence, and the rhetorical analysis elaborates on the kinds of ethos and pathos, and on the effects of stance. In effect, a combination of these approaches is occurring, yet an overt recognition of the rhetorical dimension could extend it out beyond the individual into the socio-political. There could be analyses of non-ruling relations not only within a position, but also across positions, and, with regard to ruling relations, an understanding that the negotiations of the individual are messy and broadly involved, rather than simply caught into discourse systems.

A rhetorical analysis from the standpoint of women can take the arguments of Derrida about the insistence of presence and the absolute alongside pluralist relativism, and base the images of fold, pli, seme, and so on within a situated knowledge. Derrida tried to do this through the 1980s, especially in his book on Mandela, yet every position he put himself into was still ideologically privileged. He has never, for example, discussed his own racial and cultural background. A feminist standpoint critique would first position itself in an historical immediacy, in order to look at the messy relations between people within non-ruling power, even and especially people without representation, and to look at what so many are now discussing as ethics. A rhetorical analysis adds to this an understanding of morality and ethics as engaged and negotiated best-probable-grounds-for-action, rather than as cases of relativism, where anything goes, or the absolute, in which certainty rules. Best-probable-grounds-for-action do not have to stay in a fixed position, but have strategies that can cross specific groups and address and change ruling relations.

Furthermore, there are parallel advantages of bringing together standpoint and rhetoric in both epistemology and aesthetics. Critiques of epistemology within standpoint argue for a critical reality, a critical rationality, a critical objectivity, as they uneasily defend the real while in constant tension with the absolute/relativist divide because there is no way of speaking about the probable. The rhetorical analysis of epistemology provides a vocabulary for talking about the negotiated reality, negotiated not on plausible but on probable grounds, ground worked on by people within a community and across communities through rational, analytical, syllogistic, topical, analogical, symbolic, and other logics. The approach is valuable in that it underlines the potential helpfulness in the otherwise excoriated "rational logic," and undermines attempts to define rational women as "masculine" and emotive men as "feminine." Working on probable ground necessitates an understanding of the complexity of knowledge and identity in public as neither wholly citizen (represented by state ideology), subject (represented inadequately and therefore partially repressed by ideology), or private (not represented by ideology), but is formed in terms of ethos, pathos, and stance; in other words, identity is not isolated but in relation to other human beings. Probable grounds necessitate an understanding of knowledge about reality as a matter of engagement and negotiation between ethics, or social agreement, and morality, or individual and group agency.

Just so, a critique of aesthetics within a feminist standpoint theory would argue first for the need to value the eighty percent of excluded art. Yet it would be helpful to do so not through a "critical" poetics or aesthetics that leads to a philosophical hiatus, but through a rhetorical analysis of aesthetics that offers a vocabulary for talking about the articulation of tacit knowledge with a textuality that understands limitations, a situated textuality. The work on words would not be a second-order textuality satisfied with inadequate language and reduced to encoding, nor a first-order textuality continually transgressing inadequate language toward the more nearly adequate by way of transcendent beauty, but a textuality where people work on words together to build common ground. In this attention to common ground, epistemology and aesthetics overlap, as a situated tacit knowledge becomes articulated and therefore textual.

Bringing a rhetorical dimension to standpoint theory in order to make a critique of aesthetics allows one to focus on those people who have been excluded from representation, not only as attempting to push embodiments of their lives into ideological representation, which is attempted and which discourse studies describes, but also as attempting the articulation of the not-yet represented. This is vulnerable work, but the participants know that there is only a restricted amount that can be gained by worrying about transgression and transcendence if one is not represented at all. Rhetoric can help us to explore the different aesthetics at work, understand their situated textualities, and value what is articulated.

## NOTES

1 Alison Jaggar, "Love and Knowledge: Emotion in Feminist Epistemology," in *Gender/ Body/ Knowledge: Feminist Deconstructions of Being and Knowing*, ed. Alison Jaggar and Susan Bordo (New Brunswick, NJ: Rutgers University Press, 1989).

2 See Donna Haraway, "Situated Knowledges: The Science Question in Feminism and the Privilege of Partial Perspective," *Feminist Studies* 14, no. 3 (1988): 575-99.

3 See Sandra Harding's *The Science Question in Feminism* (Milton Keynes: Open University Press, 1986) and *Whose Science? Whose Knowledge? Thinking from*

*Women's Lives* (Milton Keynes: Open University Press, 1991); Hilary Rose, *Love, Power and Knowledge: Towards A Feminist Transformation of the Sciences* (Cambridge: Polity, 1994).

4  Jane Flax, "Beyond Equality: Gender, Justice and Difference," in *Beyond Equality and Difference: Citizenship, Feminist Politics and Female Subjectivity*, ed. Gisela Bock and Susan James (London: Routledge, 1992); Flax, *Disputed Subjects: Essays On Psychoanalysis, Politics and Philosophy* (London: Routledge, 1993); see also S. Lovibond, "The end of morality?" in *Knowing the Difference: Feminist Perspectives in Epistemology*, ed. Kathleen Lennon and Margaret Whitford (London: Routledge, 1994).

5  Jürgen Habermas, *The Philosophical Discourse of Modernity* (Cambridge: Polity, 1987), and *Theory and Practice*, trans. J. Viertel (Boston, MA: Beacon Press, 1971).

6  Carole Pateman, *The Problem of Political Obligation: A Critique of Liberal Theory* (Cambridge: Polity, 1985); Dorothy E. Smith, *The Everyday World as Problematic* (Boston, MA: Northeastern University Press, 1987).

7  See Lynette Hunter, "Ideology as the Ethos of the Nation State," *Rhetorica* 14, no. 2 (Spring 1996): 197–229.

8  It is becoming more and more apparent that criticism drawing from psychoanalysis splits between the enclosing structures that take, for example, the symbolic and the imaginary as systematic, and those analyses, like Jane Flax's, that attempt to empower. Both deal with nodes of discourse.

9  Not only Haraway, Harding, and Rose, but also Fox-Keller, Longino, Hintikka, and others; see *Discovering Reality: Feminist Perspectives on Epistemology, Methodology and Philosophy of Science*, ed. Sandra Harding and Merrill B. Hintikka (Dordrecht: Reidel, 1983); Evelyn Fox Keller, "Feminism and Science," *Signs* 7, no. 3 (1982): 589–602, and *Secrets of Life, Secrets of Death: Essays on Language, Gender and Science* (London: Routledge, 1992); see also *Feminism and Science*, ed. Evelyn Fox Keller and Helen Longino (Oxford: Oxford University Press, 1996).

10  Nancy Fraser, *Unruly Practices: Power, Discourse and Gender in Contemporary Social Theory* (Cambridge: Polity, 1989); "What's Critical about Critical Theory? The Case of Habermas and Gender," in *Feminist Interpretations and Political Theory*, ed. M. Lyndon Shanley and Carole Pateman (Cambridge: Polity, 1991); see also many other contributions to Shanley and Pateman.

11  Kathleen Lennon and Margaret Whitford, *Knowing the Difference: Feminist Perspectives in Epistemology* (London: Routledge, 1994), offer several contributions to this particular critique; see also Genevieve Lloyd, *The Man of Reason: "Male" and "Female" in Western Philosophy* (London: Methuen, 1984).

12  Hilary Rose, *Love, Power and Knowledge*, 208ff; Sandra Harding, *The Science Question in Feminism*, 245; Harding also takes up the importance of metaphor (233), and expands on this in *Whose Science?* to look at literary context and the non-linearity of textual devices as democratic and womanly (301); Donna

Haraway, "A Manifesto for Cyborgs: Science, Technology and Socialist Feminism in the 1980s," in *Feminism/Postmodernism*, ed. Linda Nicholson (London: Routledge, 1990); and Donna Haraway, "Situated Knowledges"; and Evelyn Fox Keller, *Secrets of Life, Secrets of Death*, throughout chapters 6 to 9.

13 Lorraine Code, *Rhetorical Spaces in Gendered Locations* (London: Routledge, 1995), particularly in "Voice and Voicelessness," 154*ff.*

14 Rita Felski, *Beyond Feminist Aesthetics: Feminist Literature and Social Change* (Cambridge MA: Harvard University Press, 1989), see particularly 160*ff.*

15 Janet Wolff, *Feminine Sentences: Essays on Women and Culture* (Cambridge: Polity, 1990).

16 See for example R. Barthes, "The Death of the Author," *Image–Music–Text*, selected and edited by S. Heath (London: Fontana/Collins, 1977, orig: 1968), 142–48.

17 See L. Hunter, "The Puppeteer. Being Wedded to the Text," *Open Letter: Kroetsch at Niederbron*, 9th Series, Nos. 5-6 (Spring-Summer 1996), 199–218.

18 For further detail, see L. Hunter, *Critiques of Knowing* (London: Routledge, 1999), chapter 6.

19 See Andrea Lunsford, *Reclaiming Rhetorica* (Pittsburgh, PA: University of Pittsburgh Press, 1995); Susan Jarratt, ed., "Feminist Rereadings in the History of Rhetoric," *Rhetoric Society Quarterly* 22, no. 1 (1992); and Michael Billig, "Gender and the Revival of Rhetoric: Recovering the Memory of Aspasia," unpublished manuscript, 1992.

20 See, for example, the work of Christine Mason Sutherland including "Outside the Rhetorical Tradition: Mary Astell's Advice to Women in Seventeenth-Century England," *Rhetorica* 9, no. 2 (Spring 1991): 147–63.

21 Michael Billig, *Arguing and Thinking: A Rhetorical Approach to Social Psychology* (Cambridge: Cambridge University Press, 1987), and *Talking of the Royal Family* (London: Routledge, 1992).

22 See Nancy S. Struever on Jane Austen, "The Conversable World: Eighteenth-Century Transformations of the Relation of Rhetoric and Truth," in *Rhetoric and the Pursuit of Truth: Language Change in the Seventeenth and Eighteenth Centuries* (Los Angeles, CA: William Andrews Clark Memorial Library, 1985).

23 For example, Judith Rice Henderson, "Erasmian Ciceronians: Reformation Teachers of Letter-writing," *Rhetorica* 10, no. 3 (Summer 1992): 273–302.

24 For work on auto(bio)graphy, see Jeanne M. Perreault, *Writing Selves: Contemporary Feminist Autography* (Minneapolis: University of Minnesota Press, 1995).

# *Afterword*

## CHRISTINE MASON SUTHERLAND

A collection of such diversity surely needs some concluding word to draw together what has been attempted and perhaps achieved. In this final word I shall try to locate the collection within current work in rhetoric, and metarhetoric, and give some indication of how it contributes to ongoing scholarship in the study of women's relationship to rhetorical tradition.

It might appear to a traditionalist that what has characterized rhetorical theorizing for most of the twentieth century has been a quest for a definition of rhetoric; but that would be to misunderstand what has been going on. Many of those who write about rhetoric do not believe in defintions except as temporary perching places to rest before continuing a journey which has no destination, because the very idea of destination has been called into question. From a traditional perspective, then, the quest may seem bleak and the undertaking pointless.

This collection demonstrates that the journey is neither: rather, it is an adventure. We should think of ourselves as the heroes of fairy tales who set out into the world to seek their fortune. In the best fairy tales, the hero is a marginal person, the youngest brother, or the stupid one of the family, or, like Cinderella, a victim of exploitation. Cinderella, of course, does not go out into the world to seek her fortune; she has to be rescued by the fairy godmother and the handsome prince. The point of this collection is that Cinderella has grown up a bit; has decided not to sit in the ashes any more; has taken hold of her own life.

In doing so, she has joined many other adventurers. Few these days are willing to stay at home. One of the earliest adventurers was Kenneth Burke,[1] who re-envisaged rhetoric as identification, and further declared: "Wherever there is persuasion, there is rhetoric. And wherever there is meaning there is persuasion" (172). Nor did Burke confine rhetoric to speech; actions, too, carried meaning, and were therefore part of rhetorical activity. Burke's challenge to traditional ideas of what constitutes rhetoric has been seminal. We are all in his debt. What typifies the most recent work in broad rhetorical theory is the willingness to question age-old assumptions about rhetoric, to challenge traditions, to push at definitions, to test the limits, if there are any, of inclusiveness. Victor Vitanza's collection of essays, *On Writing Histories of Rhetoric*, questions not only rhetoric, but also, and most particularly, history, and what the history of rhetoric has meant, or could mean. Like many other historians, the contributors to Vitanza's collection see the traditional histories of rhetoric as too narow and exclusive, too limiting, too much grounded in a belief in objectivity.[2] James Kastely's *Rethinking the Rhetorical Tradition* takes a quite different approach.[3] He questions the Aristotelian rhetorical tradition, seeing in its commitment to persuasion a form of coercion, an insistence upon consensus that has the effect of silencing the opposition and ignoring those without a voice. However, he sees this criticism of the tradition not as something postmodern, or even modern; on the contrary, it was inaugurated, he believes, by Socrates and Plato. Contesting the central tradition from ancient times has been a kind of shadow rhetoric, a tradition of skepticism and refutation which has recognized the outsiders, the silenced, those who are forced to comply because they cannot make themselves heard. "Plato's concern with refutation follows from his belief that one can never become present to oneself, that all self-understanding is partial and deceptive – a mere play of shadows. Refutation becomes a continual political necessity precisely because well-intentioned individuals and communities repeatedly fall into the trap of believing that they understand who they are and who the Other is" (14) In tracing this tradition, Kastely considers primarily not those recognized as rhetoricians or philosophers of language but rather creative artists: in the ancient world, Sophocles and Euripides, in the modern, Jane Austen. These writers present and analyze the problems inherent in language itself: the impossibility of achieving justice, and the necessity, therefore, for an ongoing challenge to make us all aware that we have not succeeded in bringing justice about.

George Kennedy pushes out the boundaries in another way.[4] The rhetorical tradition has been exclusively western. Rhetoric has usually been thought of as "a structured system of teaching public speaking and written composition, developed in classical Greece, taught in Roman, medieval, renaissance and early modern schools, and, with some revisions, still in use today. Nothing exactly like this has existed in other cultures, though there are some partial parallels in Aztec schools and in literate cultures" (2). But this, Kennedy continues, "is only one meaning of rhetoric." His *Comparative Rhetoric* now attempts to embrace many other cultures as well. This necessarily leads him to question the traditional assumption that rhetoric is peculiarly a western phenomenon (3). Aristotle himself, who formalized the study of rhetoric, recognized that rhetorical activity had been going on for at least a century before Plato, and drew upon Greek literature for examples of it. Kennedy continues: "Rhetoric thus existed in Greece before 'rhetoric,' that is, before it had the name that came to designate it as a specific area of study. 'Rhetoric' in this broader sense is a universal phenomenon, one found even among animals, for individuals everywhere seek to persuade to take or refrain from some action, or to hold or discard some belief" (3).

Kennedy, like Kastely, then, draws on a Greek tradition going back before Aristotle, sources from which Aristotle himself drew. Rhetoricians are revisiting their beginnings, and in doing so are finding their kinship with cultures whose traditions have been quite different. Kennedy explores practices of rhetoric in non-literate cultures, including a study of aboriginal peoples both in Australia and in North America. Turning next to literate societies, he discusses rhetorical activities of the ancient Near East: ancient Egypt and Israel, from which the western rhetorical tradition ultimately derives; and also ancient China and India. In thus extending what rhetoric might mean, he dispenses with the old definitions and sees it now as "a form of mental and emotional energy" (3).

Enough has been said to demonstrate where some recent studies of rhetoric are taking us. Accepted ideas about rhetoric are being challenged on a number of different fronts: we are learning to extend our understanding of it to include practices outside the western tradition, pushing back into earlier times and other cultures. We are critiquing traditions of rhetoric, learning to see the invisible, the excluded, those outside the identification: in Burkean terms, perhaps, the scapegoated, the Other. Woman, of course, has always been the Other, and traditional rhetoric has seen her as always and necessarily excluded. Rhetorical education, for most of its history in the west, has used Latin as the language of teaching, and Latin literature as the storehouse of models of good writing. Latin was essential to the study of rhetoric. To quote Walter Ong,[5] "For well over a thousand years, it was a sex-linked language written and spoken only by males, learned outside the home in a tribal setting which was in effect a male puberty rite setting, complete with physical punishment and other kinds of deliberately imposed hardships" (113). Since women were thus normally excluded from learning the very language in which rhetorical education took place, it has often been assumed that they played no part in rhetorical activity. But this asumption, like so many others, is also being questioned. Is it true that women played no part in the rhetorical tradition? And even if it is true, does that mean that women were excluded from rhetorical activity?

This is one of the issues addressed in the present collection. We are not the first to address it, of course: the questioning has been going on for some time, and many scholars have contributed to it.[6] One of the most important of recent publications on the question is Cheryl Glenn's *Rhetoric Retold: Regendering the Tradition from Antiquity to the Renaissance*,[7] which is required reading for anyone interested in the history of women's rhetoric. As a single-authored text, however, and one which does not deal with women after the Renaissance, its approach and scope are rather different from those of the present collection. Much more similar to it are two books which have collected and focused some of the ongoing discussion: *Reclaiming Rhetorica: Women in the Rhetorical Tradition*, edited by Andrea A. Lunsford (1995);[8] and *Listening to Their Voices: The Rhe-*

*torical Activities of Historical Women,* edited by Molly Meijer Wertheimer (1997).[9] These two collections have brought the whole issue to the attention of the rhetorical community. Since our work builds upon theirs, a brief discussion of what they accomplished is in order. *Reclaiming Rhetorica* was, as its editor points out, the first of its kind. What is of particular interest, and gives great promise for the future, is that the the original impetus came in 1988, from students: "The students' approaches were marked by hesitation: hesitation because they were uncertain as to whether much material really existed; and frustration because none of their courses in rhetoric had introduced them to women or even hinted at women's contributions" (4). In response to the interest of these students, Annette Kolodny, then professor at the Rensselaer Polytechnic Institute, taught a graduate seminar on "Women Rhetoricians." It was from this group of interested women that *Reclaiming Rhetorica* grew. The aim, according to Andrea Lunsford, who took over the project and edited the volume, "was not to attempt to redefine a 'new' rhetoric . . . but to open up possibilities for multiple rhetorics."

In speaking of the archaeological project to which her volume contributes, Lunsford emphasizes a need, above all, to listen; this work of listening is continued in the book edited by Molly Wertheimer, *Listening to Their Voices.* The contributors to this volume, too, are less interested in redefining rhetoric than in opening it up and challenging "the basic conception of rhetoric as agonized debate" (3). The editor declares: "As editor of this volume, I have chosen to forego top-down pronouncements privileging any single method of revision . . . The position taken here is the promotion of pluralism" (4). This inclusivity, characteristic of much feminist scholarship, is the guiding principle of the present volume.

How then does this collection contribute to the ongoing discussion? First, by continuing the push against the accepted boundaries of rhetoric. Given the much broader sense of rhetoric that Kastely and Kennedy, among others, have opened up, we push old definitions beyond their limits. What counts as rhetoric? We have included not just the production of discourse, but also its reception. We consider, it is true, the writings of famous women, but also the reflections of one who at the time was little more than a child.

Some of the essays focus on philosophy, aesthetics, or journalism. Two essays deal not with women as either writers or receivers of discourse, but with their significance as cultural symbols, demonstrating how in the late Middle Ages and early Renaissance women were both demonized and divinized. Following the lead of Burke, we look at the rhetoric of behaviour, life as text.

We push a little, too, at received definitions of feminism. All the essays here concern women, though some of the women discussed were not historical, existing only in myth or as symbol. Moreover, by no means all of these essays are written from a feminist perspective, using feminist theory or method. In studying the relationship of women to rhetoric and its traditions, we have tried to be as inclusive as possible. The result of such an open policy has been not only to extend the scope of both rhetoric and feminism, but also to generate optimism: for as we investigate new areas of interest, we discover unsuspected presences that attest to women's underlying importance even at times when they might appear to have been absent.

Finally, this collection opens up the discussion of women and rhetoric internationally. Both the previous volumes were published in the United States, and their editors and nearly all their contributors are American. The present volume grew out of an international conference held in Canada but attended by delegates from all over the world. It includes contributions from seven different countries, and because of its international sponsorship, will be read worldwide.

These essays, then, represent something of the complexity of women's relationship with rhetoric. Partially, if not wholly, excluded throughout most of its history, women have nevertheless been present, though usually unacknowledged and unremembered. Active at the very beginning in the misty figures of Aspasia and Diotima; present in the religious tradition, which is interwoven with the rhetorical; occasionally participating fully, if only at the margins, in the male-dominated rhetorical community; challenging the tradition, co-opting it for their own ends, finally becoming fully engaged with it as equal partners with the men: women have already made an enormous contribution to the rhetorical tradition from which they were supposedly excluded. This collection celebrates that contribution and promotes its continuance into the future.

## *NOTES*

1 Kenneth Burke, *Rhetoric of Motives* (Berkeley: University of California Press, 1969).
2 Victor Vitanza, ed., *Writing Histories of Rhetoric* (Carbondale: Southern Illinois University Press, 1994).
3 James L. Kastely, *Rethinking the Rhetorical Tradition: From Plato to Postmodernism* (New Haven: Yale University Press, 1998).
4 George A. Kennedy, *Comparative Rhetoric: An Historical and Cross-Cultural Introduction* (New York: Oxford University Press, 1998).
5 Walter J. Ong, *Orality and Literacy: The Technologizing of the World* (London: Methuen, 1982).
6 For a thorough discussion of the relationship between rhetoric and feminism, see Lisa Ede, Cheryl Glenn, and Andrea Lunsford, "Border Crossings: Intersections of Rhetoric and Feminism," *Rhetorica* 13, no. 4 (Autumn 1995): 401–41.
7 Cheryl Glenn, *Rhetoric Retold: Regendering the Tradition from Antiquity to the Renaissance* (Carbondale: Southern Illinois University Press, 1997).
8 Andrea A. Lunsford, ed., *Reclaiming Rhetorica: Women in the Rhetorical Tradition* (Pittsburgh: University of Pittsburgh Press, 1995).
9 Molly Meijer Wertheimer, ed., *Listening to Their Voices: The Rhetorical Activities of Historical Women* (Columbia: University of South Carolina Press, 1997).

# Notes on Contributors

## John C. Adams
John C. Adams is the author of numerous articles on the history and philosophy of rhetoric. He is also the author, with Stephen Yarborough, of *Delightful Conviction: Jonathan Edwards and the Rhetoric of Conversion* (Westport, CT: Greenwood Press, 1993). He is currently the Dean of Graduate Studies at Fitchburg State College, Fitchburg, MA, USA.

## Linda Bensel-Meyers
Linda Bensel-Meyers is Associate Professor of English at the University of Tennessee, Knoxville, USA, where she has served as Director of Writing Programs since 1989. She teaches graduate courses in rhetorical history and practice, and chairs the Interdisciplinary Colloquy on Rhetoric for the University Studies Program. She received her BA from the University of Chicago, her MA and PhD from the University of Oregon. She has published *Rhetoric for Academic Reasoning* (1992); she was co-author of *The New Student's Guide to Research* and General Editor of *Literary Culture* (1999). She has also published articles on Renaissance Rhetoric, Twentieth-Century Rhetoric, and Composition. She is currently completing a book-length study of the cultural relationship between emblematic literature and rhetorical education and practice in Renaissance England.

## Suzanne Bordelon
Suzanne Bordelon is the Director of Composition at the University of Alaska, Fairbanks, USA. She began her study of Gertrude

Buck while pursuing her doctorate in Rhetoric and Composition at the University of Oregon.

## Hélène Cazes
Former pupil of the Ecole Normale supérieure, *agrégée de Lettres* (1986), and *Docteur ès Lettres* (1998), Hélène Cazes is presently on extended leave from the Département de Lettres of the University of Paris-X (Nanterre), France. Her doctoral thesis, under the direction of Daniel Ménager, was concerned with theory and practice of the Renaissance cento. For several years she worked in the manuscript department of the IRHT in Paris where she was concerned with the copying of classical texts and the transition from manuscripts to printing. She has also studied student compilations, collections of quotations, résumés, and critical editions of classical Latin texts of the fifteenth and sixteenth centuries. In addition, she has a continuing interest in twentieth-century literature, having co-edited *Grabinoulor*, the epic novel by Pierre Albert-Birot, and published a book about the literary critic Jean-Pierre Richard (*Jean-Pierre Richard* [Paris: Bertrand Lacoste, 1993]).

## Vicki Tolar Collins
Vicki Tolar Collins is Assistant Professor of English at Oregon State University, USA, where she teaches courses in rhetoric and composition and directs the university's Writing Intensive Curriculum. Her work has been published in *Rhetoric Review* and in collections of essays on the history of rhetoric and on composition.

## Jody Enders
Jody Enders is Professor of French at the University of California, Santa Barbara, USA. She is the author of *The Medieval Theater of Cruelty* and of *Rhetoric and the Origins of Medieval Drama*, which was honoured with the inaugural Aldo and Jeanne Scaglione Prize from the Modern Language Association. She has published numerous essays on the interplay of rhetoric, medieval literature, performance theory, and the law in such journals as *PMLA, Modern Language Quarterly, Rhetorica, Comparative Drama, Olifant*, and *Stanford Italian Review*, with others to appear in *Theatre Survey* and *Yale French Studies*.

A Guggenheim Fellowship will allow her to spend the year 1999 working on a third book.

## Erin Herberg

Erin Herberg is a Ph.D. candidate at Georgia State University, Atlanta, USA. She is currently finishing her dissertation, which continues her work with eighteenth-century women and their roles as rhetorical agents.

## Lynette Hunter

Lynette Hunter is Professor of the History of Rhetoric, University of Leeds, England, and also holds the Gresham Professorship of Rhetoric, Gresham College. She has written widely on the history of science and on the relations between literature and rhetoric. Books include *Rhetorical Stance in Modern Literature*, *Modern Allegory and Fantasy*, and the edited collection, *Topos, Commonplace, Cliche: Approaches to Analogical Reasoning*.

## Marianne Janack

Marianne Janack is Assistant Professor of Philosophy and Religion in the Department of Humanities and Arts at Worcester Polytechnic Institute, USA. Her areas of research include epistemology, feminist theory, and moral philosophy.

## Robert L. King

Robert L. King is a contributing editor and drama columnist for *The North American Review*. He has published on seventeenth-century rhetoric in *Milton Studies*, *ELH*, and *Proceedings of the Canadian Society for the History of Rhetoric*; on political rhetoric in the *Quarterly Journal of Speech*, *Southwest Review*, *Massachusetts Review*, *Washington Post*, *Cross Currents*, and *Columbia Journalism Review*; and on the rhetoric of drama in the *Chicago Review*, *Massachusetts Review*, *South African Theatre Journal*, and elsewhere. He teaches English at the Elms College in Chicopee, Massachusetts, USA.

## Brigitte Mral

Brigitte Mral is Associate Professor of Communications at the University of Örebro/Sweden. Her areas of interest are communication history and rhetoric. She is currently working on a book about women's rhetoric from ancient to present times

**Philippa Spoel**
Philippa Spoel is Assistant Professor of English at Laurentian University, Canada, where she teaches writing and rhetoric and is Co-Director of Laurentian's Centre for Academic Writing. Her main areas of interest are feminist approaches to rhetoric, the eighteenth-century elocutionary movement, the historiography of rhetoric, writing in the disciplines, and workplace writing. Her publications include "The Rhetoric of Enlightenment Rhetoric: Strategies of Ethos in British Elocutionary Handbooks," *Canadian Journal of Rhetorical Studies*, and "Disciplinary Identity and the Historiography of Rhetoric," *Proceedings of the Canadian Society for the Study of Rhetoric.*

**Margo Husby Scheelar**
Margo Husby Scheelar, a Ph.D. candidate in the Faculty of Education, is also Academic Co-ordinator of the Weekend University at the University of Calgary. This position provides opportunity for her to work with non-traditional students, a role she enjoys, as she was a mature undergraduate herself. Research interests include rhetoric, the role of women in Christianity, the history of ideas that shaped western civilization, ethics in post-secondary teaching and "Star Trek."

**Victor Skretkowicz**
Victor Skretkowicz was born in Hamilton, Ontario, Canada and educated at McMaster University, the University of New Brunswick, and the University of Southampton. He is Senior Lecturer in English at the University of Dundee, Scotland, Chairman of the Scottish Branch of the Society for Renaissance Studies, and Chairman of the body responsible for completing the *Dictionary of the Older Scottish Tongue*. He has edited *Sidney's New Arcadia* and *Nightingale's Notes on Nursing*, and is finishing a book on the Renaissance Romance.

**Rebecca Sutcliffe, Editor**
Rebecca Sutcliffe received her Ph.D. in English from Simon Fraser University and has taught composition and professional writing at

the University of Utah and the University of Saskatchewan. She has authored articles on writing for *Technical Communication Quarterly* and the Encyclopedia of Literary Biography. She is currently Associate Director of Corporate and Foundation Relations at Clarkson University, Potsdam, NY, USA. She is co-editor of the collection, having carried major responsibility for editing the documentation.

### Christine Mason Sutherland, Editor and Contributor

Christine Mason Sutherland is Associate Professor in the Faculty of General Studies at the University of Calgary, where she teaches courses in History of Rhetoric in the Communications Major Program. She has published on the rhetoric of Augustine of Hippo, and on scientific rhetoric in the seventeenth century, but in recent years has been chiefly concerned with women rhetoricians of the seventeenth century. She has published on both Mary Astell and Margaret Cavendish.

### C. Jan Swearingen

C. Jan Swearingen is Professor of English at Texas A&M University. She is the author of *Rhetoric and Irony, Western Literacy and Western Lies*, and of a number of articles and chapters on women in the history of rhetoric, including "A Lover's Discourse: Diotima, Logos and Desire," in *Reclaiming Rhetorica*, edited by Andrea Lunsford. Her most recent work includes a book on multiculturalism as an impetus behind the koine topoi in the ancient world, and a study of the influence of ancient Near Eastern women's funeral lamentations on the earliest epitaphia.

### John Ward

John Ward has taught Medieval History at the University of Sydney, Australia, since 1967, after doing his doctoral studies and teaching classics at the University of Toronto (Centre for Medieval Studies). He is the author of *Ciceronian Rhetoric in Treatise, Scholion and Commentary* (1995), together with many studies and books on medieval historiography, rhetoric, witchcraft, crusade, and other topics.

**Andrea Williams**
Andrea Williams (MA and BA, University of Toronto) is a doctoral candidate in Rhetoric and Composition at Ohio State University, USA. Her research and teaching interests include rhetorical theory, the history of rhetoric, and professional writing. She is currently writing a dissertation on the rhetoric of corporate communication.

# Index

## A
Abelard, 124–25
aboriginal peoples, 251
absolute/relativist divide, 239, 244, 245
*Account of the Experience of Mrs. H. A. Rogers*, 113, 115–16
accretion, 115–16
activism, 164
   rhetoric of, 174–78, 180
*ad hominem*, 213–23
   and argumentation, 220, 221–22
   as fallacy, 214, 220, 221
      Code's objection, 217–19, 221–23
      Walton's observations, 220, 221–23
   relevance of, 220
   and trust, 221, 223
*Advancement of Learning, The* (Bacon), 152
*Aerial Letter, The* (Brossard), 200, 203–4
aesthetics
   critique, 237, 239–42, 243, 244–46
      excluded art, 240, 246
      repositioning textuality, 237, 239, 246
      rhetoric of ideology, 243, 244, 246
   and emotion, 237, 241
   and epistemology, 237
   ethics and morality, 242, 245
   and institution, 239, 242
   and language, 239–40, 241
   and poetics, 241
   pure truth, 240
   and recipient, 239
   transgression and transcendence, 239, 241–42, 244
African-Americans, 176
*Alchemy of Race and Rights, The* (Williams), 219
anachronism, 14–15, 68-69
   in interpreting early feminists, 27–29
Anaxagoras, 41, 42
*Annunziazione* (Belcari), 88
Anselm (and Gunhild), 124
Antigone, 38
*Antonius* (Sidney), 133
apartheid, 229
argumentation, 148, 185, 188, 243
   and *ad hominem*, 220, 221–22
   and audience, 190-91
   defined, 190
   egalitarian process, 190–91, 192
   inductive method, 188, 192
   institutional setting, 221, 222
   and logic, 188, 189–90
   and persuasion, 191–92
   and psychology, 189–90
   and reasoning, 190–91
   syllogistic brief, 190
   and sympathy, 191
   and trust, 221, 222, 223

263

Aristotle, 10, 150–53, 190, 251
   and character, 223
   delivery, 200
   dialectic method, 152, 242
   and invention, 201
   rhetoric as persuasion, 10, 191, 208, 250
   science, 242, 243
artists, creative, 250–51
arts, 239
   canonical, 240
   crafts, 240
   and gender, 241
   *See also* aesthetics; narrative; poetics
asceticism, 67, 68
Aspasia, 38, 39–40, 41
   speech in *Menexenos*, 40–41
   teachings, 42, 43
Astell, Mary, 15–17, 244
   critic of Locke, 16, 22, 149–50
   as feminist, 22–23, 24, 25, 27–28
      paradox, 15–17, 28–29
      on women's rights, 16–17, 28, 149
   logical method, 150–53, 154–55
   on marriage, 23, 24–27
   philosophy, 28, 148–49
      Cartesian influence, 152–53
      echoes of Aristotle, 150–53
      echoes of Cicero, 153–56
      Platonism, 148–50
   politics, 16, 19
      political writing, 22, 28
      -religion inseparable, 22–23, 24, 28
   religious beliefs, 16, 22–23, 24, 26, 148, 149
   rhetorical theory, 147–56
   on service, 20, 21, 22, 28
   on Truth, 150, 153
   writings, 21, 22, 27, 28, 149
      *The Christian Religion*, 21, 149
      *Love's Victory*, 142
      *A Serious Proposal to the Ladies*, 17, 21, 24
      *Some Reflections Upon Marriage*, 22, 23, 24, 26–27
Athens, 38, 41, 42, 43
   women's status in, 18
Attic style, 133, 139
audience, 152, 154–55
   adapting to suit, 167–68, 174, 175–76, 229
   antagonizing, 227
   and argumentation, 190–91
   generation of knowledge, 201–2
   and persona, 162–63, 167–68, 169–70, 227
   persuasion model, 208
   position of, 243
   -speaker relationship, 174, 175–76, 208
Augustine, 87, 88
Austen, Jane, 244, 251
Austin, Gilbert, 201
Australia, 251
authority, 27
   epistemic, 216–19, 221, 222
authorship, 225
   and decorum, 233
   identity and gender, 225, 226
   and persona, 232–33
   and responsibility, 234–35
autobiographies, 103, 239, 244
Aztec education, 251

**B**

Bacon, Sir Francis, 152, 153
Baldini, Baccio, 88, 89
Barbieri, Filippo, 88, 89, 90–91, 92
Barnett, Mary Jane, 100
Barthes, Roland, 240, 244
Bath, Michael, 97, 99
Baudri of Bourgeuil, 122, 123
beauty. *See* aesthetics
Belcari, Feo, 88
Bell, Rudolph, 67

# INDEX

Benedict XV, Pope, 67
Bible, 21, 24, 26, 27, 37, 63, 87, 113
Birgitta, 65
Birken, Sixtus, 86
bodily rhetoric, 200–201
*Book of Margery Kempe, The*, 11
brank, 51–52
Brereton, John C., 192–93
Bridget, St., 170
Britain, 170, 178. *See also* England
Broner, Esther, 228
Brossard, Nicole, 199–209
  bodily memory 204, 211n.
  *écriture au féminin*, 203–4
  embodied knowledge, 201-9
  patriarchal epistemology, 202
Buck, Gertrude, 183–93
  argumentation, 188–92
  Dewey's influence, 184
  and education, 187, 192
    student interest, 188–89
  ethics, 186–88, 187, 190–91, 192
    social, 184–86
  Hegelian view, 187–88
  social Christianity, 186–87, 192
  writings, 186, 187
Burke, Kenneth, 10, 234, 250, 252, 254
Butler, Charles, 154

## C

Cambridge Platonists, 148
Campbell, George, 191
Campbell, Karlyn Kohrs, 174
Canada, 173–81
Canadian Women's Suffrage
  Association, 173
capitalism, 238
Castalio, Sebastianus, 86
Catherine (of Toulouse), 51
Catherine of Siena, St., 59–69, 117
  and Church
    advisor to, 60, 64, 66–67, 68
    challenges, 68
    commended by, 67, 68
  ethos
    of crusader, 65–69
    of daughter, 62–65, 66
    of intermediary, 61–65, 66
    of mystic, 59, 61–62
    silenced by modern scholars, 67–68
    theology, 63–64
  writings, 60, 64, 66
    political correspondence, 65–69
Catholic Church, 65, 110
  St. Catherine's advice to, 60, 64, 66–67, 68
Cavendish, Margaret, 17, 20
ceremonies
  political oratory, 43
  role of women, 37, 38
Chekhov, Anton, 229
China, 251
*Chironomia* (Austin), 201
*Choice of Emblems, A* (Whitney), 98–102
Christian Gauss lectures, 229, 230
Christianity, 65, 148, 149, 185
  love, 186–87
  public service, 21, 22, 28, 60
  revelation, 86–87, 88, 89, 90
  Sibyls, 88–90
  social, 184, 187
*Christian Religion as Profess'd by a Daughter of the Church of England* (Astell), 21, 149
Cicero, 11, 40, 153–56, 200, 227
  orator defined, 155
citizens, 245
*City of God, The* (Augustine), 87
civic responsibility, 180
Code, Lorraine, 216–19, 221–23, 239
communication, 152, 153, 154, 207
  language inadequate, 239, 241
  situatedness, 205
  speech, 214
  *See also* discourse; language

community life, 21–22
*Comparative Rhetoric* (Kennedy), 251
composition, 183–84, 188, 189, 192–93. *See also* literature; rhetoric; writing
*Concise Introduction to Logic, A* (Hurley), 214
conduct, 192
Connors, Robert, 29, 183
conscience, 103
consensus, 250
*contentio*, 10–11, 16
conversation, 167, 208. *See also* discourse; speech
cooperation, 12
Corbett, Edward, 200, 208
correspondence, 64, 65–66. *See also* writing
*Countess of Montgomery's Urania* (Wroth) *See Urania*
*Countess of Pembroke's Arcadia, The* (Sidney), 134
*Course in Argumentative Writing, A* (Buck), 184, 188, 192
credibility, 215, 230–31
  epistemic record, 219
  and speakers, 217–18
criticism, 239–40, 240–41
Crowley, Sharon, 13, 15
Crusades, 65–66, 68

### D

Dalström, Kata, 167–68
*Daphnis and Chloe* (Longus), 133, 139
daughters
  role of, 62
  treatment of, 137
Deborah, song of, 37
de Clerq, C., 88
"Decline and Fall" narrative, 183, 192–93
decorum, 227, 233
deductive method, 152–53

Delaval, Lady Elizabeth, 98, 103–5
delivery, 200–201, 230, 235
democracy
  Buck, 187–88, 189, 190–91, 192
  and education, 177, 187
  and marginalized, 238
  and women's status, 19–20
  *See also* suffrage
democratic theory of rhetoric, 183–93
demonstration, 152
Denison, Flora MacDonald, 173–81
  activism and language, 180
  editorials, 174–78, 179–80
  populism, 176–77
  style, 177, 178
*De Officiis* (Cicero), 11
*De Oratore* (Cicero), 155
depiction, 114
*De Rhetorica* (Aristotle), 150
Derrida, Jacques, 240, 244–45
Descartes, René, 152–53
Desmond, Marilynn, 225
Devil, 47, 50
Dewey, John, 184–86
  on education, 187–88, 188–89
  idealism 185, 186–87, 194n.
dialectics, 150, 151–52, 153, 192
  Hegelian, 187, 188
dialogism, 244
dialogue, 221
  and *ad hominem*, 220
*Dialogue* (St. Catherine of Siena), 60, 62, 66
diaries, 244
Diotima, 41, 43
  teachings of, 42, 43
*Discours de la vie et de la mort* (de Mornay), 133
discourse
  control by institutions, 116
  marginalized, 10, 238
  monopolized by victim, 228
  mystical, 109, 114, 116

and poetics, 241
private, 11, 114
systems, 238
*See also* conversation; language; meditation; speech
*Discrepancies between Saint Augustine and Saint Jerome* (Barbieri), 90–91
disputation. *See* argumentation
divine rights, 23, 25
domestic life, 23, 165
　as metaphor for good society, 168
　rhetoric of, 174
Dronke, Peter, 125

E
Ede, Lisa, 205
editorial genre, 174–78
education, 16–17, 251
　in argumentation, 188
　and democracy, 177, 187
　Dewey on, 187–88, 188–89
　free inquiry, 192
　inductive method (Buck), 188, 192
　rhetorical, 125, 126–27, 164, 252
　role of editorial genre, 179
　social individualism, 187–88
　and student interest, 188–89, 192
　of women, 19, 28, 103, 164
Egypt, ancient, 251
Elbow, Peter, 226–27
Eleusinian mysteries, 37, 43
Elizabeth I, Queen, 244
Elizabeth II, Queen, 244
elocution, 201. *See also* public speaking; speech
eloquence, 123, 143
Elshtain, Jean, 227
emancipation, 19–20
　female, 163
　and use of voice, 227
　*See also* suffrage; women's rights
emblem books
　*A Choice of Emblemes* (Whitney), 98–101

　　and imagistic rhetoric, 97–102, 103–5
　　meditative dimension, 101, 102, 103–5
　　as moral guides, 99–100, 101–2
　　reception of, 97, 98–102
　　tripartate form, 98–99, 103
　　　emblems, 97, 98–102, 104–5
　　　epigram, 99–101, 102, 104
　　　motto, 99, 101
emotions, 206, 207
　emotional body, 201
empiricism, 23–24, 149, 150, 151
enfranchisement. *See* suffrage
Engels, Friedrich, 215
*Engendering Power* (Morrison), 219
England
　Enlightenment, 109-16
　Jacobean, 19, 134
　Renaissance, 97–105
　suffrage, 170, 178
　*See also individual authors/speakers*
Enlightenment, the, 109–16, 219
epigrams, 99–101, 102
epistemic dependence, 216
epistemology, 190
　-argumentation relationship, 223
　embodied vision and, 204–5
　feminist, 208, 213–23
　　and *ad hominem*, 214, 215–16
　　ethical issues, 205–6
　　reformulation, 199–209, 222, 237
　patriarchal, 199, 200, 202
　rhetorical, embodied, 245
　*See also* knowledge
epitaphia, 38, 41, 42
essentialist/relativist dichotomy, 240, 243
ethical reality, and subject, 230
*Ethical Significance of 'Coriolanus', The* (Buck), 186
ethics
　of care, 12

ethics *(continued)*
    democratic, 184
    of ethos, 205–6
    and experience, 185
    social (Buck), 184–86
ethos, 17, 232, 244
    -argumentation-epistemology relationship, 223
    of crusader, 65–69
    of daughter, 62–65, 66
    definition examined, 226
    ethics of, 205–6
    of intermediary, 64–65, 66
    and knowledge, 205–6
    of mystic, 59, 61–62
    and pathos, 205, 243
    through style, 235
    and voice, 223, 225–35
    of writer, 223
Euripedes, 251
experience, 229, 244
    and ethics, 185
    and idealism, 185

**F**
faith, 151
    and morals, 24
fallacy, 213, 214, 223
    theory of, 219–20
family, 23
Fantham, Elaine, 37
feelings, 237
Felski, Rita, 239
female abuse, 133–44, 227, 230–31
    by females, 138
    rhetoric of, 140
    Wroth's advice, 134
female memory. *See* memory
female thought, traditions of, 12
feminism, 12, 170, 228
    anachronisms of early, 165, 168
    Astell, 15–17, 23, 27–29
    collective approach, 20, 179
    critics, 225
    critiques, 238
    definitions of, 254
    epistemology. *See under* epistemology
    heroines, 178–79
    inclusion, 175–76, 180
    mind-body dualism, 200
    moderate approach, 166, 170, 177
    objectivity, 206
    and rhetoric, 199, 226, 237–46
    and voice, 225–26, 227–230, 231, 235
fictions 232–34. *See also* literature; writings
figurative reasoning, 98–102, 103–5
First Amendment, 231
Fleming, Juliet, 15, 20
Foley, Helene, 37
Foucault, Michel, 116, 240
Fourteenth Amendment, 231
"free" choice, 215–16
freedom of self, 186
French Revolution, 18
frescoes, 88
Friedman, Milton, 214, 215
Frymer-Kensky, Tikva, 37
funeral rites and orations, 37, 38, 39, 40

**G**
Garnier, Robert, 133
Geoffrey of Vinsauf, 48
Germany, activism, 170
Gilligan, Carol, 12, 227, 228, 231, 232, 235
Gilman, Charlotte Perkins, 179
Glenn, Cheryl, 11, 205, 252
Goldrick-Jones, Amanda, 12
Gordimer, Nadine, 229, 232, 233–35
Gordon, Linda, 12
*Gorgias* (Plato), 148
Gorham, Deborah, 176
Great Western Schism, 68

Greece, ancient, 37, 43
  sibylline oracles, 85, 86
  women's roles in, 37, 38, 39, 169
Gregory XI, Pope, 64, 65, 66–67
Gunhild and Anselm, 124

**H**
Haraway, Donna, 29, 199–209
  conversation as metaphor, 208
  knowledge
    embodied, 203, 205
    ethical, 205–6
    scientific, 202
Harding, Sandra, 215
Havelock, Eric, 42
Hebrew scriptures, 37
Hecksher, William, 102
Hegel, Georg W., 185, 187, 215
Heinsius, 18
Hekman, Susan, 202
Heloise, 122, 123–25
Hemingway, Ernest, 232–33
Herbert, William, Earl of Pembroke, 135
hermeneutic systems, 100, 101, 104, 106
hierarchy, 22
  of epistemic authority, 222–23
Hildegard of Bingen, 122, 128–29
Hill, Anita, 218, 230–31
historians
  constructionist, 13
  essentialist, 13, 15
history of rhetoric. *See* rhetorical tradition
holism, organic, 188, 189
Holland. *See* Netherlands
*Homeric Hymn to Demeter*, 37
hooks, bell, 228, 229, 235
Howell, Wilbur, 154
Hrotsvit of Gandersheim, 122–23
Huguenot ethic, 133–34
humanism, 126–27
  and women, 17, 18
and *sermo*, 11
Hume, David, 110
Hunter, Lynette, 20, 21, 22
Hurley, Patrick J., 214, 216

**I**
iconic meditation, 98–102
iconography, sibylline, 87–90
idealism, 184, 185
  Christian, 186–87
  and experience, 185
  experimental, 185
ideal self, 185
identification, rhetoric as, 114, 190-92, 215, 250
identity, 245
ideology, and rhetoric, 243, 244, 246
ideology-subject axis, 238, 241
Ignatius, St., 98, 102, 103
imagery
  and meaning, 99
  to provoke new view, 102
imagistic rhetoric, 97, 98–102, 103–5
*In A Different Voice* (Gilligan), 227, 228, 232
inclusion, 174–78, 180, 250
*In Defence of Rhetoric* (Vickers), 121
India, 251
individualism, 20
  social (Buck), 187-88
innuendo, 220
Inquisition, 47–48
*Institutiones Divinae* (Lactantius), 86–87, 89–90
instrumentalism, 185
intelligence, 202
interest, student, 188–89
intermediaries, 62, 63, 64–65, 66
introspection, 66
invention, 201–2, 205
  and arrangement, 153–55
  embodiment, 201–2, 206
  and pathos, 207–8
Irigaray, Luce, 109, 113

irrelevance, 220
Israelite culture, 37

**J**
Jacobean period, 19, 134
Jaeger, C. Stephen, 126
Jaggar, Alison, 237
Jamesian psychology, 186
James, William, 185
Jarrett, Susan C., 199, 205–6, 230
Jesus Christ, 62, 63, 65, 112
    in the temple, 63
Johnson, Nan, 226
journalism, 174, 176–77, 178
journal-keeping, 112–14, 113–16
*July's People* (Gordimer), 233
justice, 251

**K**
Kahn, Victoria, 102
Kantian philosophy, 190
Kastely, James, 250–51
Kellner, Hans, 10
Kelly, Joan, 17
Kennedy, George, 251
Kerber, Linda, 227
Key, Ellen, 164–67, 168, 179
    public speaker, 164–67
    teaching, 165
Kinneavy, James, 113
knowledge
    acquisition, 149–51, 152
    argumentative, 190–91
    and authority, 205, 206, 216–17, 222
    cognitive practices, 217
    embodied, 200–209
    emotion and feelings, 206, 208, 237
    ethos, 205–6
    and objectivity, 203, 205, 206
    partial, 205, 217, 237, 242
    and pathos, 200, 205, 207–8
    politics of, 216–17

reformulating concepts, 202, 206
and responsibility, 203, 205–6, 222
scientific, 202
situated 202, 203, 212n., 215–16, 237, 239, 244
source of, 217–18
and standpoint theory, 217, 237–38, 245
tacit, 237–39, 240, 246
*See also* epistemology
Kolodny, Annette, 253
Krailsheimer, A.J., 24
Kramer, Heinrich, 47–48, 49–51

**L**
labour movements, 167
Lactantius, 86–87, 88, 89–90
Lagerlöf, Selma, 168–69
    "Home and State" speech, 168–69
    persona, 169
*Landmark Essays on Voice and Writing* (Elbow), 226
language
    and activism, 180
    and arts, 239–40
    critical, 239
    inadequacies of, 102, 152, 153, 239, 241
    and creative artists, 251
    Latin as rhetorical, 121-28, 252
    moral, 232
    real, 230–31
    *See also* communication
Latin rhetoric, 121–28, 252. *See also* Cicero
Lawrence, D.H., 226–27
lawyers, 230–32, 235
*Learning from the Histories of Rhetoric* (Miller), 9–10
legal hearings, 218, 220, 230–31
lesbian knowledge, 204
letter-writing, 124, 244. *See also* correspondence; writing
liberalism, 17

and feminism, 16, 20
linguistic ambiguity, 102
*Listening to Their Voices: The Rhetorical Activities of Historical Women* (Wertheimer), 253
literature, 103, 133-44, 232-35
   current protocol and, 15
   directing reader's choice, 98, 229
   emblem books, 97, 98-102
   Middle Ages, 122-28
   poetics, 100, 122-23, 239, 241, 242
   *See also* composition; writing
Locke, John, 16, 22, 28, 110, 149-50, 151
logic, 152
   and *ad hominem*, 214
   and argumentation, 188, 189-90
   -epistemology-politics, 222
   informal, 190
   and informal fallacy, 219-20
   and inquiry, 153
   and invention, 154, 201-2
   in learning, 188
   and pathos, 205-6
   and persuasion, 219
   and political reform, 175
   and psychology, 189-90
   rational, 245
   -rhetoric division, 154, 155
logical method, language in, 153
Longinus, 114
Longus, 133, 139
love, Christian, 186-87
*Love's Victory* (Wroth), 142
Lunsford, Andrea, 205
Luxemburg, Rosa, 170

**M**
MacKinnon, Catharine, 227-28, 235
   ethos, 230-32
   female abuse, 227
   as lawyer, 230-32
   on pornography, 229, 230
*Malleus Maleficarum* (Kramer), 47, 51

Mandela, Nelson, 244
Manegold, Master, 122, 125-27
   wife and daughters, 126-27
*Marc Antoine* (Garnier), 133
marriage, 134, 135, 136-37, 163
   authority in, 24-25, 26, 27
Marx, Karl, 215
Mary's Magnificat, 37
masks, 169-70
materiality, 244
maxims, 149, 190
mediation, 185, 187
Medieval period. *See* Middle Ages
meditation, 60, 154-55
   Astell on, 149
   of Elizabeth Delaval, 98, 103-5
   as imagistic rhetoric, 97, 98-102, 103-5
   *See also* emblem books
memory, 102, 204
   bodily, 205, 211n.
   collective, 169
   female
      "cutting off", 52
      demonization of, 47, 48, 50, 53
      uses, 49
   and knowledge, 206
   rhetorical function of, 48
   and social control, 49
   -speech connection, 48, 49, 51, 52
*Menexenos* (Plato), 38, 40
*Metaphor, The-A Study in the Psychology of Rhetoric* (Buck), 184
metaphors, 168
Methodism, 109, 110-16
   journal-keeping, 112-14
   problems with mysticism, 115
   publishing, 113, 115-16
methodology, 238
Meun, Jean de, 124
Michigan, University of, 184, 185
Middle Ages
   ethos, 59, 61-62
   Latin rhetoric, 121-28

Middle Ages *(continued)*
  mystics of, 59, 61–62, 169
  poetry, 122–23
  Sibyls, 85–92
  women's status, 17–18, 19, 125, 127
    female politicians, 170
    religious role, 127
    violence, 52
Mildmay, Lady Grace, 103
Miller, Thomas, 9–10
Milton, John, 19, 21
mind-body dualism, 200
misogyny, 18, 138, 163
moderation, 177
modes of understanding, 151
Moore, Dorothy, 20–21, 22
morality, 24
  in emblem books, 99–100, 101–2
  ethics, and poetics, 242
  public and private, 25
  and voice, 227, 232
Mornay, Philippe de, 133
Morrison, Toni, 219
mothers, 17, 165, 167, 169
motto (emblem books), 99, 101
mourning, 38
Muriel (poet), 123
Murphy, J. J., 121
"mysterique, la", 109
mystics and mysticism, 68, 109, 110–16, 170
  Birgitta, 65
  Catherine of Siena, 59, 60, 61–62
  discourse of, 109, 116
  Hester Rogers, 109–116
  mystical experiences, 59, 60, 61–62, 110, 111
  narrative, 113–14, 115
    threatens church, 115
  repackaging, 115–16
  view of world, 61
  ways of, 110, 111, 114
mythology, sibylline oracles, 85, 86

**N**
Nagler, Michael N., 61, 68
narrative, of mystic, 113–15
narrator, 233–34
Near East, 251
  roles of women, 36–37, 37–38, 39–40
Neo Aristotelian movement, 12
neo-Hegelianism, 185, 186, 187, 188
Netherlands, 18, 19, 20
networks, 166–67, 174
Newton, Isaac, 154
Nicholls, William, 26
Nietzsche, Friedrich, 53
Nightingale, Florence, 179
Noffke, Suzanne, 68, 69
Norris, John, 148, 149
North America, 222
  aboriginal people, 251
*Novum Organon* (Bacon), 152

**O**
obedience, 26, 62–63, 64
objectivity, 14, 205, 206, 238, 243, 250
  and knowledge, 203
  reformulating concepts, 202
Ong, Walter, 252
*Only Words* (MacKinnon), 230–31
*On Writing Histories of Rhetoric* (Vitanza), 250
opinion, 151
oppression, 229
opuscles, 92
*Oratoriae Libri Duo* (Butler), 154
orators, 155, 242–43
oratory, 43, 176, 227
  divisions of classical, 200–201
*Organic Education: A Manual for Teachers in Primary and Grammar Grades* (Buck), 187, 189
Orsini palace, 88, 91
Osborn, Michael, 114

**P**
paganism, 88, 90
Pamphilia (Wroth), 135–39, 140-1
Pankhurst, Emmeline, 178
parable of the talents, 21
paralogism, 220
Parker, Francis W., Col., 187
Pascal, Blaise, 24
past, learning from, 29–30
Pateman, Carol, 238
pathos, 200, 201, 205, 207–8, 243, 244
patriarchy, 17
   'objectifying gaze' of, 204
   strategy for participation in, 170
   and vision, 207
Paul, St., 26, 27, 37
Paul VI, Pope, 67
Pericles, 40, 41
persecution, 51, 53
persona, 227
   acceptable, 170
   and author's voice, 232–33
   and choice of masks, 170
   of Dalström, 167–68
   editorial, 175–76
   importance of, 169–70
   of Key, 165
   of Lagerlöf, 169
   in public speaking, 162–63, 174
persuasion, 250
   and argumentation, 191, 192
   and audience, 208
   bodily, 200–201, 205
   classical model, 208
   delivery, 200–201
   editorial genre, 180
   and logic, 219
   in public arena, 229
*Phaedrus* (Plato), 148
phylacteries, 90
*Pistis*, 113
Pius II, Pope, 66

plainness, 133–34, 137, 138, 139–41, 142–43
Plato, 38, 40, 49, 148–50, 242, 250
   Aspasia, 41, 42
   defines rhetoric, 10
   Diotima, 41, 42–43
Plutarch, 41, 139
poetics, 100, 122–23, 239, 241, 242
Pogge, Paul, 89
"poisoning the well" argument, 220, 221
*Poissance d'amor*, 49
political reform
   and content, 229
   and logic, 175
   strategies, 174
   and voice, 228–29
politics, 174–75
   and communication, 239
   feminist critique of, 238
   in novel, 234
   political writing, 28, 65-69, 165, 177
   -religion, 22–23, 28, 116
   women's roles, 37
   removing subject, 230
   women in, 162, 163, 167, 168
popes. *See individual names*
populism, 177
   adverse effect of, 176
pornography, 230, 231
power
   abuse, 202
   elaboration, 238
   female
      attributed to Devil, 50
      Middle Ages, 17
   and knowledge, 237
   loss of, with liberation, 17
   and love, 138
   of the mind, 102
   non-ruling, 238
   relations, 12

power *(continued)*
    and rhetoric, 205, 243
*Pragmatic Theory of Fallacy, A* (Walton), 214
pragmatism, 185
Praz, Mario, 99
preaching, female, 69, 115
*Principles of Psychology* (James), 185
private
    identity, 245
    life, 17, 18
privilege, and knowledge, 217, 245
probable grounds, 245
Proba, Falconia, 92
prophecies, repetition, 91–92
prophet(esse)s, 87, 88, 89, 90, 165, 169. *See also* Sibyls
propriety, 227
Protestantism, 109, 110–16, 133–34
    and women 19, 27. *See also* Astell; Rogers
psychoanalysis, 238
psychology
    functional, 184, 186, 194n.
    and logic, 190
public life, 161–70
    separate from private, 17, 18
    and women, 155
    public service, 20, 21, 28
    religious, 28, 60
public speaking
    acceptable subjects, 164, 165, 170
    and *ad hominem*, 214
    and argumentation, 190–91
    and decorum, 166, 169–70, 227
    Denison, 173–74, 175–76
    ethos, 229–30
    and persona, 162–63, 169–70
    political speech, 228–29
    rhetorical questions, 168
    story-telling role, 169
    style, 162
    Swedish women, 161–70, 168
    testifying, 219
    voice metaphor, 225–26, 228, 230–31
    *See also* rhetoric
purgations, 111, 112

## Q
Quintilian, 155, 191, 200

## R
*Race-ing Justice* (Morrison), 219
racial harassment, 230, 232
racism, 222
Ramus, 153, 154
Raspa, 102
rationalism, 23–24
    dispassionate, 202
rational mind, 201
readers, 229
realism, 237
reason, 103, 149, 202
    and emotion and body, 202
    reformulating concepts, 202, 205
reasoning, 150, 151, 232
    dialogic, 221
    figurative, 97, 98–102, 103–5
    informal, 192
    and moral problems, 232
    syllogistic, 152, 153
reception
    emblem books, 97, 98–102
    as rhetoric, 253. *See also* identification
*Reclaiming Rhetorica: Women in the Rhetorical Tradition* (Lunsford), 18, 252–53
Reformation, 110
    and women, 18, 19
refutation, 250
relativism, 239, 244, 245
religion
    and emblem books, 99, 101, 102
    hermeneutics, 100, 101, 104, 106
    Methodist theology, 110

and moral behaviour, 24
mystical experience, 59, 60, 61–62,
    110, 111
-politics interrelationship, 22–23,
    28, 37, 116
rituals, 38, 39, 41
Sibylline art, 87–90
spiritual journals, 112
suffering, 68
theology, 63, 125
union with God, 110, 113, 114, 116
Renaissance, 48
    Ciceronian revival, 154
    drama, 15
    novel, 133–44
    rhetoric, 11
    syncretism, 98, 105, 106
    treatise on Sibyls, 89–90
    women's meditations, 97–105
repentance, 103
repetition, and sibylline books, 92
republicanism, 134
responsibility, 180, 187, 205, 234–35
    Ciceronian, 155
    epistemic, 216–19
*Rethinking the Rhetorical Tradition*
    (Kastely), 250–51
revisionism, 68
Reynolds, Nedra, 205–6, 230
rhetoric, 14
    of accretion, 115–16
    Astell's attitudes, 147–56
    of behaviour, 59–69, 250
    classical, 41, 230, 242–43, 251
        Aristotelian. *See* Aristotle
        Greco-Roman schema, 134,
            136, 137, 139
        Latin, 121–28, 153–56, 252
    and communication, 152, 153
    as conversation, 191, 208
    definition, 9–10, 121, 242, 249,
        251, 253–54
    education, 125, 126–27, 164, 252

embodied, 200, 201–3, 204
and ethos, 225, 226–27
feminism,
    thoughts on, 237–46
    strategy, 199, 226
functions of, 109–10, 114, 191
as identification, 114, 190–92, 215,
    250
imagistic, 97, 98–102, 103–5
-logic, 153, 154, 155
-philosophy boundary, 222, 223
populism, 176–77
redefining, 191, 199, 253
self-rhetoric, 113
of social justice, 184, 186–88
of writing. *See* writing
rhetorical epistemology. *See*
    epistemology
rhetorical tradition, 199
    activist rhetoric, 174–78, 180
    and *ad hominem*, 213–23
    anachronism, 14–17, 23, 27–29,
        68–69, 165, 168
    and argumentation, 189–92
    and critique of arts, 239–40, 242
    "Decline and Fall" narrative, 183-93
    delivery, 200–201
    emblem books, 97, 98–102
    female, 12, 38–39, 41, 113, 121–28,
        133–44
    and feminism, 14–17, 67–69, 165,
        168 174, 199
    gender bias, 9-11, 13, 15, 35, 174,
        199, 252
    Latin, 121–28, 252
    private (*sermo*), 10, 11, 12, 97–98,
        113–16
    religious. *See* intermediaries;
        mystics
    revisionist, 37, 68, 180, 244
        opening up to women, 10–13,
            35–36, 38, 68, 116, 121–28,
            251–55

rhetorical tradition *(continued)*
   silencing opposition, 51–52, 67–68, 250–51, 252
   within epitaphia, 42
*Rhetoric* (Aristotle), 223
*Rhetoric in the Middle Ages* (Murphy), 121
*Rhetoric Retold: Regendering the Tradition from Antiquity to the Renaissance* (Glenn), 252
rhetors, 176, 205. *See also* orators; speakers
rituals, role of women in, 37
Rivet, André, Dr., 20, 21
Roberts, Josephine, 135
Rockefeller, Steven C., 185
Roe, Hester (later Rogers), 110–13. *See also* Rogers, Hester
Rogers, Hester Ann (née Roe), 113, 114–16
   mystical experience, 109–116
   public testimony, 113–16
   *See also* Roe
Roman Catholicism. *See* Catholic Church
Romantic poets, 241
Rousseau, Jean-Jacques, 18
Royster, Jacqueline Jones, 174

**S**
sacrifice, 63–64
Sappho, 38
Sayers, Janet, 202
Schiner, Olive, 178–79
science, 151, 202, 238
   accounts of reality, 206
   authority, 203
   critique of, 243
   and institutions, 242
   objectivity, 203
Scott, Harriet M., 187
Seibers, Tobin, 227
self-consciousness, 186–87
self-denial, 111, 112
self-realization, 186

self-righteousness, 227
self-understanding, 250
*Serious Proposal to the Ladies, A* (Astell), 17, 21, 24, 147, 153–54, 155
*sermo*, 11, 122
service, 22
   of God, 28, 62
   of mystics, 112
   public, 20, 21, 28, 60
sexism, 222
sexual harassment, credibility and, 230–31
sibylline oracles, 86, 87
   destruction of, 85, 86
   two traditions established, 86
Sibyls, 85–92
   in art, 87
   Christian, 87, 88–89
   established by Lactantius, 86–87
   pagan, 88
   predictions, 91, 92
   repetition, 91
   thirteenth added, 92
   visual images change, 87–90
Sidney, Mary, Countess of Pembroke, 133
Sidney, Sir Philip, 134
silenced groups, 123, 124, 227, 250–51
silent modesty, vs. civic responsibility, 155
situatedness, of arts, 239
Smith, Dorothy, 238
Smith, Hilda, 23
social control, and memory, 49
*Social Criticism of Literature, The* (Buck), 184
Social Democracy, 167, 168
Socrates, 38, 40, 42, 43, 250
   solidarity, 207
   shift in, 215
   and testimony, 219
*Some Reflections Upon Marriage* (Astell), 22, 23, 24, 26–27
sophists, 40, 42, 43, 148

Sophocles, 251
South Africa, 234
Southern, Richard W., 124
sovereignty, and family, 23
speakers
    and audience, 174, 175–76, 208
    and control, 208
    and credibility, 218
    epistemic character of, 218
    public, in Sweden, 161–70
    *See also* orators; rhetors
speaking. *See* public speaking;
    rhetoric
*Speculum of the Other Woman* (Irigaray), 109
speech
    communication, 214
    figurative, 102
    and memory, 48, 49, 51, 52
    plainness in, 133–34, 137, 138, 139–41, 142-43
    *See also* communication; linguistics; rhetoric
speeches
    and *ad hominem*, 220
    and delivery, 200
    editorials, 174–78
    privileged acts of speaking, 228
    suffrage, 174, 176
    *See also* public speaking
Spies, Marijke, 18
spiritual discourse, 116
*Spiritual Exercises* (Ignatius), 98, 102
spiritual perfection, 110, 114
Springborg, Patricia, 22, 23, 27
stance, 243, 244
standpoint epistemology, 215–16, 237–38, 239, 244–46
    and *ad hominem*, 216–17
    critiques, 237–38
    poetics, 241, 242
    and rhetoric, 237, 239, 241–42, 244, 246
stories and story-tellers, 169, 175, 239

Stowe, Dr. Emily, 178
student interest, 188–89, 192
*Study of Ethics, The: A Syllabus* (Dewey), 185–86
style, ethos through, 235
subject, 237, 238, 240, 245
    removing, 230
subjection, 26, 63
subjectivity, 219, 243
submission, 207
subordination, 25–26
    use of voice, 227–28
suffering, religious, 68
suffrage, 167, 170, 173–81
    editorial genre, 174–78
    history of, 180
    moderate approach, 177
    rhetoric of, 173–81
    universal, 168
    women's, 164, 174, 180
suffragettes, 170, 178
Sundén, Hjalmar, 162
Swearingen, C. Jan, 229–30
Sweden
    public speaking, 161–70
    suffrage, 170
    women's activism, 164
syllogistic brief, 190
sympathy, and argumentation, 191
*Symposium* (Plato), 42
syncretism, 98, 105

T

*Taleus* (Butler), 154
Tarquin the Proud, King, 86
teachers, 164, 167, 169
teaching, 126–27, 165, 173–74
Teresa of Avila, St., 112
testimony, 217, 221, 222
textuality
    of arts, 239
    repositioning, 237
    situated, 237, 246
    and words, 246

theology. *See* religion
Thomas, Clarence, 218, 230–31
thought, emotional, 207, 209
Tinkler, John, 10–11
Toronto, 176, 178
*Toronto World*, 174
torture, 51
transgression and transcendence, 241–42, 244, 246
*Treatise on Rhetorical Delivery, A* (Austin), 201
trust, 218, 221, 222, 223
truth, 150
    assumptions about knower, 216–17
    classical rhetoric, 242–43
    critique of pure, 240
    Dewey, 185
    philosopher neutral, 216
    in poetics, 241
    search for, 148–9, 150
    use of plainness, 134, 141, 143
    in writing, 229
Truth, Sojourner, 36, 176
Twelfths, 166, 167
tyranny, 134

## U

Underhill, Evelyn, 110, 111
understanding, 151
United States, 184, 185, 218
    feminism, 228
    suffrage, 170, 176, 178
    women's rhetoric, 173
    *See also individual authors/speakers*
unity, 187
*Urania* (Wroth), 133–44
    autobiographical elements, 135
    female abuse, 133, 134–38
    rhetorical style, 134, 136, 137, 139–44

## V

Vickers, Brian, 121
victims, voice of, 227, 228

*Vindication of the Rights of Women* (Wollstonecraft), 18
violence
    philosophical model for, 48, 49–50
    *See also* female abuse
Virgil, 92
    and Sibyls, 87
vision, 207
    embodied, 203, 204
    and reality, 204
    and standpoint theory, 216
visionaries, 169, 170. *See also* mystics
visual images, of Sibyls, 87–90
Vitanza, Victor, 13, 250
vocabulary. *See* language
voice, 235
    abstracted, 229
    appropriate, 232
    authentic, 226, 233–34
    authority given to, 225
    author's, 232–33
    and content, 229
    defensible use, 227
    development of political, 228–29
    emphasizing, 235
    and ethos, 223, 225–35
    and experience, 229
    expressing pain, 227
    in legal trials, 230–31, 232
    metaphor, 226
    and moral purity, 227
    and privilege, 225
    to oppression, 229
    of victim, 227, 228

## W

*Waiting for Godot* (Beckett), 29
Walker, Cheryl, 225
Walton, Douglas, 214, 221–23
    theory of fallacy, 219–20
Waswo, Richard, 101
wedding rituals and songs, 37, 38, 39
Wells, Ida B., 174

Wesley, John, 110, 112–13, 115
Whately, Richard, 191
Whigs, 17, 23
Whitney, Geoffrey, 98–102
Williams, Patricia, 219
wisdom, 155
witches, 48, 50, 51, 52–53
Wolff, Janet, 239
Wollstonecraft, Mary, 18, 235
women's movement
  elitism, 176
  inclusion, 174–78
  origins of, 14, 175, 180
  rhetoric of, 173–81
  symbols, 168
  transnational, 178–79
  *See also* feminism
*Women's Power Misused* (Key), 165
women's status
  acceptable roles, 165, 167
  and democracy, 19–20
  and liberalism, 20
  Middle Ages. *See under* Middle Ages
  Renaissance/Enlightenment, 18, 19, 20
  rights, 163, 168, 229
Woolf, Virginia, 14
writing, 60, 154, 155, 174, 251, 253–54
  and *ad hominem*, 214
  argumentative, 188
  autobiographical form, 103, 239, 244
  correspondence, 60, 64, 65–66
  and ethos, 223
  journalism, 176–77
  letter-writing, 66, 124, 244
  narrative of mystic, 112–14
  novel, 133–44, 229, 232–34
  poetic, 122-23
  political, 22, 28, 65–69, 165, 177, 235
  responsibility, 234–35
  stories and story-tellers, 169, 175, 239
  student interest, 188–89
  and vision, 207
  *See also* composition; literature; poetics; rhetoric; and *see also individual authors*
*Writing Histories of Rhetoric* (Vitanza), 13
Wroth, Lady Mary,
  exposé of abuse, 133, 134–38
  Limena, 136–37
  on love, 135–36
  on misery, 135, 140, 143
  Pamphilia, 135–39, 140–1
  style
    classical, 134, 136, 137, 139
    plain speech, 133–34, 137, 138, 139–41, 142–43
    variations, 139–43
  *Urania*, 133-44
Wroth, Sir Robert, 135

Z
Zetkin, Klara, 170